SIR GEOFF HURST

Eighty at Eighty

SIR GEOFF HURST

Eighty at Eighty

with Norman Giller

An A-Z of Masters from Ali to Zola

England's 1966 World Cup Hat-Trick Hero
Selects the Greatest Sportsmen of his Lifetime

A Norman Giller Books Publication
In association with Pitch Publishing
and Terry Baker, A1 Sporting Speakers

First published by Pitch Publishing, 2021

Pitch Publishing
A2 Yeoman Gate
Yeoman Way
Worthing
Sussex
BN13 3QZ
www.pitchpublishing.co.uk
info@pitchpublishing.co.uk

ISBN 978 1 80150 128 6

Typesetting and origination by Pitch Publishing
Printed and bound in Great Britain by TJ Books, Padstow

CONTENTS

In loving memory of my two great
club and country team-mates,
Bobby Moore and Martin Peters.

AUTHORS'
ACKNOWLEDGEMENTS

SIR GEOFF Hurst and Norman Giller thank the indefatigable Terry Baker for his encouragement and the Pitch Publishing brother-and-sister double act, Paul and Jane Camillin, for their expertise and enthusiasm.

Thanks, too, to number one son Michael-Alan Giller and sports fanatic David Guthrie for their in-depth knowledge and safety-net checking, Duncan Olner for making us suitably jacketed; also skilled editor Gareth Davis, proofreader Cath Harris, and layout guru Graham Hales.

We have rifled through all sorts of reference points for our extensive 'For the Record' facts and, in particular, the *Guinness Book of Records, Wisden Cricket Almanack, The Ring Boxing Encyclopaedia*, various *Rothman's Football Annuals* and the irreplaceable modern friend of authors, Wikipedia. The revered Alamy picture agency has provided many of the photographs and several have come from the private collection of the authors.

Thanks chiefly to the 80 sporting superstars featured in the following pages. They have made world history so much richer and enjoyable.

Finally, from Geoff, a public word of thanks to Judith, for always being there.

Enjoy.

INTRODUCTION BY
SIR GEOFF HURST MBE

'My great sporting heroes,
and there is actually one over the 80!'

EIGHTY! I cannot believe it. How did that happen? It seems like only yesterday that I became something of a celebrity by being lucky enough to bang in three goals to help England clinch a World Cup victory. 1966 and all that. It remains the only hat-trick ever scored in a World Cup Final. Sorry if it sounds as if I'm boasting, but it is a fact of which I am rather proud. And the longer the record lasts – 55 years and counting – the prouder I get.

I entered this mortal coil on Monday, 8 December 1941, and little did I know it but the world was in turmoil and shaking with fright and fear. The day before – US president Franklin D. Roosevelt called it 'a date that will live in infamy' – Japanese bombers attacked Pearl Harbor and brought the United States into a war they had been studiously avoiding. And there was little Geoffrey Charles Hurst, cuddled in his mother's arms in a hospital in Lancashire, unaware that he had come into a world that had gone barmy.

All of this was 80 years ago. Where on earth has that time gone? I wondered how I could mark this special time in my life – four score years, with the emphasis on score. It was my good friend and long-term agent Terry Baker who came up with the idea of this book, and we brought renowned author and sports historian Norman Giller in to lend his expertise to the project. He has written more than 100 books, 20 of them with my old pal Jimmy Greaves, and describes himself as 'a boring walking record book' on sport. I have talked the book to Norman and while the facts are his, the *feelings* are mine, as I speak from deep in my soul about the 80 sportsmen who have given me most pleasure and inspiration in my 80-year journey through life. Eighty at 80 has a nice ring to it, don't you think?

There are plenty of sportswomen who also merit a mention, but the publishers have a project under way to give them a special platform, so I shall just concentrate on the sportsmen who have most impressed and enchanted me during my mere 80 years on this planet.

Norman knows me better than most. He is one of the few people still around who reported my 1960 West Ham debut for the local paper, the *Stratford Express*, where he was sports editor. Back in those days I was an old-fashioned wing-half, wearing the number six shirt. It was omniscient manager Ron Greenwood who converted me to the striker role that was to bring me my fame and a little bit of a fortune, but nothing compared with what top footballers earn now. I promise I am not complaining and have never ever envied today's young footballing millionaires. I like to think I lived and played through the golden days of the game.

My writing partner Norman was also in the Wembley press box to see me enjoying FA Cup and European Cup Winners' Cup success with the Hammers in 1964 and 1965. He then completed the hat-trick – yes, another hat-trick – by being the only reporter, then on the *Daily Express*, to get into the England dressing room after the 1966 World Cup triumph before Alf Ramsey turfed him out.

Even in that moment of wild euphoria, Alf believed the dressing room should be as private as a woman's boudoir. Have you seen

Goal!, the official film of the 1966 World Cup? You will notice there are just a few snatched seconds of us celebrating in the dressing room because the cameraman came up against Alf's strict 'no outsiders' rule and he and his sound and lighting man were dispatched along with Norman. The bar had been put up by the Wembley minders after skipper Bobby Moore had complained to Alf before the match that the dressing room was like Piccadilly Circus at rush hour. Alf knew that if he let one journalist in, the place would become flooded with prying pressmen, so Norman was politely shown the door and we celebrated our victory as the close-knit team of players we had become in the build-up to the match of our lives.

Goodness knows how Alf would have coped with the demands of today's media, which takes in television, newspapers, radio, bloggers, vloggers, and every Tom, Dick and Harriott who expects at least soundbite quotes from the manager. I had a small taste of management with Telford, Chelsea and Kuwait, but wouldn't want the pressures that are on the men in charge today. I bow the knee to Gareth Southgate, who proved during the wonderfully exciting Euro 2020 finals that he was a master at not only football tactics but also handling the media. Alf would have blown a gasket at the sight of a forest of cameras, microphones and notebooks. I laugh at the thought of people going up to Alf and asking for a selfie. No, sorry, the imagination will not stretch to that.

Let me tell you the rules for this special book. I put my head together with Norman – from the same golden oldie generation as me – and came up with a list of 80 of the sportsmen who have done most to motivate me during my long lifetime. I have placed them in A to Z – Ali to Zola – order. I kicked into touch the temptation to name them in order of preference, because there is no way you can judge whether a basketball wizard like Michael Jordan is superior to a golfing great such as Jack Nicklaus.

My list consists of only the best, the crème de la créme. It is a completely personal choice and I apologise if I have left out any of your favourites. Perhaps I can put it right when we publish *90 at 90*!

I have never been blinkered about football and love watching superstars from all sporting spheres. In fact, at one time it was a toss-up as to whether I would choose cricket rather than football as my professional sport. I was a promising batsman with Essex and managed one County Championship match before I realised there was no way I could combine both sports in the style of one of my all-time great heroes, Denis Compton. He played in an era when there was a definite punctuation mark that separated the football and cricket seasons, and when I was a kid growing up dreaming of being an all-round sportsman there were plenty who earned a living from both sports. As well as Compo I can think of Bill Edrich, Arthur Milton, Phil Neale, Willie Watson, Leslie Compton, Brian Close, Graham Cross and Chris Balderstone.

I remember Jim Standen, our goalkeeper at West Ham, was an excellent bowler with Worcestershire, and the inimitable Ian Botham – one of my great 80 – was a solid centre-back with Scunthorpe.

It got to the stage when I had to choose cricket or football, and I was induced to select the winter game when the then West Ham manager, Ted Fenton, offered me terms at a princely £7 a week plus a huge £20 signing-on fee. It was football on another planet compared with now.

If I could make it 81 heroes, I would add just one: my late dad, Charlie Hurst, who I idolised when I was a kid growing up first in Ashton-under-Lyne in Lancashire and then Chelmsford, now a city in Essex but back then a small town. Dad, a proud son of the red rose county, was a have-boots-will-travel professional footballer, who played as a workmanlike centre-half for Hyde United and then Bristol Rovers, Oldham Athletic, Rochdale, Chelmsford and Sudbury Town.

Dad was one of those from a golden generation who lost their peak playing years to the war, and was among the British

Expeditionary Force rescued from Dunkirk. At the age I was helping England beat West Germany to win the World Cup, he was shooting at the Germans in a real war. He excelled as a sporting all-rounder with his regiment but was nearing 27 by the time of his demob and any chance of footballing fame with a major club had passed him by.

A cheerful, life-and-soul-of-the-party type, he could light up any room with his self-taught piano playing and used to fill my head with tales of his football playing days that lit the touchpaper to my dream of one day becoming a professional sportsman. He had a cast-iron, work-hard-for-what-you-want ethic that he passed on to me and I think there is plenty of evidence to show that I never ever shirked my workload on the football pitch. That was down to my hero, my dad.

So I have got this far without my writing partner Norman Giller bringing up the subject of THAT goal. If I had a pound for every time somebody had mentioned to me the second of my 1966 World Cup Final goals over the past 50-something years I would have enough pound notes and coins to build a castle. Even now, more than 55 years after the deed, I have people come up to me who honestly think they are the first to ask, 'Was it over the line?' I try hard to be friendly and put on a face that masks the fact that this is the millionth time I have been asked the question, but as I slip into grumpy old git territory it is becoming increasingly hard to bite my tongue. I remember an episode of *Father Ted* in which the priest sees actor Richard Wilson (Victor Meldrew in *One Foot in the Grave*) resting privately on a beach, and he goes up to him and shouts as if he has come up with an original thought, 'I don't believe it!' Well, that is how it has been for me for more than half a century.

'Was it over the line?'

Just in case you have arrived from Mars and have not heard about it, let me tell you that in the 11th minute of extra time with the score at 2-2, Alan Ball scampered past tortured left-back Karl-

Heinz Schnellinger for the umpteenth time and found me with a cross from the right. I had my back to the goal, collected the ball, swivelled and all in one movement fired a right-foot shot over the head of goalkeeper Hans Tilkowski. The ball smashed against the underside of the bar.

I could not see what happened as the ball bounced down because my view was obstructed by Tilkowski. What happened next turned it into the most hotly debated moment in World Cup history, which continues to rumble on to this day, and I am always at the centre of it.

The ball came down off the bar, on to or – as I believe – just behind the goal line and spun out. Roger Hunt, following up, instantly raised an arm to celebrate a goal as Wolfgang Weber hurriedly kicked the ball behind the goal for what he insisted was a corner.

On the line or behind it?

Referee Gottfried Dienst at first, I feared, appeared to signal no goal, but then decided to consult 'the Russian linesman' Tofik Bakhramov.

With three quick, vigorous – and for me, wise and wonderful – nods of his head and a wave of his flag towards the centre circle, Bakhramov signalled that it WAS a goal, to trigger an argument that has lasted for 55 years and to which there can never be a satisfactory answer.

Early in 2016 Sky Sports, using state-of-the-art camera techniques, declared that it was definitely a goal and that the whole of the ball had crossed the line, conveniently forgetting to mention that just a few months earlier a team of specialist engineers at Oxford University – also using 'state-of-the-art' measuring devices – had declared that the ball had NOT crossed the line. At the last count, German television had investigated the incident at least 30 times and had always come to the conclusion that the ball had hit the line and come out. These days, of course, the referee would have known instantly whether the ball had crossed the line because of the tracking device officials now wear on their wrists. Back then, it was down to eyesight alone.

According to the Laws of the Game the definition of a goal is when 'the whole of the ball passes over the goal line'.

How linesman Bakhramov managed to see it clearly enough to give a goal remains a mystery to some. His angle from level with the 18-yard line seems all wrong on television and film replays, and he was surrounded by German players screaming protests at him.

It all got nasty, to the point where he was accused of getting revenge for wartime atrocities, and it was claimed that – asked on his death bed why he gave the goal – he replied, 'Stalingrad.' It's apocryphal, of course. Stalingrad was one of the most bitter battles of the war, but Bakhramov, who fought with the Red Army on the Eastern Front, was nowhere near it.

Crazily, it reached the stage where Judith and I were reluctant to go out socially because we knew at some point a complete stranger would come up to me and ask the dreaded 'Was the ball over the line?' question.

I created the stock answer, 'What was the score before the ball hit the bar? 2-2. And afterwards 3-2. So it must have been a goal.'

All I know is that the always honest and fair Roger Hunt had the best view and he immediately and instinctively raised his arm and turned around celebrating. It definitely was a goal. Just look in the record books.

At least it has given people something to talk about for all these years, and even fairly recently German football legend Franz Beckenbauer gave social media new ammunition during an out-of-season visit to Wembley. The groundsmen were digging up part of the pitch and both goals had been taken to the Wembley workshop for general repairs. 'Ach,' said Franz, mischievously. 'I see they have removed the evidence.'

I was a guest of honour when the national stadium in Azerbaijan was renamed after Bakhramov following his passing in 1993. The

'Russian linesman' was not Russian after all! But I will always be grateful to him for nodding his head at the right time.

Credit the Germans for swallowing their disappointment and dragging their weary limbs back into the contest in a bid to come from behind again. They had to gamble everything on snatching an equaliser, and this meant pushing everybody up into the England half during the second draining period of extra time. Could they come up with a repeat of the Wolfgang Weber goal that had dragged us into the additional 30 minutes? An equaliser would have meant everybody coming back to Wembley the following Tuesday for a replay.

There was a last-minute German raid on the heavily defended England net, but they lost possession and the ball broke loose to the imperious Bobby Moore five yards from his own goal. He calmly exchanged passes with Roger Hunt as if in a training match while behind him Jack Charlton was screaming, 'Get rid of the f***ing thing. Put it in the stands.'

Bobby, blessed with ice in his veins, strode forward with the ball at his feet as I went motoring into the German half. He stroked the ball with his right foot and it arrowed 30 yards into my path. Human dynamo Alan Ball – by my reckoning, the man of the match – was running parallel with me and demanding a pass in his high-pitched Clitheroe Kid voice. But I had adopted tunnel vision and at the end of that tunnel was the German net. I had made up my mind to strike the ball with all my might in the hope it would hit the net, or at least go so far that precious seconds would be eaten up before the ball boys retrieved it.

The BBC's Kenneth Wolstenholme was keeping pace with me with his commentary as half a dozen spectators started to run past stewards on to the pitch, thinking the referee had blown the final whistle. I've heard it hundreds of times and know it off by heart.

'And here comes Hurst. He's got ... some people are on the pitch, they think it's all over.'

I let fly with a ferocious left-foot shot from 15 yards that whooshed past Tilkowski.

'It is now! It's four!'

I had completed the perfect hat-trick. Head, right foot, and now left foot. And the first – still the only – hat-trick in a World Cup Final!

It was the dream end to a dream World Cup for me. To have my West Ham club-mates Bobby and Martin in the team was the icing on the cake.

Now choking back tears as it hits me that they are no longer with us, I dedicate this book to their memory. They are, of course, among my 80 at 80.

Enjoy.

1

MUHAMMAD ALI

'He floated like a butterfly,
stung like a bee and shook up the world'

ONLY ONE person slept at Wembley on 30 July 1966, the day that changed my life. As I completed the hat-trick that won England the World Cup, my hero Muhammad Ali was fast asleep in his complimentary VIP seat at the back of the press box, oblivious to the roar of the crowd as he dozed and I danced with my team-mates in celebration of our 4-2 victory over West Germany.

The great man later explained that he was on Pacific Daylight Time and drifted off as the final went into extra time. 'I had no interest in soccer, didn't even understand it,' he later explained. 'I was just there to try to drum up publicity for my world title defence the following month against Brian London at Earls Court. It was one of my few fights that was a financial flop for the promoter but I made sure I got paid up front. Back home, soccer was a game for gals and young boys. I had no idea what a hat-trick was but when it was explained to me as being the equivalent of three home runs in baseball I was impressed by what Geoff Hurst had achieved. But it still didn't keep me awake!'

Ali was into the early days of telling the world he no longer answered to his 'slave name' of Cassius Clay. He had mixed feelings about Wembley Stadium, which was where in 1963 'Our 'Enery' Cooper knocked him down with his hammer of a left hook before he won on a cut-eye stoppage in the fifth round, just as he had predicted.

He was never burned by the flame of fame, but used it to publicise his fights, and – more important to him – his sincere but controversial religious and civil rights beliefs. I was first aware of him as an Olympic champion when I watched the 1960 Games from Rome on a small black-and-white TV set. Back then, I was just starting out on my adventure as a professional sportsman with West Ham, and my main interests were in football and cricket. I considered boxing a brutal game for mugs.

But by the mid-1960s Ali had captured the planet's interest and imagination by taking the world heavyweight title from 'big, bad' Sonny Liston. We all looked on open-mouthed as he seemed to throw away his title and promised riches by refusing to join the US Army for active service in Vietnam. 'I ain't got no quarrel with them Vietcong,' he told the media. 'Why do I want to kill my brown brothers? They ain't never called me a nigger.'

The incendiary words almost set the United States on fire and got Ali stripped of his boxing championship, and he was handed a jail sentence for insisting he would not join the armed forces.

His worldwide fame – or notoriety – transcended boxing and he became even more recognisable and famous than popes, presidents, princes and prime ministers. As he started touring the world fighting all comers after getting his prison sentence turned over in court, I joined the millions who wanted to see him in action.

There was an Ali admirers club at West Ham led by boxing fan Bobby Moore, and we used to go to Gants Hill Odeon for the midnight live screenings of his fights on the revolutionary ViewSport cable shows.

You could not help but be won over by Ali's charisma and larger-than-life personality, and we supported him through his boxing journey that took in the 'Fight of the Century' with Joe Frazier at Madison Square Garden in New York in 1971, the extraordinary 'Rumble in the Jungle' with George Foreman in Zaire, the 'Thrilla in Manila' return fight with Frazier and winning the world title for a third time with a revenge victory over Leon Spinks. My co-author Norman Giller worked as a publicist with Ali on several of his European fights and says he needed a PR like Einstein needed a calculator.

Ali had the world at his feet, but then came the darker moments when he went to the well far too many times, taking a hammering from his former sparring partner Larry Holmes and being stopped for the only time in his glorious career; then, finally, losing a heartbreaking fight against Trevor Berbick, an opponent who would not have laid a glove on him when at the peak of his powers.

Was there a sadder, more moving sight in sport than when, shaking uncontrollably with Parkinson's disease, he lit the flame to open the 1996 Olympic Games in Atlanta? He had paid a terrible price for his success in the ring, but never once complained about his fate after a career in which he won all but five of his 61 fights.

At his best, Ali was a brilliant and inventive ring craftsman: built like a black Mr Universe and perfectly proportioned, he could move as fast as a featherweight and boxed off a foundation of natural skill and talent. He would use his cutting tongue to give himself a psychological advantage over more powerful opponents, and his Ali shuffle was, for me, like seeing George Best-style footwork in the ring. Unbelievable! 'Float like a butterfly, sting like a bee,' became his anthem of aggression, and for several years he shook up the world.

As age started to catch up with him he adapted his style, and showed he could tolerate pain by adopting kamikaze rope-a-dope tactics and then unleashing two-fisted counter-attacks after his opponents had punched themselves out. I used to watch these superhuman performances and offer up a silent prayer of gratitude that I had chosen football as my sporting career.

I was supposed to have met the great man along with the rest of the England boys for a photo shoot during the build-up to the 1966 World Cup final. We all gathered at the British Boxing Board of Control gymnasium in Haverstock Hill two days before the final. Only one man was missing, Ali! He had overslept. But he was wide awake against Brian London at Earls Court the following month and knocked him out in three rounds.

From Liston to Frazier, Floyd Patterson, Ken Norton, Earnie Shavers, Larry Holmes and George Foreman, Ali operated in the golden era of heavyweights and emerged – as he continually told us – as 'The Greatest'.

There has never been a showman to touch him, and I considered it a privilege to have been around on the sports scene at the same time as the 'Louisville Lip'. He would have greatly approved of the Black Lives Matter movement of recent times and would undoubtedly have been a leading spokesperson, preaching a message that was at the very core of his life.

The world mourned the loss of a unique and universally admired personality when Ali died on 3 June 2016 aged 74. I am presenting my selection alphabetically. If it had been in one-to-80 order of greatness, he would still have been my number one choice.

MUHAMMAD ALI FOR THE RECORD:

- Born: 17 January 1942, Louisville, Kentucky
- Name at birth: Cassius Marcellus Clay
- Olympic light-heavyweight champion: Rome 1960
- Professional debut: 19 October 1970, Louisville, v. Tunney Hunsaker; won on points, six rounds
- World heavyweight champion for the first time in 20th fight, v. Sonny Liston, 25 February 1964, Miami Beach; won when Liston retired in the interval between the sixth and seventh rounds
- Changed named to Muhammad Ali: 1964
- 1967–70 forced out of boxing after refusing to join the US Army
- Loses 'Fight of the Century' on points after 15 rounds v. Joe Frazier
- World heavyweight champion for the second time in 47th fight v. George Foreman, 30 October 1974, Kinshasa, Zaire; won by knockout in eighth round
- World heavyweight champion for the third time in 59th fight, v. Leon Spinks, 15 September 1978, New Orleans; won on points, 15 rounds
- Final fight v Trevor Berbick, 11 December 1981, Nassau, Bahamas; lost on points, 10 rounds
- Total fights: 61; 56 wins (37 inside the distance), five defeats
- Died: 3 June 2016, Scottsdale, Arizona, aged 74

2

GORDON BANKS

'A goalkeeper who soared like Superman and
had hands that could catch pigeons'

A BIT morbid, I know, but I had the privilege of giving Gordon's eulogy at his funeral, which brought the streets of Stoke to a standstill in February 2019. I told the capacity congregation that he was the Superman of goalkeepers, who could actually fly and while in mid-air grab the ball as if catching pigeons. In all my 80 years I have not seen a better England goalkeeper; Gordon was even a fingertip ahead of Peter Shilton, his brilliant successor at Leicester and in the England jersey.

Gordon, a smashing bloke as well as a goalkeeping genius, was a treasured team-mate in the 1966 World Cup-winning side, and four years later I was on the pitch as witness of arguably the greatest save ever made in a World Cup game. We were playing probably the finest Brazilian team there has ever been – which means the greatest football team ever. The match took place in Guadalajara in Mexico in June 1970, and we'd been sent out in the scorching midday sun to satisfy the TV gods who virtually run international football.

I clearly remember the move starting with an astonishing pass from their skipper Carlos Alberto. He struck the ball with the outside of his right foot from just beyond his penalty area and it swerved round our left-back Terry Cooper and into the path of the sprinting Jairzinho. I knew they could perform banana free kicks, but this was a banana pass! Poor old Terry had been left for dead.

The magnificent Tostão drifted to the near post and the alert Gordon properly went with him as he sensed that Jairzinho would try to hit him with a diagonal pass. What none of us saw, including Gordon, was Pelé running beyond his marker Alan Mullery at the far post.

Jairzinho lofted a dipping centre high in the direction of Pelé and Banksie suddenly had to scamper back across his goal in a blur of action.

Pelé got above the ball and powered it low and hard towards the corner of the net. It was the perfect header. Gordon was now into a dive to his right and as the ball hit the ground just in front of the goal line he flicked it with his outstretched right hand as it came up. Somehow, he had managed to divert it up and over the bar. Alan told me later that Pelé had been shouting 'Goal' as Gordon reached the ball.

The peerless Pelé later told the press, 'It was the greatest save I have ever seen. I was convinced I had scored.'

I agreed with his assessment. I recall watching it from 30 yards away, and thinking, 'Oh well, we're a goal down.' I had to blink several times before I could believe what I was seeing. Somehow Banksie got himself from one side of the goal to the other to pull off the most amazing save I ever saw. It was the closest you will get to having a miracle happen before your eyes.

Gordon told me some years later, 'To this day, when I see an action replay of the save on the TV, I think to myself, "How on earth did I manage that?" To be honest, it looks impossible. I remember Mooro whacking me on the backside and saying in that deadpan way of his, "Next time, Banksie, for gawd's sake catch the bloody thing!'"

It was astonishing, and reminds me of Gordon saving a penalty from me in a League Cup semi-final when West Ham were playing Stoke at Upton Park. I liked to whack the ball as hard as I could from the penalty spot. No messing about trying to place it, just leather it. Against Stoke that night I hit the ball with sledgehammer power and somehow Gordon pushed it over the bar. I knew what Pelé felt like!

I am convinced that Gordon would have won many more than his 73 caps but for the car smash that robbed him of the sight in his right eye in the autumn of 1972, just a few weeks after he'd been voted Footballer of the Year. Even with only one eye he managed to get himself voted the 'Most Valuable Goalkeeper' in the United States soccer circus after he had failed to get back into league football in England because of his handicap and not being able to judge angles, such a vital part of his art.

His record with the national team was phenomenal. He let in only 57 goals in his 73 appearances, a miserly average of just 0.78 goals per game. And he kept a remarkable 35 clean sheets, and was never on the losing side for a sequence of 23 matches between 1964 and 1967, which embraced the 1966 World Cup.

What I do know for sure is that when Gordon was between the posts in international matches the defence was as safe as the Bank of England. I always felt assured when I looked back to see him patrolling in goal. I knew we were in safe hands. Pelé was always tongue-in-cheek-amused that the Banks save remained such a talking point for so many years after the match. 'I have scored more than a thousand goals in my life,' he told me, 'and the thing people always want to talk to me about here in England is the one I didn't score.'

I always wonder how far England might have gone in that 1970 World Cup had Banks been able to play at Léon in the quarter-final against West Germany. We had been so careful about what we ate and drank that we could not believe it when Gordon, of all people, went down with what we took to be Montezuma's Revenge, a tummy rot often experienced by people travelling south of the US border, especially to Mexico. Gordon had to pull out of the West Germany tie at the last minute and Peter Bonetti, woefully short of match practice, was called in. Poor Peter was like a cat on a hot tin roof and had a disastrous game. We lost 3-2 after leading 2-0. I think it was just about the worst I ever felt on a football pitch when the final whistle blew. That was a great England team and I honestly believed we were going to get into the final to defend our world title.

Gordon wondered in later years why it should have been him and no other member of the England squad who contracted a bug. We had all eaten exactly the same food. There were unproven stories that he had been nobbled with a doctored drink, but we will never ever know.

In the 1966 World Cup, Gordon played a major part in our success. He kept three clean sheets in the group stage and another against Argentina in the quarter-final when I made my World Cup debut, and he was only prevented from making it five shut-outs in a row when Eusébio thumped home a penalty for Portugal in the semi-final.

We used to call him Fernandel because he had the same comic-lugubrious look as the French comedian. He would continually have us in fits in training sessions when doing a Freddie Frinton drunk act, and he used to light up the dressing room with his droll Yorkshire humour. A lovely bloke, and the greatest of all England goalkeepers.

GORDON BANKS FOR THE RECORD:

- Born: 30 December 1937, Sheffield, Yorkshire
- Youth career clubs: Millspaugh, Rawmarsh Welfare, Chesterfield
- Professional clubs: Chesterfield (23 appearances, 1958–59); Leicester City (293, 1959–67); Stoke City (194, 1967–73); Cleveland Stokers (loan, 7, 1967), Hellenic (loan, 3, 1971); Fort Lauderdale Strikers (37, 1977–78; voted Most Valuable Goalkeeper); St Patrick's Athletic (loan, 1 game 1977)
- England under-23s: two caps 1961
- England: 73 caps 1963–72, conceded 57 goals and kept 35 clean sheets
- World Cup winner 1966, League Cup winner with Stoke 1972
- Lost sight of right eye in a 1972 car crash
- Managed Telford United 1979–80
- Died 12 February 2019, Stoke-on-Trent, aged 81

3

SIR ROGER BANNISTER

*'The modest man who broke the four-
minute mile barrier and saved lives'*

THURSDAY, 6 MAY 1954 is a date that sits happily in the memory of anybody sports-mad like me and who was around in the '50s. This was the day Roger Bannister entered the land of sporting legend by becoming the first man to run the mile in under four minutes.

These days, with the record brought down to a swift 3:43.13 by Moroccan Hicham El Guerrouj, people will probably wonder what all the fuss was about. But back then the four-minute barrier was considered unconquerable after a procession of the world's top runners had found it impossible to break.

I was 13 and at my most impressionable when Bannister broke through the barrier and I recall that with my mates at our Rainsford Secondary Modern School in Chelmsford we raced each other round the sports field in a re-enactment of the historic run on the Iffley Road cinder track at Oxford. At that time Bannister was the most celebrated sportsman in the land but did his best to avoid all the fuss and fanfare.

A scholarly man of superior intellect, he planned the record attempt like a military operation along with his old Oxford University pals Chris Chataway and Chris Brasher (the man who launched the London Marathon). To add to the fairytale story, Roger had helped lay the track when he was an undergraduate and at the time of the race was a 25-year-old medical student at St Mary's Hospital and could only spare 45 minutes a day for training.

On that momentous evening – just before 6pm and in front of BBC news cameras – Brasher led for a metronomic two laps in breezy, blustery conditions that almost caused the race to be called off. Chataway, later postmaster general in the Ted Heath government, took over as pacemaker for the next 500 yards. The gangling Bannister then spurted into the lead, battling against the clock as he raced for the finishing line. He collapsed exhausted as he burst through the tape and revived to hear his close friend, the *Guinness Book of Records* founder Norris McWhirter, teasingly announce over the public address, 'A track record, English native record, British national, British all comers, European, British Empire and world record; the time: three [the rest drowned out by cheering] minutes, 59.4 seconds.'

It brought the nation to its feet, all of us dancing with delight and disbelief. Roger Bannister had beaten the impossible barrier and had completed the magic four-minute mile. More than 67 years on, the memory still raises the hairs on the back of my neck.

In later years I met Sir Roger several times at various sporting dinners and functions and found him a shy, 'terribly English' and extremely modest man who wanted to deflect all talk about himself to the achievements of others. My writing partner Norman collaborated with him on a book called *The Golden Milers*, and said that as he got older Roger grew more and more annoyed with himself that he had committed so much of his university time to athletics.

He was totally obsessed with medical matters and was berating himself for getting caught up in what some would consider the trivial pursuit of sport. But all I know is that this 13-year-old schoolboy along with the entire nation was pumped with pride over his historic performance on the cinders of Oxford, a track that ran clockwise until Roger demanded they change it to an orthodox circuit during its refurbishment in 1949.

It was in 1954 that the BBC introduced its Sports Personality of the Year award and you would have thought that Bannister was a shoo-in after going on to beat Aussie ace John Landy in the 'Mile of the Century' in the 1954 Empire Games in Vancouver and then winding up his career by taking the European 1500m title in Berne, Switzerland.

But the award went to his good companion Chris Chataway after he had captured the public imagination by beating Russian iron man of the track, Vladimir Kuts, in a floodlit race at London's White City while also breaking the world 5000m record. It was Chataway who, the month after the first sub-four-minute mile, paced John Landy to a new world record in Finland, the second time the barrier had been beaten. But even so, it was a nonsense that Bannister was beaten to the inaugural award in the postcard-vote count.

But the rather aloof Bannister could not have cared less. All he was interested in was his medical research and trying to make the world a healthier, safer place. Awards and public acclaim were way down on his list of priorities.

Born in Harrow to a Lancastrian dad (so we had that in common), Roger was disappointed to 'only' finish fourth in the 1952 Olympic 1500m final in Helsinki. He had made up his mind to hang up his spikes after the Games but then set his sights on the 'impossible' four-minute mile. He filled out a newspaper questionnaire before competing in Helsinki, and listed his role models as Louis Pasteur and Marie Curie. Not your usual sports competitor.

During his delayed national service, he volunteered to go out to Aden, using his physiological experience to investigate deaths among young soldiers. He found that they were susceptible to potentially fatal infections if they were put through strenuous exercise before they had acclimatised. To prove this hypothesis he conducted research at the London School of Hygiene and Tropical Medicine, and published the outcome in two *Lancet* papers. All this while carrying out his Army duties.

He recovered from a near-fatal car crash in 1974 to become one of the world's leading neurologists. In 1975 he was knighted, and ten years later he returned to Oxford as master of Pembroke College, where he served until his retirement in 1993. How fitting that the Iffley Road track on which he broke the four-minute mile barrier is named after him.

In 2014 he revealed that he was suffering from Parkinson's disease, one of the brain-related illnesses he had done so much to try to conquer. He died four years later, survived by Moyra, his renowned artist wife of 60 years, two sons, two daughters and 14 grandchildren. A full life.

The world will always remember him for those three minutes and 59.4 seconds.

SIR ROGER BANNISTER FOR THE RECORD:
- Born: 23 March 1929, Harrow, Middlesex
- 1950 European Championships, Brussels: bronze medal, 800m bronze
- 1952 Olympic Games, Helsinki: fourth, 1500m
- First man to break four minutes for a mile: Oxford, 6 May 1954
- 1954 Empire Games, Vancouver: gold medal, one mile
- 1954 European Championships, Berne: gold medal, 1500m
- Died: 3 March 2018, Oxford, aged 88

4

FRANZ BECKENBAUER

'Der Kaiser ruled the football pitch with what
was almost regal splendour'

FRANZ BECKENBAUER – known throughout the world
of football as Der Kaiser – was on the pitch facing me in the
highest and lowest moments of my playing career. In the 1966
World Cup Final he was the fresh face of the future of German
football, a hugely skilled, dynamic young player who could dictate
a match from his midfield position. Fortunately for us, but not
the spectators, he and our world-class schemer Bobby Charlton
cancelled each other out with meticulous man-to-man marking. I
was the one who benefited most from them stifling each other and
came away with a hat-trick (have I mentioned that before?) and a
World Cup winners' medal.

Fast forward four years and there was Beckenbauer wearing a
winning smile as he helped dismantle us after we had taken what
seemed a conclusive 2-0 lead in our World Cup quarter-final in
the high altitude of Léon in Mexico.

It was Franz who brought West Germany back into the match
with a spectacular goal in the 69th minute. This was when Alf

Ramsey made one of his rare blunders and took Bobby Charlton off to save him for the semi-final. It was unheard of for Alf to take things for granted.

'We could not believe it when we saw Ramsey call Charlton off the pitch for Colin Bell,' Franz told me some time later. 'It gave us all a sudden flood of confidence. We now felt a foot taller and believed we could go on to win. Bobby was very big in the German psyche.'

In fairness to Alf, I should point out that in his long career as player and manager he had never experienced the substitute rule, and when it was introduced in time for the 1970 World Cup finals it was foreign and unfamiliar to him. That day in Mexico, I'm afraid he got it hopelessly wrong.

It's sad history that the under-prepared Peter 'The Cat' Bonetti had kittens every time the Germans attacked, and from almost strolling to what we thought would be victory we were suddenly on the back foot, with the flying substitute Jürgen Grabowski running our overworked left-back Terry Cooper to exhaustion. Clearly, it was the out-on-his-feet Terry who needed to be taken off but Alf compounded his error by withdrawing Martin Peters and replacing him out on the right with the notoriously left-footed Norman Hunter.

West Germany made us pay for Alf's misguided substitutions and went through to the semi-finals for an unforgettable match with Italy that they lost 4-3, with Beckenbauer bravely playing through much of the second half with a dislocated shoulder. He was not only a class act but courageous with it.

His most memorable moments were still to come. He took over as team captain for what were some of West Germany's most glorious conquests, lifting the European Championship in 1972 and then, the peak of football's Everest, capturing the World Cup in 1974 with a memorable victory over Johan Cruyff's Netherlands in Munich.

Franz turned the sweeper role into a work of art, and was expert at switching defence to attack with deliciously placed passes and clever changes of pace and direction. A complete master of the Beautiful Game.

European Footballer of the Year twice, he remains the only 'defender' to win the prestigious Ballon d'Or on two occasions. Franz is one of three men (with Mário Zagallo and Didier Deschamps) to have won the World Cup as player and as manager, and he is the first man and one of only two (with Didier Deschamps) to have won the title as team captain as well as manager. That's some record!

At the back end of his trophy-laden playing career, he had two periods with New York Cosmos, teaming up with Pelé in the North American Soccer League. He held his Germany passing-out parade with Hamburger SV, where he collected yet another Bundesliga title, making five in all. It was inevitable that at the end of his playing days he would turn to coaching and management, and – naturally – this born leader was successful. He steered West Germany through the 1990 World Cup in Italy, where they beat Argentina 1-0 in the last final before Germany's reunification.

Beckenbauer then briefly managed Marseille before returning to take charge of the Bayern Munich team for which he had been such an influential player, later becoming the powerful club president.

In 1998 he climbed even higher, taking on the role of vice-president of the German Football Association and heading the successful bid by Germany to host the 2006 World Cup finals.

I know Franz professionally and socially and have always found him likeable, suave and sophisticated. Judith and I have been out partying with him and one of his three wives! But he has too often got involved in the politics of football and has had a long-running feud with the barons who boss the game. They have often tried to bring him to heel and he has been enmeshed in controversies over alleged bribery and corruption.

But let's judge him purely as a footballer, and I believe there have been few finer all-round players in the history of the game. He continually played with an intelligence and style that bordered on arrogance, and seemed to have complete control of what was going on around him.

He has always been quite the philosopher, and he captured exactly what I think about our great game of football with this quote that he can, of course, deliver in several languages: 'Football is one of the world's best means of communication. It is impartial, apolitical and universal. Football unites people around the world every day. Young or old, players or fans, rich or poor, the game makes everyone equal, stirs the imagination, makes people happy and makes them sad. It brings everybody together, and sometimes tears them apart. But in the final analysis it truly is the Beautiful Game.'

I was last with Beckenbauer in Barcelona in 1999 for a warming and emotional date when he and I jointly announced that the late, great Bobby Moore was being installed into the FIFA Hall of Fame. Also there to receive the FIFA memorial trophy on behalf of Bobby was his widow Stephanie. Franz told the audience: 'Bobby was not only an exceptional player but a wonderful sportsman who I was proud to call a friend. We played many times against each other and also as team-mates in the United States, and I was always in awe of his talent and his composure. His name deserves to be emblazoned in the FIFA Hall of Fame.'

Sadly, Beckenbauer's health has not been so good in recent years and he has twice had cardiac surgery and, like so many of my old colleagues and opponents, has had to have an artificial hip inserted. I am also a member of that club. It's the price we old-timers pay for all that running around in the springtime of our lives.

Franz, certainly a man of substance, epitomised the professional way Germany always approach their football and had a winning mentality that motivated the players around him.

I'm just glad Der Kaiser did not spoil England's party in 1966.

FRANZ BECKENBAUER FOR THE RECORD:

- Born 11 September 1945, Munich, Germany
- Youth career: SC Munchen (1951–59); Bayern Munich (1959–64)
- Professional clubs:
- Bayern Munich (427 appearances, 60 goals, 1964–77)
  - Bundesliga: 1969, 1972, 1973, 1974
  - European Cup: 1974, 1975, 1976
  - European Cup Winners' Cup: 1967
  - Intercontinental Cup: 1976
- New York Cosmos (80 appearances, 17 goals, 1977–80; 15 appearances, 2 goals, 1983)
  - North American Soccer League: 1977, 1978, 1980
- Hamburger SV (28 games, 1980–82)
- Bundesliga: 1982
- Total games: 560 (79 goals)
- West Germany: 103 caps (14 goals)
- World Cup: 1974
- UEFA European Championship: 1972
- Teams managed:
  - West Germany (1984–90)
    World Cup: 1990
  - Marseille (1990–91)
    Ligue 1: 1991
  - Bayern Munich (1996)
    Bundesliga: 1994
    UEFA Cup: 1996
- Ballon d'Or: 1972, 1976
- German Footballer of the Year: 1966, 1968, 1974, 1976

5

GEORGE BEST

*'What a pity George was not born ugly. He
chased the girls as much as defenders'*

WITHOUT A shadow of a doubt, George Best was one of the
greatest British footballers of my lifetime; of any lifetime in fact.
To paraphrase what Joe Mercer said about Stan Bowles and betting
shops, 'If only George could have passed a pretty girl like he passed
the ball.' If just half the stories we used to hear about George and
his, uh, flirting and philandering were true it was a miracle that
he could so often be magical with a ball at his feet. At his peak, he
was one of the great untouchables. How his managers and team-
mates must have wished he had been born ugly!

If I had to pick anybody in the game who was a complete
contrast to my goody-two-shoes lifestyle it would have to be George.
Sorry to sound precious, but the way he burned the candle at both
ends and also, it seems, in the middle was completely foreign to me.
For six or so years from when he first burst on the scene at the age
of 17 in 1963 he was one of the world's great footballing talents,
but his 'boozing and birding' gradually caught up with him and it
was heartbreaking to see him finish up a wreck of a man.

There has not been a more dynamic trio in club football than Best, Denis Law and Bobby Charlton in full flow for Manchester United. I played against this Holy Trinity of the game for several years and often felt like applauding their artistry and ability on and off the ball. I have good memories of the first time I played against the three of them. It was in the 1964 FA Cup semi-final at Hillsborough on a mud heap of a pitch. We won 3-1 against all the odds, with Ron 'Ticker' Boyce scoring twice for the Hammers and me banging in the third goal (from a pass by Bobby Moore; sound familiar?).

But West Ham were usually second best to them, and in particular in 1967 in a First Division match at Upton Park. United needed a victory to clinch the championship and Best, Law and Charlton ran riot. They were 4-0 up inside the first 20 minutes and finally finished 6-1 winners and champions with a performance that left us shell-shocked. I seem to recall that our young stand-in goalkeeper Colin Mackleworth's third appearance was his final one for us after what can only be described as a nightmare game against a Manchester United side at full throttle.

George looked a genius that day, and during the season he picked up the nickname of the 'Fifth Beatle' and started getting into the headlines as much for his behaviour off the pitch as his performances on it.

He possessed dribbling skills which, in the words of his team-mate Pat Crerand, could leave opposing defenders with 'twisted blood', and he had a gymnast's balance which enabled him to ride or avoid the most ruthless tackles. This was in an era, remember, when it was common for defenders to threaten to break his leg if he continued taking the mickey out of them with his bewildering ball control and insatiable appetite for nutmegging opponents.

Bobby Charlton once confided, 'He is an absolute genius of a dribbler but can be infuriating to play with. While team-mates are getting into positions to receive a pass, George hangs on while he gets even with markers trying to kick him by holding on to the ball and humiliating them. A great individualist but sometimes not a team player.'

Best's goalscoring record was phenomenal for a winger. He was lightning quick, brave as a lion, and a sublime passer of the ball when he could curb his natural inclination to hold on to it for as long as possible. At his best, he gave the impression that he was on another planet compared with us mere mortals. But he could have achieved so much more with a less cavalier approach to life.

George was a charming man to talk to and oozed warm Irish wit and friendliness, but I used to wince when I saw the company he kept and the newspapers were continually featuring him in photographs with beautiful girls on his arm. They often finished up in his bed. My long-term agent Terry Baker used to feature George in his theatre roadshows in the company of the one and only Jimmy Greaves, who could tell mind-blowing tales privately about George's antics.

Jimmy managed to beat the bottle after his well-publicised battle with alcoholism, but George said he had no intention of stopping drinking 'because it gives me even more pleasure than sex'. How could you argue with that sort of logic?

There is one Bestie story Terry tells me that I can share: George was in Leeds with Greavsie for a theatre show and, says Terry, not for the first time, he failed to turn up. But for once, he had what he reasoned was a good excuse. He and Jimmy had stopped to eat in a pizza restaurant and spotted the former Leeds player Albert Johanneson walking past. George did not know the black, South African-born man that well – but he knew he was an alcoholic and lonely. Bestie called him in, bought him a pizza and they left Jimmy behind and got 'on the sauce', with Johanneson staggering home about midnight with George in tow. 'I know I shouldn't have done it,' Best told Terry, 'but I thought Albert needed a night out. I brought a little light back into his life. No regrets.' Jimmy and Terry did the show minus George. This is an anecdote that in an off-beat way shows the caring side of Best, who was always looking to do favours for hard-up people down on their luck.

My favourite George Best tale, one he often told at the celebrity dinners I used to attend with him, was of the night he won £20,000 in cash at a Manchester casino. He just happened to have the current Miss World as his companion bringing him luck. It was 1973, when he was making headlines over a bust-up with Manchester United.

They returned to their plush hotel and George slipped the night porter – like him, from Belfast – a £20 note as a tip for bringing up a bottle of iced champagne.

When the small, elderly porter brought the champers to their room he found Miss World draped on George's bed in a negligé, and the £20,000 scattered loose on the bed cover.

The porter put the champagne in its ice bucket on the table at the side of the bed, and as he was backing out of the door summoned up the courage to say, 'I hope you don't mind me asking, Mr Best, but where did it all go wrong?'

When I asked George if it was a true story, he gave his rascal's smile and said, 'Of course not. It was the previous year's Miss World.'

There are hundreds of similarly bizarre and unbelievable stories about George, but he insisted he was enjoying his life and he left the worrying to the rest of us.

He was an outstanding talent in the United side that won the European Cup in 1968, the season he won the Ballon d'Or and was named Football Writers' Association Footballer of the Year.

People seem to think he had a short career, but he made a total of 466 appearances for United, scoring 178 goals, before becoming a have-boots-will-travel nomad who saw action in Los Angeles, Cork, San José, Fort Lauderdale, Edinburgh with Hibs, Hong Kong, Stockport, Brisbane and Bournemouth, and he teamed up with Rodney Marsh for a wonderfully entertaining interlude with Fulham. In all he played 588 club matches and scored 207 goals.

It was football's loss that he did not make it on to the World Cup stage with Northern Ireland. He deserved to be on the same platform and pedestal as the Pelés, the Maradonas and the Cruyffs so that people could see that he was in their class and fit to be compared with any of them as a master of the Beautiful Game.

Back in the 1990s, George and I went to a London sculptor's studio together to have our feet set in plaster moulds for a boot company promotion about famous footballing feet. A footnote: I wore a size eight and a half boot, George half a size smaller. It was Judith who said I was always too big for my boots.

Shortly after his premature death, an old pair of George's boots found in an attic sold for £3,000 and were later exhibited at the National Football Museum in Manchester.. George once told me he earned more from boot sponsorship than he did in wages for playing the game. He was happy to go along with the quote attributed to him: 'I spent much of my money on birds, booze and fast cars. The rest I squandered.'

In his later years, before succumbing to alcoholism at the age of 59, George said that he hoped he would be remembered not for his drinking or the women he had dated, but for his football. One of his favourite quotes was, 'Pelé called me the greatest footballer in the world. That is the ultimate salute to my life.'

Best was simply the best.

GEORGE BEST FOR THE RECORD:

- Born: 22 May 1946, Belfast
- Manchester United (466 appearances, 178 goals)
  - First Division: 1965, 1967
  - European Cup: 1968
  - Ballon d'Or: 1968
  - FWA Footballer of the Year: 1968
- Other clubs, from 1974 to 1984:
  - Jewish Guild (5 games, 1 goal)
  - Stockport County (3/2)
  - Cork Celtic (3/0)
  - LA Aztecs (55/27 over two spells)
  - Fulham (42/8)
  - Fort Lauderdale Strikers (28/6)
  - Hibernian (17/3)
  - San José Earthquakes (56/21)
  - Sea Bee (2/0)
  - Hong Kong Rangers (1/0)
  - Bournemouth (5/0)
  - Brisbane Lions (4/0)
  - Osborne Park (1/1)
  - Dee Why (1/1)
  - Nuneaton Borough (3/1)
  - Tobermore United (1/0)
- Northern Ireland: 37 caps, 9 goals
- Died: 5 November 2005, London, aged 59

6

SERGE BLANCO

'The smoking gun of rugby who brought flair
and fire to the French try machine'

YOU COULD write what I know about rugby on the back of a
postage stamp, but French full-back Serge Blanco transcended his
sport and was a magician who attracted attention even if you did not
know a flanker from a flunkie. He would have to be in anybody's
top list of sportsmen for the spirit and style in which he played the
game. His fleet-footed performances used to be spotlighted on
television and it was easy to see why he was known as rugby's Pelé.

He played when the sport was for amateurs only, and people who
know these things tell me he would today be valued in millions of
euros as rugby union franchises become huge business, particularly
in France where the 15-a-side game has a massive following.

While he was mostly famous for playing at full-back for Biarritz
Olympique and the French national side, Serge used to often switch
to the wing, where he mixed subtlety, speed and power to score
spectacular tries that earned him legendary status in rugby circles.
He won 81 of his then world-record 93 international caps in the
number 15 shirt, and the other 14 as a wing.

I was surprised to find that a player idolised by the French public was in fact born in South America. The son of a Venezuelan father and a Basque mother, he moved to south-west France from Caracas in 1960 after his dad died of a heart attack. While learning the rugby arts in his adopted home city of Biarritz, Serge trained as an engineer with the aerospace giants Dassault and played his first matches with St Jean de Luz, then a top-division club. He eventually joined Biarritz Olympique, where he is still regaled and revered as a national treasure.

Something that set Serge aside from most sportsmen apart from his natural talent is that throughout his career he was a chain smoker, going through an average of 40 cigarettes a day! We had several smokers in our 1966 World Cup squad, notably Bobby Charlton and Jimmy Greaves, but the only footballer I knew who could have matched Blanco's habit was Dutch master Johan Cruyff, who was infamous for puffing in the dressing room at half-time.

But it was Blanco's smoking runs through opposition defences that brought him his reputation as one of the great rugby try scorers, and he was voted France's top player for four consecutive seasons.

He was continually the star man in the French Grand Slam victories of 1981 and 1987 and was prominent in four further title triumphs. More than anybody he represented the flair and joy of the great French sides that captured the interest and admiration of even non-rugby people like me.

I have deliberately downplayed my knowledge of rugby because any expert could pull me apart, but since moving with Judith to Cheltenham I have taken more than a passing interest in the exploits of our outstanding local club Gloucester, and am no stranger to the club's famous 1873 lounge. I kept a close watch on Ben Cohen – nephew of my England team-mate, George – when he was playing in the 2003 Rugby World Cup Final. What a family double when he joined George as a World Cup winner. I know that Jimmy Greaves, even while fighting his health crisis, is an avid rugby fan and never misses an England or British and Irish Lions match on television.

One of my most fascinating days in recent years was when Mike Atherton got me together with rugby great Will Greenwood to discuss our various World Cup final experiences for a Sky Sports special.

Will and I discovered we had loads in common through our World Cup adventures, even though they were two decades apart. We found that the common denominator between the football winners of 1966 and the rugby champions of 2003 is that each England squad had a club-type spirit. This all came from the organisational work and discipline of the two managers, Alf Ramsey and Clive Woodward, both of whom were rightly knighted for their services to sport. Each understandably wanted things done their way, with everybody pulling in the same direction. There was no room for prima donnas and all the players in each squad were given equal treatment.

The shape of the balls may have been different, but the aims and the preparation were the same. In fact, Sir Clive was so sure that management was the same across all fields that he later had a spell as director of Football at Southampton.

Will astonished me by confessing that he considered feigning an injury to get him out of England's rugby final. 'I felt utter terror during the build-up to the match,' he told me. 'It took me ten years to admit to anyone that on the Wednesday or the Thursday before the final, I genuinely contemplated pulling my calf. I didn't want to be the skinny bloke that let the lads down.'

It was an amazing admission, but it underlines the mental pressure on sportspeople before major events when they are assailed by self doubts. I was a born competitor, greedy for action, but I knew many team-mates who used to be eaten up with nerves and losses of confidence. So much of all sport is in the mind and it is only in recent years that clubs have started to pay proper attention to the psychological side of the game.

Will and I both agreed on the importance of strong captaincy. He said that he continued to worship the hugely impressive Martin Johnson, calling him 'my God and the man I still turn to for advice and guidance'.

I had similar feelings about Bobby Moore, but I will wait for his entry before paying my dues.

There's a happy ending to the Serge Blanco story. Following his retirement, Blanco became a fabulously wealthy hotelier and sportswear manufacturer before taking up a position as the head of the governing body of French club rugby and also president of his beloved Biarritz club.

And he still has plenty of puff.

SERGE BLANCO FOR THE RECORD:

- Born: 31 August 1958, Caracas, Venezuela
- Position: full-back and wing
- Major teams: France 'A', World XV, France, Biarritz Olympique
- Test career span: 1980–1991
- Test caps: 93 (including 42 in Five Nations, 9 in Rugby World Cup)
- Grand Slams: 1981, 1987
- Five Nations: 1983, 1986, 1988, 1989
- Test record: won 54, lost 36, drew 3
- Captain of France: 17 times
- Test tries: 38

7

USAIN BOLT

'The fastest man on the planet would have
loved my football World Cup medal!'

BACK IN my professional playing days I fancied myself as being able to get up quite a gallop. I've worked it out that in a 100m race with a peak-power Usain Bolt – 'the fastest man on the planet' – I would have finished 20 metres in his wake. And I was considered one of the faster strikers.

He was a phenomenon, blitzing all the sprint records and winning enough gold medals to set up his own Fort Knox. Yet I know for sure that he would have swapped much of what he won for my achievement in helping win the football World Cup.

When he was a kid growing up in Jamaica's rural parish of Trelawny he had the same two dreams that motivated me when I was in short trousers – to be an all-round star in football and cricket. He was a quick bowler in the mould of his idol Courtney Walsh and an enthusiastic centre-forward for his school football team. His ambition was to play for Manchester United or Real Madrid. Usain only had lofty dreams. But coaches recognising his natural speed on the cricket and football pitches persuaded him to concentrate on athletics, and the rest is very rapid history.

The son of parents who ran a grocery store, he first made headlines in the 2002 World Junior Championships staged in Jamaica's National Stadium in Kingston. At just 15 years old he became the youngest male world junior champion in any event when winning the 200m. His career was off and running.

There was a theory that very tall sprinters are disadvantaged when going down into their starting blocks, but the 6ft 5in (1.96m) Bolt very quickly disproved this by leaving opponents trailing at the sound of the gun.

At 17 he became the youngest sprinter to break the 20-seconds barrier for the 200m and was installed as a favourite for the Athens Olympics in 2004, but a hamstring injury prevented him from making the expected impact. Four years later he was unbeatable in the Beijing Games when he became the first man since American speedster Carl Lewis in 1984 to win gold medals in the 100m, 200m and 4x100m relay. He, with his team in the relay, set world records (9.69s, 19.30s, and 37.10s respectively) in all three events, but many years later had to surrender his relay gold when one of his team-mates failed a drugs test.

Bolt shattered the 100m record at the 2009 World Championships, winning in a blistering 9.58s. Defending the title two years later he was controversially disqualified for a false start. Bolt recovered to capture golds in the 200m and the 4x100m relay, helping to set a new world record in the team run.

This all whetted our appetite for his appearance in the 2012 London Olympics in the stadium where West Ham now play their football. He did not disappoint, successfully defending his titles in the 100m and 200m, and becoming the first person to win both races in consecutive Olympiads. He won a huge following outside the world of athletics with his, at times, eccentric showboating and his trademark 'Lightning Bolt' celebration. I am always concerned about the element of drug taking in modern athletics, but Usain always seemed 'clean' and won his races on his amazing natural ability.

In 2013 he collared his customary three gold medals at the World Championships and two years later he again won gold medals in his three signature events.

Bolt confirmed his status as the best sprinter in history at the 2016 Rio Olympics, capturing golds in the 100m, 200m and 4x100m relay, so becoming the first athlete to win titles in the two individual sprints in three straight Olympics. He hung up his spikes after the 2017 World Championships, at which he won a bronze medal in the 100m and finished in eighth place as a member of the 4x100m relay team after injuring a hamstring in the final.

For all his success on the track, the great man was still not fulfilled. He had that dream nagging him from his childhood of becoming a professional footballer. Bolt trained with Norwegian team Strømsgodset and German Bundesliga side Borussia Dortmund, and then turned down an offer to play for Maltese club Valletta in favour of trying his luck in Australia.

There is, of course, a lot more to football than running the legs off defenders. You need to have positional sense, ball control, physical strength, stamina and the ability to ride tackles. Usain could out-sprint any opponent but his technique and passing ability were questionable during a trial run out with the Central Coast Mariners in New South Wales, and eventually the eight-time Olympic champion, by then a creaking 32, had to concede that he was not going to realise his dream of becoming a professional footballer.

Bolt's stride length was an extraordinary 2.47m and when he set the world record for 100m at 9.58s in Berlin in 2009, he covered the distance in just 41 steps. This stat made me smile because I remembered how my dad had always taught me to move with short strides, as he said it was easier to adjust your feet to receive a pass. Perhaps that's why Usain failed as a footballer, and I was not an Olympic champion!

There is unlikely to be an athlete to touch him as a sprinter, and like Muhammad Ali, his fame transcended sport because he had a strong, jovial personality to go with his sensational speed. But he never won a football World Cup medal!

USAIN BOLT FOR THE RECORD:
- Born: 21 August 1986, Sherwood Content, Jamaica
- World Championship gold medals: 11
- Olympic Games gold medals: 8
- World records:
  - 100m (9.58s)
  - 200m (19.19s)
- 'Triple triple' Olympic gold medals in the 2008, 2012 and 2016 Games (a 2008 sprint relay gold medal was taken away after one of his team-mates tested positive in a drugs test)
- Individual awards include:
  - IAAF World Athlete of the Year: 2008, 2009, 2011, 2012, 2013, 2016
  - Track & Field Athlete of the Year: 2008, 2009
  - Laureus Sportsman of the Year: 2009, 2010, 2013, 2017
  - Jamaican Sportsman of the Year: 2008, 2009, 2011, 2012, 2013
  - *L'Equipe* Champion of Champions: 2008, 2009, 2012, 2015
- BBC Overseas Sports Personality of the Year: 2008, 2009, 2012

8

BJÖRN BORG

'The "IceBorg" who only melts when he watches
Charlton Athletic play!'

IN ALL my years being involved in professional sport, whether
playing, managing, coaching or just looking on from the sidelines,
I have never seen a cooler, more laid-back champion than tennis
legend Björn Borg. Back in the 1970s and going into the '80s, he
had a spell when he seemed just about unbeatable

He did not seem to know the meaning of nerves or pressure
as he became the first man since the Edwardian era to win the
Wimbledon singles crown five successive times, from 1976 to
1980. On top of that he captured the French Open title for a then
unprecedented four years in a row and six times in all.

His ice-cold demeanour on court earned him the nickname
'IceBorg' and contrasted hugely with that of a young upstart
from New York who loudly started to make a name for himself
– of course, John McEnroe. We spectators looked on entranced
as these two titans of tennis clashed in a series of duels that
captured the world's attention, even if you were not a fan of
the sport.

They met 14 times, ending with an irritatingly inconclusive 7-7 record. Their duels were so compelling that more than a quarter of a century later Hollywood made a gripping movie based on their rivalry, *Borg vs McEnroe*. The fourth set of the 1980 Wimbledon final is at the heart of the film. I've rarely seen sporting combat like it.

They slogged to a tie break, with the poker-faced Borg trying all he knew to land the championship point against the stubborn, brash McEnroe who shared every emotion with the crowd, while the Swede hid whatever was going on in his calculating mind. McEnroe saved five match points before finally winning a sensational set 18-16. The drama continued in the deciding set, the controlled Borg retaining his title with an 8-6 victory. Then, and only then, did he let his mask slip as he memorably dropped to his knees, overwhelmed by what he had achieved. He was human after all.

Nobody could read Borg's intentions and the sports world was stunned when suddenly he quit tennis right at the peak of his career, aged just 26. Years later, he reappeared on the veterans' circuit, but we all wondered what he might have gone on to achieve if he had continued to play through the 1980s.

Borg and McEnroe shared one thing off the court. Both were lovers of my game, football. Björn was never shy of shocking people and it came as a surprise to learn that he was a massive fan of Charlton Athletic. It became general knowledge when an interviewer at one of his comeback tournaments asked him if it was true the he supported Charlton. Many in the audience thought this meant either Bobby or Jackie Charlton, or even Heston.

'It is very true,' Björn replied. 'My love for Charlton Athletic goes way back, with my father's father. Granddad was a massive fan of Charlton and used to go to England as many times as possible to watch them play. He passed this love on to my father, who became equally fanatical, and our house was stacked with club memorabilia and red flags. Then I became the third generation of

Charlton supporters carrying on the Borg tradition. Come on you Addicks! I have often been to The Valley to see them play, and no matter where I am in the world I check on their results and am always with them in spirit. I have a collection of Charlton shirts that I often wear.'

I can truthfully say that is one of the more surprising anecdotes in this book.

Björn Borg getting excited!

BJÖRN BORG FOR THE RECORD:

- Born: 6 June 1956, Stockholm, Sweden
- Prize money: $3,655,751
- Grand Slam victories: 11
  - French Open 1974, 1975, 1978, 1979, 1980, 1981
  - Wimbledon: 1976, 1977, 1978, 1979, 1980
- Davis Cup with Sweden: 1975
- BBC Overseas Sports Personality of the Year: 1979
- Voted Sweden's greatest ever sportsman: 2015
- Won 77 singles titles during his career and four doubles
- Ranked No 1 in the world for 109 weeks between 1977 and 1981

9

IAN BOTHAM

*'The larger-than-life cricketer who
now Lords it over us all '*

IAN BOTHAM was the sort of swashbuckling, flamboyant
all-round cricketer and character we would all liked to have
been, winning matches with bat and ball and taking brilliant
slip catches with a mixture of audacity and bravery. Real *Boys'
Own* stuff; a hero of heroes. He was one of the last to manage to
straddle the seasons and play cricket and football professionally,
and while he was a genius at the white flannelled game I think
he would admit to having been only an average defender with
Scunthorpe United.

Nobody who was around in 1981 will ever forget the match of
Ian's life when he turned the Headingley Ashes Test on its head to
snatch an unlikely victory against the Aussies. I was between jobs
at the time and needed cheering up after getting the boot from
Chelsea and before trying my luck out in Kuwait, in between
learning new skills as an insurance man. Yes, it was a strange period
for me, and those Botham performances during that Ashes series
helped take my mind off the turmoil in my life.

Ian was born in Heswall, Cheshire, in 1955 – the year before I joined the West Ham ground staff – and later moved to Somerset, where he made his name alongside the Master Blaster Vivian Richards. His footballing career with Yeovil and then Scunthorpe was brief because England needed him for their overseas tours outside the League season.

In a glorious international career he took 383 wickets at an average of 28.40 and scored 5,200 runs at 33.54. These figures on paper do not tell the story of how Botham frequently made a vital impact on the pitch. He didn't just decorate games; he decided them. Both possessed prodigious power and could bludgeon the ball out of the ground, but he also had good technique when required. His swing bowling was often effective, deceiving a procession of batsmen with his ability to move the ball either way.

Both – also known as 'Beefy', and 'Guy the Gorilla' because of his huge frame – was a larger-than-life character who made as many headlines off as on the pitch. He was short on patience and once deliberately ran out the cautious Geoff Boycott for scoring too slowly in New Zealand. Several of the stories that hit the front pages involved alleged extra-marital affairs, but he remains married to the long-suffering Kathy. One of his autobiographies was called *Don't Tell Kath*. I don't think I'd be here to tell the story if I had treated my lovely Judith in the same way!

That 1981 series made him a household name. He resigned the captaincy after the first two disappointing games, including getting a pair in the second Test at Lord's. For the third Test at Headingley, the cricketing intellectual Mike Brearley was made captain. Australia scored a whopping 401-9, and England replied with a 174 whimper. Botham top scored on 50 not out. England's frontline batsmen again flopped in the follow-on and on the Saturday evening bookmakers were offering 500/1 for England to win. It is claimed that several Aussie players took the odds.

On the Sunday, Botham came to the crease when England were 105-5 before England then lost Boycott and Bob Taylor, leaving them tottering on 135-7. Defeat looked inevitable. But, with Graham Dilley and then Chris Old joining Both, we were treated to one of the all-time great innings. Knocking the ball all round the Headingley ground, Botham scorched to 149 not out. Still, England's lead was just 129, but then Bob Willis took over and with 8/43 bowled the Australians out for 111. Ian has always insisted that Bob deserved a share of the man-of-the-match honours.

In the next Test, England won by 29 runs – helped by a mesmerising spell of bowling from Botham, who took five wickets for one run. With a sublime 118 he was again outstanding in the fifth Test as England claimed the Ashes.

Naturally, he was named the man of the series, scoring 399 runs and taking 34 wickets.

After a fall-out with Somerset, he wound up his county cricket career with Worcestershire and then Durham, the closest club to his North Yorkshire estate where he follows his pursuits of hunting, fishing and shooting on his exclusive grouse moor. Never afraid of a battle, Botham has had a long and bitter dispute with the Royal Society for the Protection of Birds, and he lost a high-profile libel case against former cricketer and now Pakistan president Imran Khan who had accused him of ball tampering.

Superman Botham was not content with setting records with the bat and ball. He then took to the road to put action where his mouth was, walking hundreds of miles to raise millions for children's charities. He quite rightly joined me as a knight in 2014, and then after a long career as a Sky Sports commentator and pundit he was elevated to the House of Lords (Baron Botham of Ravensworth), with all his past demeanours clearly forgiven and forgotten.

In the summer of 2021, Lord Botham was appointed the UK's Trade Envoy to Australia. We all had a good chuckle at the thought of Beefy negotiating with his Aussie nemesis Ian Chappell, his huge rival on and off the pitch in his playing days.

He really had something to tell Kath, now Lady Botham.

IAN BOTHAM FOR THE RECORD:

- Born: 24 November 1955, Heswall, Cheshire (now Merseyside)
- Counties: Somerset, Worcestershire, Durham
- Tests: 102
    - Runs: 5,200 (33.54)
    - Wickets 383 (28.40)
    - Top score: 208
    - Five wickets in an innings: 27 times
    - Ten wickets in a match: four times
    - Best bowling return: 8/34
- First-class career: 402 matches
    - Runs: 19,399 (33.97)
    - Top score: 228
    - Wickets: 1,172 (27.22)
    - Five wickets in an innings: 59 times
    - Ten wickets in a match: eight times
- BBC Sports Personality of the Year: 1981
- *Wisden* Cricketer of the Year: 1978

10

DON BRADMAN

'The Don was the nearest thing to sporting perfection there has ever been'

EVERY SPORTS-SILLY schoolboy 'in my day' grew up with the legend of Don Bradman written large in their minds. He was the closest thing there has ever been in sport to complete perfection, and there are stats and facts to prove it. All he had to do in his final Test was score four and that would have given him an astonishing career average of 100 runs.

It is part of cricketing folklore how he walked to the Oval wicket for the last time along an avenue of England players applauding him. Rival skipper Norman Yardley stepped forward and shook his gloved hand. The thunderous applause lasted for several minutes before play resumed. Just one boundary and he would become the one and only batsman to average 100 runs an innings. Facing his second ball, he played forward to a googly from Eric Hollies, misjudged it and was bowled for a duck. 'He didn't see the ball for the tears in his eyes,' Hollies said after The Don departed to another standing ovation from a crowd, who knew they would never see his like again. He had ducked out.

Bradman finished his extraordinary career there and then with 6,996 Test runs to his name at an average of 99.94. He scored 29 Test centuries between 1928 and 1948, including what was then a world-record innings of 334 on his first 1930 visit to England (309 of his runs coming in just one day!).

It was fairytale stuff for the kid from Cootamundra in the Australian outback, where he used to perfect his timing and coordination by using a cricket stump to hit a golf ball against an old water tank. This helped him develop a quick eye, balanced footwork and a never-surpassed judgement of bowling. He was also a tactical master as captain and a brilliant fielder who inspired his team-mates with his agility, catching and throwing. As he started to gather runs at a prodigious rate, he became known as 'The Boy from Bowral'.

Though a quiet, unassuming character, he could when necessary be a fierce competitor as he showed in the infamous 1932/33 'Bodyline' tour when England's martinet of a captain, Douglas Jardine, ordered his fast bowlers (and they didn't come faster than our Harold Larwood) to target the bodies of the Aussie batsmen while he set an aggressive leg-side field. This was in the days before helmets and extra padding. The mayhem almost caused a diplomatic war between English and Australian politicians, and through it all Bradman remained stoical and determined.

His peak performance away from the Test arena came in a Sheffield Shield match between New South Wales and Queensland at the Sydney Cricket Ground in January 1930. He broke the world record for the highest score in first-class cricket with 452 not out in just 415 minutes. Bradman was chaired off at the end – by his opponents.

It was a different game then from today's 'Big Bash' culture, and the MCC textbook style which I was taught was to rarely hit the ball above knee height. Bradman had a staggering 618 fours in his Test collection but scored only six sixes.

Many considered his most impressive knock was when, suffering from influenza and coming in at number seven, he scored 270 to guide Australia to victory against England in a 1937 Test, later described by the sport's bible *Wisden* as the best Test innings of all time. In 1948 he became the only Australian cricketer to be knighted but was already recognised as the king of the game.

When I started playing with Essex juniors eight years after Bradman's retirement, our county skipper, Trevor Bailey, used to mockingly boast that he captained the Essex team that was the only side to get The Don's 1948 'Invincibles' all out during their tour. It was at Southchurch Park in Southend in May 1948. Trevor would pause after giving the good news that Essex had dismissed the untouchable Aussies and then add, 'The bad news is that they scored a world record for a single day's first-class cricket of 721 runs. We all finished with sunburned tongues.' Bradman amassed 187 of the runs and Trevor got just the one wicket, bowling Keith Miller first ball for a duck. 'Keith shouldered arms and surrendered his wicket,' Trevor revealed. 'He said he wanted no part of the slaughter and returned to the dressing room and his game of poker.' The Aussies, who famously went through their tour undefeated, won by an innings and a mere 451 runs!

Like many boys back then, I had ambitions to follow The Don's run-making example. But I only got to play one county game before opting for a full-time role in football and, as they say, I failed to trouble the scorers. My grand contribution in a match against Lancashire in 1962 was 0 and then 0 not out. But at least I can shout that I played in the same team as the legendary spin bowler Jim Laker, who took the little matter of 19 wickets in a Test against the Aussies at Old Trafford in 1956. One D.G. Bradman, by then an Australian Test selector, looked on in wonder.

Bradman became a leading cricket administrator after working as a successful stockbroker, and it was calculated that he attended 1,713 meetings of the South Australia Cricket Association committee during his half-century of service. For The Don, life was a long innings that finally ended at 92. He inspired a new word for sporting perfection: Bradmanesque.

DON BRADMAN FOR THE RECORD:

- Born: 27 August, 1908, Cootamundra, New South Wales
- State teams: New South Wales, South Australia
- Tests: 52
  - Runs: 6,996 (99.94)
  - 29 centuries
  - Highest score: 334 v. England at Headingley, 1930
- First-class career: 234 games (1927–49)
  - Runs: 28,067 (95.14), 69 centuries
- World record of 12 double centuries
- Highest first-class score: 452 not out, for New South Wales v. Queensland, 1930
- Died: 25 February 2001, Adelaide, aged 92

11

DAVID CAMPESE

'Australia's goose-stepping Campo was
the Muhammad Ali of rugby'

DASHING DAVID Campese was the nearest thing the Australians had in rugby to a Don Bradman. Many rate him as the greatest – and certainly the most entertaining – player to light up the rugby union stage. While preparing this book, I considered my favourite sports. Rugby came fourth after football, cricket and tennis. It was Campo who captured my interest more than most with his quick and inventive play either at full-back or out on the wing.

Campese always took the eye with spectacular runs and I was attracted to his almost cocky confidence. It was the sort of swagger I saw in great footballing team-mates of mine such as Budgie Byrne, Alan Ball and Greavsie.

Sport at top level is very much a mind game and this often arrogant Aussie used to know how to generate psychological advantages over his opponents. He was unmerciful with his long-running verbal blows against the England approach to rugby, all of it designed to wind up the enemy. He loved being the pantomime villain and it was all aimed at getting under the opposition skin.

He had a touch of Muhammad Ali about him, making outrageous comments but then providing action to go with his words. And like Ali had his shuffle, he had the 'Campo goose-step', suddenly striding past his markers with a hitch-kick acceleration that left defenders tackling his shadow. He also had a trademark way of holding the ball, in one hand like a silver salver waiting to be delivered over the line.

The facts speak for themselves about his astonishing ability. He represented Australia for 15 years and New South Wales for 11 years, and set the then world record for tries by downing the ball an amazing 64 times. He was the first Aussie to play 100 Tests for his country and had rugby followers across the world acclaiming his speed and style. Rugby sevens was another speciality of his and he notched up dozens of tries at club and international level.

From the small town of Queanbeyan near Canberra, Campo was originally a rugby league disciple but switched codes in his late teens to become a legend in the 15-a-side game. He divided his time between playing in Australia and Italy, home of his ancestors and where he was a huge favourite while with Petrarca Padova, inspiring them to three successive Italian championships. He later switched with equal success to Amatori Rugby Milano, which was then under the umbrella of AC Milan.

He was supremely fit throughout his career, following a punishing daily programme of weights, sprints and aerobics. There was often criticism of him that he was too much of an individualist and not enough of a team player. I would liken him to George Best, but he was much more disciplined with his behaviour off the pitch where he kept himself to himself and allowed nobody into his private and family life.

His six tries in six matches in the 1991 World Cup helped Australia lift the Webb Ellis Cup at Twickenham at the expense of England, and this performance was highlighted when he travelled to London in 2008 to collect a 'Legends' Oscar du Midi for being voted the best winger in the world by French rugby newspaper *Midi-Olympique*.

But he has not always been the hero. His spectacular gaffe in the third Test against the British and Irish Lions in 1989 was a scar on his reputation. The series was tied at 1-1 and the Wallabies were desperately protecting a lead in the Sydney decider. Mr Cool Campese suddenly lost his composure and threw a suicidal goal line pass to his full-back, who had no chance of collecting it. Lions winger Ieuan Evans hungrily pounced on the error and downed the ball in what became known as 'Campo's Corner'. It was a nightmare moment that went down in Australian history. A well-known electronics manufacturer used a replay of Campese's mistake to advertise a new video recorder, with the cutting slogan, 'Now you can watch Campo cock up as often as you like!' The Wallabies lost 19-18, narrowly missing out on a long-awaited first victory over the Lions. Former Aussie skipper Andrew Slack fumed, 'You don't play Mickey Mouse rugby like that in the green and gold of Australia.'

Campo eventually recovered from the sort of nightmare all sportspeople dread and by the end of his eventful career in 1998 was established as one of the greatest players ever to set foot on a rugby pitch. This round ball football man salutes him.

DAVID CAMPESE FOR THE RECORD:
- Born: 21 October 1962, Queanbeyan, New South Wales
- Position: full-back and wing
- Major teams: Queanbeyan Whites, Canberra Vikings, Petrarca Padova (Italy), Randwick District, New South Wales, Amatori Rugby Milano
- Test career span: 1982–1996
- Test caps: 101
- Test tries: 64
- Rugby World Cup: 1991
- Player of the Tournament: 1991
- Oscar du Midi: 2008

12

WILT CHAMBERLAIN

'A tall sports story about Wilt the Stilt'

NO QUESTION about who has been the biggest of my heroes. I give you all 7ft 1in of Wilt 'The Stilt' Chamberlain, the basketball giant who created more records than Elvis Presley. It was not until I went to America on football tours that I realised just how massive the sport is on that side of the pond. Basketball players are really looked up to (an attempt at a joke there), and their top performers earn salaries that make the wages paid to our footballers seem like chicken feed.

Few were bigger in the game – and not just physically – than Chamberlain, whose career ran parallel to mine, so I was always aware of his extraordinary exploits. When I was just starting out with West Ham in the late 1950s he was leaving the University of Kansas, where he had been a prolific points scorer on the college circuit. NBA rules prevented him from going pro for a year, so he spent 12 months on the road with the world-famous Harlem Globetrotters.

Now I can show off a bit of my basketball knowledge. I took Judith to see the Globetrotters at Wembley Arena in 1965, the year after we got married, and I have rarely been so entertained in a sports environment. From the moment they came on court to their 'Sweet Georgia Brown' theme song, everything was choreographed to show off their skill and amazing ability at putting the ball in the basket. Our favourite player was the clowning genius Meadowlark Lemon, who had more tricks than Paul Daniels. A little trivia for you: the Globetrotters were formed in 1926 by a Whitechapel-born character called Abe Saperstein, who emigrated to the United States and became a basketball coach and team booking agent who saw the potential of a touring squad of great exhibitionists. They went nowhere near Harlem until 1968, but Abe chose the name to show they were an all-black team.

But back to Wilt the Stilt. In 1959 he played his first professional game for his hometown Philadelphia Warriors against the Knicks in New York City, scoring 43 points. He finished his first season as NBA Rookie of the Year. Wilt was having a ball and for the next three seasons was selected for the All-NBA first team. His most astonishing campaign came in 1962 when he became the first NBA player to score 100 points in a game, setting a league record for the highest number of points scored in a single game (which he still holds to this day). By the season's end, Chamberlain had racked up more than 4,000 points, becoming the first NBA player to pass that magic mark and scoring a staggering average of 50.4 points per game.

Chamberlain stayed with the Warriors when their franchise moved out to San Francisco in 1962, but returned to his home town three years later as star man for the Philadelphia 76ers, steering them to an NBA championship win over his old Warriors team. On the way to the championship, he also inspired the Sixers to defeat the mighty Boston Celtics in the Eastern Division Finals to end a run of eight consecutive championship wins by the team from Massachusetts.

Traded to the Los Angeles Lakers in 1968, Chamberlain again proved he was the king of the court by helping the Lakers win the

1972 NBA championship, triumphing over the New York Knicks in five straight games. Wilt was named the Most Valuable Player in the finals.

By the time he retired in 1973, the big man had played in 1,045 games and achieved an average of 30.1 points per game – the NBA record until Michael Jordan came along. His cumulative career tally was a then record 30,000-plus points.

After his retirement, all his teams retired his number 13 vest. He produced a best-selling autobiography titled *Wilt: Just Like Any Other 7-Foot Black Millionaire Who Lives Next Door*. In another book, *A View from Above*, he added an extra interesting statistic to all the facts and figures when he claimed that he had slept with more than 20,000 women. Even George Best would have to bow the knee to him. It was Judith who said, 'That's a lot of slam dunks.' She has always had a sharper sense of humour than me.

Chamberlain died of heart failure on 12 October 1999, at his Los Angeles home. He was just 63. What a life. A truly tall story.

WILT CHAMBERLAIN FOR THE RECORD:
- Born: 21 August 1938, Philadelphia
- Position: Center
- Major teams: Philadelphia Warriors, San Francisco Warriors, Philadelphia 76ers, Los Angeles Lakers
- Coached San Diego Conquistadors
- Career points: 31,419 (average 30.1 per game)
- Rebounds: 23,924
- Assists: 4,643
- NBA champion: 1967, 1972
- NBA Most Valuable Player: 1960, 1966, 1967, 1968
- Seven times NBA leading scorer (1960–66)
- Died: 12 October 1999, Bel Air, California, aged 63

13

JOHN CHARLES

*'The Gentle Giant from Swansea who
became King John of Juventus'*

WHENEVER THE subject comes up as to who has been the
greatest British footballer of all time, the name of John Charles is
too often left out of the debate, simply because he spent his peak
years out of sight in Italy. Talk to any pro from the 1950s and you
will hear the same line, 'He was THE king of football.'

He could have walked into any team at either centre-forward
or centre-half and been hailed as a master of the footballing
arts. I don't mind admitting that he was a far better striker than
me, and there was no better centre-half on the British – or even
world – stage.

Standing 6ft 2in and weighing around 14st, a heavyweight
yet with slender hips and broad shoulders, he had perfect balance,
effortless touch and the spring of a gymnast. Big John was an
exceptional sight to behold when either scoring or stopping goals:
the complete all-rounder.

He remains a footballing god in Italy where he is remembered
for the 93 goals he scored in 155 league games for Juventus

between 1957 and 1962, helping them to three Scudettos. But more significantly, he sits in memories for his refusal to use his awesome strength unfairly. In an era when tackling was fierce and frightening, he was never sent off or cautioned and would never stoop to petty fouling. His immaculate behaviour and sportsmanship earned him the nickname that most clearly defines his career, 'Il Gigante Buono' – The Gentle Giant.

A proud son of Swansea, along with his younger footballing brother Mel, he had to travel to find his fame, first of all to Leeds where he made his league debut in 1949 as a 17-year-old centre-half. The following year, at the age of 18 years and 71 days, he became the youngest player to proudly wear the red shirt of Wales, winning the first of 38 caps, a total that would have trebled but for Juventus insisting he put club before country.

The turning point in King John's career came in the 1952/53 season when he was tried as an experimental centre-forward. He quickly proved he was a natural striker and scored 27 goals in 30 matches. The following season he was the league's top marksman with 42 goals, still a club record.

Having helped Leeds to promotion in 1956 he caused as much havoc in the First Division, his 38 goals attracting the interest of Juventus, who paid an incoming British record fee of £65,000 to sign him in 1957.

If you wanted to get Jack Charlton started, you just had to mention John to him. Jack was a young pro at Leeds, often playing under John's wing. Jack used to love talking about him, and once told me during an England get-together, 'In those days none of us really knew much about the game over there in Italy but John would have made it anywhere. He was the greatest thing on two feet. Majestic. Whenever I'm asked at dinners about the most effective British player of my time, of any time, I'm sure people expect me to say George Best or maybe our kid [brother Bobby], but they forget about John. While everybody else just played the game, he went out and won matches on his own. As a young player

I learned more from him than anyone: how he positioned himself in defence, his reading of the game. It was all instinctive.

'As a defender I'd put him right up there with Bobby Moore. As a centre-forward he was sensational, as good if not better than Lawton, Lofthouse, Wor Jackie Milburn, any of the greats. He had a powerful shot and, in the air, well, he was on his own, a different class. If there's been a better all-round player then I've not clapped eyes on him.'

You didn't argue with Jack, you just listened. He was a great judge of players and I joined the John Charles fan club even though I was not lucky enough to see him at his best. In his first season in Italy his tally of 28 goals was remarkable in the then ultra-defensive Italian league. He shot Juventus to their first championship for six years, was voted the league's Italian Footballer of the Year and named as the most valuable player in Europe, ahead of the Real Madrid maestro Alfredo Di Stéfano, and valued at £400,000, a staggering figure at that time.

Charles helped Wales reach the quarter-finals of the World Cup in 1958 but because of injury missed the match against eventual champions Brazil, who won the game 1-0 with a goal scored by an unknown 17-year-old debutant called Pelé.

In 1962 John made an abortive return to Leeds, then went back to Italy with Roma. His career went into a nosedive as he got caught, as we all do, by the unstoppable march of time. He was sold to Cardiff City at the end of that season. There followed spells in non-league football as the player-manager of Hereford and Merthyr Tydfil, then coaching at Swansea and with the Canadian club Hamilton Steelers.

He is unfairly represented in the 'greatest' arguments because there is little television and film evidence to show just how powerful and dominating he was in two key positions.

In retirement he was asked whether he preferred to play centre-half or centre-forward. He replied in the bass-baritone voice that had earned him a following as a singer, 'Without doubt, centre-forward. A defender can kick five shots off the line but it's the goalscorers who get the glory. And that's what the game's all about, boyho. Glory.'

King John had more than his share of it, but out of sight of British spectators. It's unlikely there has ever been a better player from these shores.

JOHN CHARLES FOR THE RECORD:

- Born 27: December 1931, Swansea
- Leeds United: 297 games, 157 goals (1949–57)
- Juventus: 155 games, 108 goals (1957–62)
- Leeds United: 11 games, 3 goals (1962)
- Roma: 10 games, 4 goals (1962–63)
- Cardiff City: 69 games, 18 goals (1963–66)
- Hereford United: 173 games, 80 goals (1966–71)
- Merthyr Tydfil: player-manager 1972–74
- Awarded a CBE in 2001
- Voted the greatest overseas player ever to wear a Juventus shirt in 1998
- Wales: 38 caps, 15 goals (1950–65)
- Died: 21 February 2004, Wakefield, aged 72

14

SIR BOBBY CHARLTON

*'The name known and
revered around the world'*

I WAS fortunate to travel the world with Bobby and wherever we were, everybody knew who he was. Many could only speak two words of English, 'Bobby Charlton'. Yet for all his fame and instant recognition, his head never got a centimetre bigger. He was the most modest and sporting of superstars, and it hurts like hell that as I write he is going through a worrying health decline.

He and big brother Jack were as alike as grass and granite. There was no doubt that Bobby was the better footballer, an all-time great, but Jack was the more powerful and persuasive personality, which is why he was one of the few 1966 World Cup heroes who had any success as a manager.

Jack, of course, has left us and now Bobby is suffering that same curse of dementia that claimed his big brother. It's none of my business, but it was sad to see the two siblings drift apart after achieving so much together on the playing fields of England. Families, whether of famous people or just plain ordinary folk, get locked in disputes for all sorts of reasons and none of us should try to judge why the Charlton brothers fell out. That's all I want to say on the subject.

I considered it a privilege to be on the same pitch as the pair of them, particularly Bobby who was, along with Gordon Banks, Ray Wilson and, of course, Bobby Moore, one of the truly world-class players in our 1966 World Cup squad. There was one other who would have walked into any other team in the world, Jimmy Greaves. More of that later.

Bobby was already making a name for himself when he survived the horrific Munich air crash on 6 February 1958. It was one of those 'What were you doing when John F. Kennedy was shot?' moments that you just don't forget. I was 17 at the time and playing table tennis in our local youth club in Chelmsford and was just about to serve when somebody listening to the wireless shouted, 'Man United's plane has crashed.'

The haunting words stopped the football world for a while, and it is nothing short of miraculous what Bobby – Sir Bobby – has achieved since he was hauled from the wreckage. He went on to play 106 times for England, was for a long time our top scorer with 49 goals and always played the game with grace and style, walloping shots with either foot and – until the final – was the general of our World Cup team with his precision passes, intelligent positioning and sniper shooting.

As I mentioned in the Franz Beckenbauer entry, he and Bobby cancelled each other out in the final by man-marking each other. That meant the two most skilful players on the pitch were neutralised, and so – let's be honest – without the drama of extra time it was hardly the most spectacular final in history.

If I wanted to show people Bobby at his best I would direct them to the film of the classic semi-final against Portugal when he was just majestic. He scored two superbly taken goals and was so exceptional that the watching West Germany manager Helmut Schön reacted by sacrificing the brilliant Beckenbauer to shadow-mark him in the final. Meantime, Alf Ramsey had ordered Bobby to keep an eye on the young German star. I felt sorry for the spectators, but then looking at it through selfish eyes I had more space in which to manoeuvre.

Bobby is a deep-thinking, ultra sensitive person, no doubt an overlap from the trauma he suffered in that air disaster. He has always cried easily, and was in tears again at Wembley in 1968 when he helped fire Manchester United to the European Cup in a dramatic match against Benfica that again went to extra time.

He, along with the deadly Denis Law and the magical George Best, made United the team everybody wanted to watch through the 1960s, and as an opponent I used to consider it a privilege to be on the same pitch. I would willingly have paid to watch them play.

Like me, Bobby has been lucky in the partner he found. While Judith is the rock in my life, Bobby has always had Norma by his side during a wonderfully solid 60-year marriage. Her maiden name is Ball, and you can guess the stick we used to give him when Alan Ball was in the squad. No relation, of course.

Bobby has never asked for it, but we all tend to put him up on a pedestal. He is uncomfortable when he is the centre of conversation and he looks to deflect praise as something he feels he has not earned by doing what came naturally to him.

He comes on his mother's side from a great footballing family, the Milburns, including north-east idol 'Wor' Jackie Milburn. Throughout his schoolboy years he used to travel by bus every other Saturday to watch Newcastle play at St James' Park and it was assumed that after winning England schoolboy honours he would join the Magpies. But, after being approached and sweet-talked by famous scout Joe Armstrong, he joined 'the other' United at Old Trafford, where he remains revered and respected by everybody who had the pleasure of watching him play in the famous red shirt. He left a lasting mark on Old Trafford where there is a stand in his name, but his most permanent memory will be of his 249 goals in 758 games and, above all, the sporting spirit in which they were accumulated.

Let Franz Beckenbauer have the last word on his great rival and even greater friend. He once told me, 'People quite properly talk about Bobby's skill, his shooting power and his intelligent passing. What people don't talk about is his stamina. I know better than anybody from having had to mark him in the 1966 World Cup Final that he can run all day. He wore me out and I was relieved to hear the final whistle even though we lost. You don't often hear this said but Bobby has the lungs of a horse.'

A thoroughbred, of course.

SIR BOBBY CHARLTON FOR THE RECORD:

- Born: 11 October 1937, Ashington, Northumberland
- Manchester United: 758 games, 249 goals (1956–73)
- European Cup: 1968
- European Footballer of the Year: 1966
- FWA Footballer of the Year: 1966
- Preston North End: 38 games, 8 goals (1974–75)
- Waterford: 3 games, 1 goal (1976)
- Newcastle KB United: 1 game (1978)
- Perth Azzuri: 3 games 2 goals (1980)
- Blacktown City: 1 game 1 goal (1980)
- Knighted in 1994
- England: 106 caps, 49 goals (1958–70)
- World Cup: 1966

15

JIM CLARK

*'The sheep farmer who came over
the hill, very quickly'*

I LOST interest in motor racing when too many of the F1 drivers finished up in the morgue. You needed to be around in the 1950s to know what I mean. Like most schoolboys, I started getting captivated by the excitement and exhilaration of the sport but back then it was chillingly common for drivers to be tragically killed at the wheel, and my passion for races was slowly stifled. Fifteen competitors lost their lives in the 1950s alone, and one of my idols, Mike Hawthorn – the first British driver to win the world title – died in a crash on the A3 Guildford bypass in 1958 soon after lifting the championship trophy.

By the early 1960s I was drawn back to the sport by the exceptional exploits of Jim Clark, a quiet, unassuming sheep farmer from Scotland who had started out driving as a hobby and was suddenly proving himself the greatest thing on four wheels. He had made a name for himself in local hill club events, driving a Sunbeam-Talbot, and quickly caught the eye of the Border Reivers team who encouraged him to drive Jaguar D-Types and

Porsches in rally events throughout the UK. Soon he had chalked up ten victories, which attracted the attention of Lotus chief Colin Chapman. They had first met on the Brands Hatch track when Colin, then an enthusiastic driver, had to push his foot flat to the floor to hold off the challenge of the determined young Scot.

He was promoted to the Lotus F1 team in 1960 and within two years was proving himself one of the most accomplished drivers on the circuit. The media shone the torchlight of publicity on him but they found the reclusive Clark reluctant to talk about his precocious talent. He was a man of action, not words.

In 1963 he won seven of the ten F1 races and was an impressive winner of his first world championship. Two years later he regained the title from John Surtees, a remarkable achievement because he missed the Monaco Grand Prix to compete in the prestigious Indianapolis 500. He was the first driver to win both the F1 championship and the Indy 500 in the same year.

Clark had won a record 25 F1 races but changes in the regulations were weighted against Lotus, and he agreed to drive in a Formula Two race at the Hockenheimring in Germany to keep his eye in for an all-out challenge to regain the world championship.

I remember the day well: Sunday, 7 April 1968. I was resting at home with an injury the day after West Ham had beaten Newcastle 5-0 at home without me. Trevor Brooking, then just 19, had taken my place and scored the one and only hat-trick of his career. As I was watching highlights of the match there was a news flash that Jim Clark had been killed when his car left the track and hit a tree at 170mph. He was just 32. What a waste of a life. I watched the rest of the West Ham triumph with tears in my eyes.

We had lost the man who at the time was regarded as the driver's driver. He had won 25 of his 72 Grand Prix races, achieved 33 pole positions and people said of him that he was an artist at the wheel who controlled races thanks to his great reflexes, his courage and ice-cold temperament. An inconsolable Colin Chapman later paid this tribute, 'Jimmy will always be the best.

I'm sure in time someone else will come along and everyone'll hail him as the greatest ever. But not me. For me, there will never be another in his class. He was The Master.'

Jim Clark deserves his place in my list because in his all-too-short life he made the world sit up and take notice of his speed and daring. But was it really worth his life?

JIM CLARK FOR THE RECORD:

- Born: 4 March 1936, Kilmany, Fife
- Career span: 1960–68
- World F1 champion: 1963, 1965
- Team: Lotus
- Indy 500 winner: 1965
- 25 F1 Grand Prix victories from 72 starts
- Pole positions: 33
- Podiums: 32
- Career points: 274
- Died: 7 April 1968, Hockenheimring, Germany, aged 32

16

SEBASTIAN COE

'The elegant running pride of Britain'

IF I had to choose one person to represent the pride of Britain and the elegance of sport it would have to be Sebastian Coe, now Baron Coe of the House of Lords. He has cemented himself into sporting history with his exploits on the running track and, since hanging up his spikes in 1990, has become one of the world's leading administrators and the voice of sense and reason in the international arena.

This Renaissance man has walked the tightrope as a Conservative member of parliament, represented world athletes, led (unsuccessfully) England's bid to host the FIFA World Cup, is chancellor of Loughborough University, and now sits in the House of Lords but is mostly lauded for his role in the phenomenally triumphant 2012 London Olympics. He is also an obsessive Chelsea supporter. Phew, and I've not mentioned his running yet!

He makes my list because of his achievements as an athlete, when he was poetry in motion on the track, always running with elegance and style that you could have set to an Elgar composition. At his peak he won four Olympic medals, including 1500m golds at the Games of 1980 in Moscow and 1984 in Los Angeles. Unusually, he was elevated to the House of Lords six years before being knighted in 2006.

This made-in-Britain running machine set nine outdoor and three indoor world records, burning up the track in 1979 with three in the space of just 41 days. He was on fire, yet never looking as if he was trying that hard. When I look back at footage of me playing football flat-out I had a physical tension about me that showed I was putting in full effort – stiffening the sinews, summoning up the blood, as the Bard put it. But for Seb it was if he was running on air and with a grace from the gods.

Like me, Seb was coached by his father and so both of us experienced that special bond that lays a foundation of discipline that lasts a lifetime. Peter Coe gave his son a punishing training schedule that made demands that other coaches could not have matched. From the moment he arrived as a student at Loughborough University, Coe – with a strong Indian pedigree on his mother's side – quickly proved himself physically and mentally superior to his peers and began to build a reputation for having stunning speed and stamina.

His track rivalries with first Steve Ovett and then Steve Cram put British athletics on the map in the 1980s. Coe and Ovett actually duelled on the track only seven times in 17 years, competing in opposition with each other, swapping records and (quite often) barbed insults from a distance. The races that grabbed the world headlines were in the 1980 Moscow Olympics.

Coe went to Russia as world 800m record holder and was favourite for that event. Ovett was unbeaten in 43 races at 1500m or the mile, held the world mile record and was expected to triumph in the 1500m. The two deadly adversaries – the almost aristocratic Coe and the 'Brighton brawler' Ovett – also came into the Games with a share of the world record at a distance over which they had never met, 1500m.

For a master tactician, Coe got his race plan completely wrong in the 800m and it was his nemesis Ovett who took the gold, with Seb an anguished second. Five days later with all the experts selecting Ovett to complete the double, Coe ran out of his skin and took the gold in what is recognised as the blue riband event of the track. Ovett was well beaten back in bronze medal third.

The two races went down in the annals as the greatest head-to-head battles in Olympic history.

There was a new force to be reckoned with when Steve Cram – the Jarrow Arrow – emerged, setting world records in the 1500m, 2000m and the mile during a 19-day spree in the summer of 1985. The three Brits were expected to battle for the gold in the 1500m in 1984 and all was going to plan at the bell when suddenly Ovett stepped on the curb and walked out of the race. This left Coe and Cram to battle it out, and Seb moved up a gear to win by eight yards and so become the only male athlete to win back-to-back 1500m gold medals.

The media had written Coe off before the race and he stepped out of character by letting his feelings be known with a flurry of finger gestures in the direction of the press box.

This old footballer looked on in sympathy, and I reckon that Gentleman Coe had learned that sign language on the terraces of Chelsea, where I had taken my share of abuse during my brief managing stint.

As my dear mate Greavsie used to say, it's a funny old game.

SEBASTIAN COE FOR THE RECORD:

- Born: 29 September 1956, Hammersmith, London
- Career span: 1974–90
- Clubs: Hallamshire Harriers, Sheffield, Harringey AC
- University: Loughborough
- Major titles:
  - Olympics:
    800m silver 1980 and 1984
    1500m gold 1980 and 1984
  - European Championships:
    800m gold 1986, silver 1982, bronze 1978
    1500m silver 1986
  - World Cup: 800m gold 1981, silver 1989
  - Career best times:
    800m: 1m 41.73s (1981)
    1500m: 3m 32.53s (1984)
    Mile: 3m 47.33s (1981)
- President of the IAAF: 2015
- Chairman of the British Olympic Association: 2012
- BBC Sports Personality of the Year Lifetime Achievement Award: 2012
- Knighted: 2006
- Life peer: 2000

17

DENIS COMPTON

*'Compo enjoyed the summer wine of cricket and
the mixed fortunes of football'*

ALONG WITH most schoolboys in the 1940s and early '50s, Denis Compton was the all-round sportsman I wanted to be. In the playground you chose to be either the dashing, dancing Denis or the more composed, dogged Len Hutton. As a Lancashire lad I could not possibly go for the Yorkshireman, so in my imagination I became the cricketing/footballing hero Compo.

In the years after the war, Denis was just the icon the nation needed to help lift spirits during what were often tough and bleak ration book days. When I arrived in Essex at the age of six he was already established as a sporting god of cricket and with his footballing skills as a second string to his golden bow. It is written large in the record books that in the glorious summer of 1947 he accumulated the little matter of 18 centuries. There has never been consistency to match it and every run was gathered for Middlesex or England with a spirit of adventure that captured the attention even of people who had no interest in 'the game of flanneled fools'.

In the winters, he and his big brother Leslie played football for the Arsenal, and here's a fact I bet most people don't know: he played more times at Tottenham's White Hart Lane ground than at the Highbury home of the Gunners. Throughout the war and for two years after they shared the Lane while the Arsenal stadium was requisitioned as an Air Raid Precaution centre.

He shared many of his batting partnerships with his 'twin', Bill Edrich, another who enjoyed the double life of cricketer in the summer and footballer in the winter; a Norfolk man, he played for Norwich City and then Tottenham. During their run blitz of 1947 Edrich scored 3,539 runs to Compton's astonishing 3,816. They made runs while the sun shone in one of the hottest summers on record, inspiring this young boy down in Chelmsford to take a close interest in both cricket and football. A cricketer in the summer and a footballer in the winter. Paradise. That will do nicely, Geoffrey. AND getting paid for it.

While I was being taught the straight-bat MCC batting technique by the Essex coaches, Compo went his own way. If he ever read a coaching manual he must have been dyslexic because he rarely did anything by the book. He would continually take risks, standing outside the crease even to the quicker bowlers, playing all around the wicket but hardly ever hitting straight. His specialities were a late cut – a very late cut – and a sweep shot played with an audacious skill admired by cricket fans and dreaded by fielders around the world.

He was also a sometimes unplayable left-arm spin bowler, taking 622 wickets, mostly with his confusing 'chinamen' deliveries, a great skill that Compo casually regarded as a bit of a fairground sideshow. His occasionally haphazard 'yes-no-yes-no' running between the wickets was the source of a thousand after-dinner anecdotes. Our skipper at Essex, the inimitable Trevor 'Barnacle' Bailey, described a call from Denis as 'a basis for negotiation'. He was impossible to bowl against if he got his eye in, as evidenced by a merciless knock of 278 against Pakistan at Trent Bridge in

1954, and the fastest triple hundred in first-class history, collected in just 181 minutes for MCC against North East Transvaal in Benoni in 1948/49. He also had a safe pair of hands, holding 416 catches during his career.

Born on 23 May 1918 in Hendon, Middlesex – just a stroll from the England hotel headquarters for the 1966 World Cup – Denis and the older Leslie learned their cricket and football in the backstreets with dustbins as wickets and rolled-up coats as goalposts. He progressed to the Lord's ground staff and then, bridging the war, played some of the most entertaining and exciting cricket ever witnessed.

Denis was a dribbling left-winger who won 14 wartime caps for England and an FA Cup winners' medal with Arsenal against Liverpool in 1950 (fortified, he later revealed, by a large glass of scotch just before leaving the dressing room). A pre-war football injury plagued him for much of his career and the 'Compton knee' was a constant worry for England Test cricket fans. When his kneecap was removed in 1955 his surgeon kept it as a souvenir before giving it to Lord's for their archive. The kneecap became more celebrated than any of Compton's cricket caps.

And how about this for a family double: the Compton brothers achieved the unrivalled feat of winning cricket's County Championship and the Football League title together. Incredible.

My writing partner Norman was a colleague of Denis for ten years on Express newspapers and once asked him if he had to choose between cricket and football for a career which sport would get his vote. 'Without doubt, cricket,' he said instantly. 'I could have made more money playing football, but there is nothing to beat going out to bat in front of a full house at Lord's, or scoring runs against the Aussies Down Under. Cricket every time.'

Lucky old Denis had the best of both worlds. The perfect sporting life.

Famous as the pin-up 'Brylcreem Boy', Denis was handsome in a Cary Grant kind of way and attracted a legion of women spectators to cricket. He remained popular throughout his sometimes boisterous life and after he died at the age of 78 on St George's Day 1997 there was a record application for tickets to his memorial service at Westminster Abbey. Just as it was at the peak of his cricket career, the house was full.

We won't see his like again.

DENIS COMPTON FOR THE RECORD:

- Born: 23 May 1918, Hendon, Middlesex
- County: Middlesex (1936–58)
- Tests: 78 (1938–1955)
  - Runs: 5,807 (50.08), 17 centuries
  - Highest score: 278 v. Pakistan at Trent Bridge, 1954
- First-class career: 515 games (1936–58)
  - Runs: 38,942 (51.85), 123 centuries
- Fastest triple century: 300 in 181 minutes for MCC v NE Transvaal in Benoni in 1948/49
- Scored 3,816 runs in the summer of 1947, including a record 18 centuries
- Balls bowled in Tests: 2,710 (wickets 25)
- Best Test bowling return: 5/70 v. South Africa 1948/49
- Best bowling return: 7/36 MCC v. Auckland 1946/47
- Football: First Division championship winner with Arsenal, 1948
- Awarded CBE: 1958
- Died 23 April 1997, Windsor, Berkshire, aged 78

18

SIR HENRY COOPER

'Our 'Enery hooked first place
in the popularity stakes'

FOR A man who made his living trying to flatten people, Henry Cooper was one of the most charming and likeable people ever to cross my path in the world of sport. Gentle Giant was the nickname given to football Goliath John Charles. It would have sat just as comfortably on 'Our 'Enery's' wide shoulders. Mind you, that was *outside* the ring. Once the bell rang he was like a bomb waiting to go off, and his ferocious left hook – 'Enery's 'Ammer – left a procession of opponents in a heap on the canvas.

Most famously, the potent punch dropped Muhammad Ali in the closing seconds of round four of their 1963 battle at the same Wembley Stadium where three years later I had a match to remember. It's painful history how Ali, then known as Cassius Clay, was saved by the bell before stopping Cooper in the fifth round with a gashed eye. When they met in a return at Highbury in that eventful year of 1966, Henry was stopped in six rounds, again with a severely cut eye. It was his one tilt at the world championship.

Despite the cut-eye curse Cooper won a record three Lonsdale Belts outright and also the Empire (later Commonwealth) and European crowns. He had the character to overcome three successive title fight defeats in 1957 by Jamaican Joe Bygraves, Sweden's Ingemar Johansson and Welsh stylist Joe Erskine. Seven of his 14 defeats in a 55-fight career were the result of eye injuries.

Henry was massively popular with the public, who warmed to his genial nature and pleasant, sporting demeanour. We often used to meet at various functions, and he always radiated friendliness and happiness, a man at peace with himself – until that bell rang.

We were once comparing weights while sitting together at a book-signing session when – talking as ever in the royal 'we' – he told me this fascinating, little-known story, 'We knew we had to be built for speed in our first fight with Clay and I overdid the training. On a check weigh-in at the gym the day before the fight, my manager Jim Wicks nearly swallowed his cigar. "Goodness gracious," he said, or words to that effect. "You've become a bloody flyweight. Twelve stone 12 pounds. My dog's heavier than you." Don't forget, Ali was a six foot three, 15-stoner. A monster compared to me. At the official weigh-in the next day I got on the scales with jockey handicap weights hidden inside my shoes and my weight was announced as 13 stone four pounds. We didn't want Ali to have the psychological advantage of knowing I was just a light-heavyweight. When I hit him with my left hook in that fourth round he knew for sure I punched like a genuine heavyweight.'

His knighthood in 2000 was awarded more for his prodigious charity work than what he achieved in the ring, and 20 years earlier he had been honoured with a papal knighthood. He converted to the Roman Catholic religion after his marriage to his Italian-born wife Albina and sincerely followed his new vows for the rest of his life. His popularity was underlined by the fact that he was the first to win the BBC Sports Personality of the Year award twice.

Henry's identical twin George (who fought as Jim Cooper) was also a heavyweight boxer and he, too, suffered cut-eye problems that prevented him from making as big an impact as his brother. They were mirror twins, George right-handed and Henry left.

Henry's long ring career ended in controversy when at the age of 37 he was considered by referee Harry Gibbs to have been outpointed by 21-year-old Joe Bugner. Most people watching the fight at Wembley Arena and later on television thought the verdict should have gone to the veteran Cooper, who immediately retired from boxing in disgust at the decision.

For the next three decades Henry was looked on as a national treasure, increasing his popularity with television appearances as a team captain on *A Question of Sport*, as a public speaker and on a series of roadshows with Jimmy Greaves, promoted and compered by our agent Terry Baker. He lost much of the fortune he won in the ring when he became a victim of the 1990s Lloyd's Names scandal but shrugged off the calamity, downsized his home and got on with his life in the old jovial manner that had earned him widespread acclaim. After retirement from the ring he played golf with the same enthusiasm as he tackled boxing and, as he admitted in that humorous way of his, with just as big a hook.

There have been better fighters than Henry, but none so beloved.

SIR HENRY COOPER FOR THE RECORD:

- Born: January 3 May 1934, Lambeth
- ABA light-heavyweight champion: 1952, 1953
- Professional debut: 14 September 1954, Harringay Arena, v. Harry Painter; won by knockout in first round
- Commonwealth title fight: Joe Bygraves, 1957; lost by knockout in ninth round
- British and Commonwealth title fights:
  - Brian London, 1959: won points, 15 rounds
  - Joe Erskine, 1959: won ref. stopped fight, 12th round
  - Joe Erskine, 1961: won ref. stopped fight, 5th round
  - Joe Erskine, 1962: won ref. stopped fight, 9th round
  - Dick Richardson, 1963: won. knockout, 5th round
  - Brian London, 1964: won points, 15 (also for the European title)
  - Johnny Prescott, 1965: won, retired 10th round
  - Jack Bodell, 1967: won ref. stopped fight, 2nd round
  - Billy Walker, 1967: won ref. stopped fight, 8th round
  - Jack Bodell, 1967, won points, 15 rounds
  - Joe Bugner, 1971 lost points 15 rounds (also for European title)
- Other European title fights:
  - Ingemar Johansson 1957, lost knockout, 5th round
  - Karl Mildenberger. 1968: won, disqualified 8th round
  - Piero Tomasoni. 1969, won knockout, 5th round
  - Jose Urtain, 1970, won ref. stopped fight 9th round
- World heavyweight title: Muhammad Ali, 1966, lost ref. stopped fight 6th round
- TOTAL FIGHTS: 55, 40 wins (25 inside the distance), 14 defeats
- Died 3 1 May 2011, Limpsfield, Surrey, aged 76

19

COLIN COWDREY

'The Master artist used a cricket bat
like Goya used a brush'

IT'S AMUSING talking about Colin Cowdrey just a couple of pages after Denis Compton. There could not be more contrasting characters and cricketers. I said how Denis had seemed never to have read an MCC coaching manual. Well Colin lived by it from day one of his birth on Christmas Eve 1932 in India, where his extremely proud English father ran a tea plantation. He was cricket-mad and deliberately gave his son the initials M (Michael) C (Colin) Cowdrey to put down a marker for the future.

It was Cowdrey and his England batting partner Peter (P.B.H.) May who my Essex coaches used to tell me to study when I was learning the game, dreaming of one day playing for England with their sort of imperious style. Both were full of guile and grace and along with 'Lord Ted' Dexter gave England an almost aristocratic aura during the stiff late 1950s going into the swinging '60s. In those days. many cricketers were still true-blue amateurs – 'gentlemen' who had their own entrance on to the playing fields of England to separate them from the oik professionals.

From the first day that Colin picked up a cricket bat it was like a magic wand in his hands. He never used to smash the ball to the boundary. He stroked it, glanced it, caressed it. For we spectators it was like watching a Goya of the game, using brush strokes rather than cricket strokes to bring bowlers to their knees.

When I was trying to choose between football or cricket for my career, I used to play as a batsman-wicketkeeper and I would imagine bending down behind the stumps while Cowdrey was at the wicket. Not once did I see him give even a whiff of a chance to the man with the gloves. He played textbook cricket, invariably scoring in front of him as if batting was the simplest thing in the world.

After taking eight wickets for 117 with his leg-spin bowling for Tonbridge against Clifton at Lord's, it was thought his future lay as a spin bowler. He was just 13. But Colin preferred to concentrate on batting and was in the engine room of the game for half a century, as a batsman with Oxford University, Kent and England and then as a very positive cricket administrator, picking up a knighthood on the way and then becoming the first cricketer to be awarded a peerage, becoming Baron Cowdrey of Tonbridge. He also managed to fit in a highly successful career as an executive with Barclays Bank.

In an era of exceptional English batsmen, he was the most enduring, with a Test career spanning more than two decades. He was the first man to play 100 Tests, captained England 27 times and scored almost 43,000 first-class runs – 7,624 of them in Tests. His collection included a century in his 100th Test. Oh yes, and he was a natural at golf, rackets and squash, as well as cricket. Makes you feel inferior, but he never once boasted about his considerable talents. He was Mr Modesty.

I have warm memories of watching on television when he and the peerless Peter May came together at 113-3 in the second innings of the opening 1957 Test against the West Indies at Edgbaston, with England facing an innings defeat. A little over eight hours later they had added 411 runs to the total in one of the most pulsating partnerships ever witnessed. In the same year Colin became captain of Kent, a job he proudly held for the next 15 seasons and led them to the County Championship in 1970.

His chip-off-the-block sons Chris and Graham followed in his famous footsteps to give Kent more than 50 years of Cowdrey influence.

He answered an emergency call to arms at the age of 42 in 1975 when he hurried down to Australia for his sixth Ashes tour, this time to help out an England team being blasted by the typhoon twins Lillee and Thomson. He arrived in time for the second Test and, broad of beam and smile, he ambled out to the crease and introduced himself to the feared Thomson, 'I don't believe we've met. My name's Cowdrey.' It was unnecessary. Everybody in the cricket world knew M.C.C.

Thomson the Terror was unimpressed and his two word response to Cowdrey has to be censored. Suffice to say the second word was 'off'.

In later years, Colin chuckled over the famous welcome he got from Thommo and said: 'He kept calling me Fatso, which I found quite endearing. I was pleased to have the extra padding as Lillee and Thomson made things fairly hostile. It was great fun!'

That summed up the Cowdrey approach to the game he was born to play. He always preached that cricket was a game to be enjoyed. The spectators who witnessed him in full flow at the crease certainly enjoyed seeing a master at work and play. G.C.Hurst would have loved to have had a tenth of his batting technique and talent. Cricket the Cowdrey way was a joy to behold

Baron Cowdrey died on 4 December 2000 just short of his 68th birthday after suffering a stroke earlier in the year. His only disappointment is that he was never trusted with the England captaincy Down Under for the Ashes battles. He was considered too nice. How about that for an epitaph.

COLIN COWDREY FOR THE RECORD:

- Born: 24 December 1932, Ootacamund, Madras, India
- County: Kent (1950–78)
- Tests: 114 (1954–75)
  - Runs: 7,624 (44.08), 22 centuries
  - Captain: 27 times
  - Highest score: 182 v Pakistan at The Oval, 1962
- First-class career: 892 games (1950–78)
  - Runs: 42,719 (42.89), 107 centuries
  - Highest first-class score: 307 v. South Australia in Adelaide
- Test catches: 120
- First to score a Test century against six different nations: Australia, South Africa, West Indies, New Zealand, India and Pakistan
- Knighted: 1992
- Ennobled: 1997
- Died 4 December 2000, Littlehampton, West Sussex, aged 67

20

JOHAN CRUYFF

'Cruyff turned football into a total triumph'

JOHAN CRUYFF was footballing royalty. He has plenty of supporters for the title of greatest footballer of all time, certainly from Europe. I have seen few better club sides than Ajax of the early 1970s when they won the European Cup three times in a row, and it was the creative Cruyff who was their chief orchestrator. He then took his magic boots to Barcelona and got the Catalans challenging the long supremacy of mighty Real Madrid.

In England we looked on with interest and a little bewilderment as Cruyff inspired a new style that they called 'Total Football'. Every outfield player took responsibility to drop into a team-mate's position if they went on the attack, so you saw full-backs playing as wingers, central defenders in striking roles and centre-forwards filling in at the heart of the defence.

Plenty of clubs had tried it in the past, but Ajax got it working to perfection because they had the highly skilled midfield partners Cruyff and Johan Neeskens to make it work with their quick, accurate passing and intelligent running off the ball. It was like watching ten versions of my dear old mate Martin Peters.

The twin pistons of Cruyff and Neeskens were also at work for the Dutch national team and with Ruud Krol in solid support they were narrowly beaten 2-1 by West Germany in the 1974 World Cup Final after they had electrified the tournament with their Total Football. Holland reached the final again four years later in Argentina, but Cruyff was mysteriously missing from the squad. It was later revealed that he had pulled out because of threats by a gang to kidnap his children.

An England football philosopher called Vic Buckingham first gave Cruyff his chance at Ajax. Buckingham had been in on the ground floor with Alf Ramsey when Tottenham first put into practice the push-and-run ideas of manager Arthur Rowe, and when injuries forced his retirement from playing he then coached West Bromwich Albion to the FA Cup in 1954.

He also had spells in charge at Fulham and Sheffield Wednesday sandwiched between two reigns at Ajax and then moved on to Barcelona. The Dutchwoman who cleaned his office at Ajax told him about her son who was in the youth squad. Her married name was Cruyff. Vic watched him in training, saw rich potential and promoted him to the first team at the age of 17 and the rest as they say is history.

Buckingham was soon replaced by Dutch coach Rinus Michels, who took over where the Englishman left off and worked in close co-operation with Cruyff on developing a new formation. Total Football was born.

After he had steered Ajax to three Dutch titles, Michels moved to Barcelona where Buckingham had been forced to stand down because of a back problem caused by his playing days at Tottenham. He had been trying to bring Cruyff to Barcelona when he had to surrender his position. Michels completed the deal and the Dutch master powered the Catalan club to their first La Liga title in a decade.

Cruyff scored 402 goals in 702 games during his 19-year career and would have retired in 1978 but for losing much of his fortune to a con artist who convinced him to put his money into a pig farm. It was a complete scam, and Johan had to continue playing to avoid bankruptcy. No wonder the man who had smoked throughout his career increased his intake to the daft levels that led to his early death from cancer.

Speaking as somebody who has had conmen and chancers trying to fleece me, my heart bled for Cruyff when he confessed he had been taken to the cleaners. It is a statutory lesson to all footballers (anybody for that matter) to be wary who you trust. The young millionaire players of today are sitting ducks for the crooks and scammers out there. Take the advice of an old battered and cynical footballer, don't trust a soul you have never met before or even some alleged friends.

Johan was young, energetic and determined enough to recover from his shattering experience of being conned by somebody close to him, but it left a bitterness that dropped a black cloud on what should have been the summertime of his life. He started to rebuild his fortune, much of it made from the commercialisation of his favourite No 14 shirt and his personalised Puma football boots in which he performed magical moments beyond we mere mortals.

His signature 'Cruyff turn' was copied by footballers the world over, and he inspired a procession of Dutch players to rise to the top including Marco van Basten, Patrick Kluivert, Ruud van Nistelrooy and Dennis Bergkamp.

In a bid to build up his bank account again, he became a globetrotting player at the back end of his career with Los Angeles Aztecs, Washington Diplomats, Levante and back to the Netherlands for winding-down seasons with Ajax and Feyenoord.

He then took all his knowledge into management and coached Barcelona to 242 victories in 387 matches, with 75 draws and 70 defeats.

When Johan was going through the nightmare of being conned out of his money, feelers were put out for him to join Chelsea where

I was the manager having a rough ride. It didn't come to anything, and I was shown the door soon after.

You could say it was a Bridge too far.

JOHAN CRUYFF FOR THE RECORD:
- Born: 25 April 1947, Amsterdam
- Ajax: 240 games, 190 goals (1964–73)
- Barcelona: 142 games, 48 goals (1973–78)
- Los Angeles Aztecs: 23 games, 14 goals (1978–79)
- Washington Diplomats: 30 games, 12 goals (1980–81)
- Levante: 10 games, 2 goals (1981)
- Ajax: 36 games, 14 goals (1981–83)
- Feyenoord: 33 goals, 11 goals (1983–84)
- European Cup: 1971, 1972, 1973
- European Footballer of the Year: 1971, 1973, 1974
- Holland: 48 caps, 33 goals (1965–77)
- World Cup runner-up: 1974
- Manager: Ajax (1985–88), Barcelona (1988–96), Catalonia (2009–13)
- Died: 24 March 2016, Barcelona, aged 68

21

ALFREDO DI STÉFANO

'The Blond Arrow from Argentina hit the bullseye'

I WAS into my debut season as a professional footballer when I got my first glimpse of 'Saeta Rubia', as Alfredo Di Stéfano was known in all Spanish-speaking countries – the 'Blond Arrow'. The 1960 European Cup Final between Real Madrid and Eintracht Frankfurt was being shown live from Hampden Park and even in black and white on our small screens Alfredo the Great came across as if from another planet.

It was almost as if we were watching footballing ballet, as Di Stéfano floated across the turf in beautifully choreographed movements in a match that has gone down in history as one of the finest ever played. Real won 7-3 in front of a Glasgow crowd of 127,000 and another 70 million watched on television across Europe.

Even now, more than 60 years later, the game stands out in my memory, and as a raw young pro it made me realise I had chosen the right sport after my struggle as to whether to concentrate on cricket or football. By the time Di Stéfano came into view his famous blond hair had receded but there was no lessening of his smooth power, his balance and his skill as he pulled the strings for the masterly Real Madrid side that was lifting the European Cup for a fifth successive year.

I will go into the amazing politics surrounding the match when I come to the Ferenc Puskás entry, but on the pitch Di Stéfano and Puskás were as near to perfection as playing partners as you will ever see. This lean, hungry-for-action boy back home in Chelmsford watched in wonder as they scored all seven Real goals between them, four to Puskás and a hat-trick to schemer-in-chief Di Stéfano.

Both players had been rebels without a pause, Puskás an exile from what had been war-torn Hungary and Di Stéfano a nomad born in Argentina where he started his glittering career with River Plate before joining Millionarios of Bogotá in the outlawed Colombian league. Wherever he went he lay his international hat and played for Argentina, Colombia and later Spain after joining Real in 1953 following a dispute as to whether he had also signed for Barcelona.

The pity for all football aficionados is that Di Stéfano – like George Best – never got to play on the World Cup stage, but he achieved enough at club level to prove that there have been few more artistic and supreme players ever to step gracefully on to a football pitch. My Irish friends will want me to point out that his mother had heritage in County Mayo. Maradona and Messi have taken over as better known Argentinian-born players but to my generation and those who watched the Real–Eintracht match Di Stéfano is up there with the true greats of the game.

He scored a then club record 216 league goals in 282 games for Real. His 49 goals in 58 matches was the all-time highest individual total in the European Cup. Di Stéfano scored in five consecutive European Cup finals for Real between 1955 and 1960 including that treble against Eintracht, and he added another 11 goals in a wind-down period with Espanyol before finally hanging up his golden boots at the age of 40.

His fame made him a target for nutters and fanatics, and while on a playing tour to Venezuela in 1963 he was kidnapped at gunpoint by a revolutionary group. He was later released unharmed and without a ransom being paid. How could you put a price on the blond head of a footballing god?

In 2008 Di Stéfano was given the recognition he deserved as a giant of the game. At a special ceremony in Madrid, he was guest of honour at an unveiling of his statue, and making a presentation on behalf of world and European football, UEFA President Michel Platini described him as 'a great among greats.'

Speaking as somebody awestruck by his skill as a schoolboy, I could not think of anybody more worthy of such an accolade. He was a poet of the game who talked with his feet and everything rhymed, and he made the Beautiful Game even more beautiful. If he were playing today, you would be talking about the first £200m footballer.

ALFREDO DI STÉFANO FOR THE RECORD:

- Born: 4 July 1926, Buenos Aires, Argentina
- River Plate: 66 games, 49 goals (1945–1949)
- Huracán (loan): 25 games, 10 goals (1945–1946)
- Millonarios: 101 games, 90 goals (1949–1953)
- Real Madrid: 282 games, 216 goals (1953–1964)
- Espanyol: 47 games, 11 goals (1964-66)
- Total: 521 games, 376 goals
- European Cup: 1956, 1957, 1958, 1959, 1960
- La Liga: 1954, 1955, 1957, 1958, 1961, 1962, 1963, 1964
- Spanish Cup: 1962
- La Liga top scorer: 1954, 1956, 1957, 1958, 1959
- Scored 49 goals in 59 European Cup matches
- International football:
  - Argentina 6 caps, 6 goals (1947)
  - Colombia 4 caps (1949)
  - Spain 31 23 goals (1957–1962)
- Teams managed:
  - Elche (1967–1968)
  - Boca Juniors (1969–1970)
  - Valencia (1970–1974)
  - Sporting CP (1974)
  - Rayo Vallecano (1975–1976)
  - Castellón (1976–1977)
  - Valencia (1979–1980)
  - River Plate (1981–1982)
  - Real Madrid (1982–1984)
  - Boca Juniors (1985)
  - Valencia (1986–1988)
  - Real Madrid (1990–1991)
- Died 7 July 2014, Madrid, aged 88

22

DUNCAN EDWARDS

*'Tragic Busby Babe Duncan lives
on in the memory'*

I NEVER had the satisfaction of seeing Duncan Edwards play in the flesh but I know for sure that he was something very exceptional. Bobby Charlton is one of the most honest men I know and he told me that the young giant from Dudley in the West Midlands was the greatest British footballer he ever played with. 'He was the only player who made me feel inferior,' Bobby said. 'If I had to choose one footballer to play for my life, it would have to be Duncan. Yes, he was *that* special.' Duncan's death came in a Munich hospital 15 days after the tragic air disaster, which Bobby survived. He was 21 and already considered potentially the finest all-round footballer England had ever produced.

I often hear people say that if it had not been for the Munich tragedy, Bobby Moore would never have won an England cap. Sorry, but I do not go along with that theory. A place would have been found for Mooro AND Edwards, which would have meant two of the greatest English footballing heroes playing in the same team. The mind boggles.

Duncan was such an outstanding prospect that he was trusted with First Division football at the age of 16 with the Busby Babes, and he became the then youngest England international at 18 years and 183 days. This was against Scotland at Wembley on 2 April 1955. England won 7-2, and Wolves striker Dennis Wilshaw scored four goals. Duncan played alongside one of his heroes, Wolves and England skipper Billy Wright, who told him, 'With that accent, Dunc, you should be with us at Molineux.'

It was well known that Wolves manager Stan Cullis had been keen to sign local boy Edwards before he was snapped up by Manchester United.

Billy said that Duncan gave him a rueful smile and replied in his thick Black Country voice, 'Aye, Mr Wright, but Mr Busby called at my house before Mr Cullis.'

Yes, he was that respectful. 'Mr Wright.'

He famously used to ride to Old Trafford from his digs on a bicycle, and he would faithfully send home two-thirds of his £15-a-week wages to his mum. 'A perfect model for any young footballer,' was how Matt Busby described him. The nearest he got to a scandal was when he was stopped by police for riding an unlit bicycle at night. He was fined ten bob (50p) by the local magistrate, and it made huge headlines.

My England team-mate Bobby knew Duncan better than most and came up with this memory that captures the awe in which he was held,

'Duncan was the complete player – good with both feet, strong in the tackle, commanding in the air, had a powerful shot, the physique of a bodybuilder and was an accurate passer of the ball no matter what the distance. He could play in any position and had the ability to dictate and dominate any match.

'I remember one particular game when I was playing with Duncan for the Army against the RAF during our national service. Duncan received the ball from our goalkeeper deep in our half, passed it to the full-back and took the return pass. Then he exchanged passes with me, stroked the ball to another forward, quickly demanded it back and unleashed the hardest shot you're ever likely to see from the edge of the box.

'The ball rocketed towards the goalkeeper's head. He ducked out of the way and the ball crashed into the net.

'Quite a few years later I was walking down a street in Cambridge when a chap stopped me. "You don't remember me, do you, Bobby," he said. "I played against you some time back when you were in the Army team."

'The game came back to me, and I asked him which position he played. "Goalie," he said.

'When I reminded him how he had ducked out of the way of Duncan's shot, he replied, "Yes, that was the proudest moment of my life."'

Billy Wright, England captain 90 times and the first player in the world to win 100 international caps, once described a goal Duncan scored against West Germany in Berlin in 1956. 'Three German defenders just bounced off him as he surged forward from midfield to shoot from 25 yards,' he recalled. 'The ball went into the net like a guided missile. It was one of the most spectacular goals I ever saw and the Germans gave him a nickname, "Boom Boom".'

In his short career Duncan played a key role in Manchester United's back-to-back league championships, and they were going for the hat-trick at the time of the Munich disaster.

There is, of course, no telling how good he might have become. But it's fair to surmise that he would have been right at his peak at the time of the 1966 World Cup. Old pros who saw Duncan in action used to say he and Bobby Moore together would have been the perfect combination, with Bobby concentrating on defence and big Duncan prompting the attack. There would have been plenty of room in the team for both of them, so let's put to sleep forever the notion that Bobby Moore would never have played for England but for Munich.

How about this for a statistic: in the 1956/57 season Duncan played a total of 94 – I repeat, 94 – competitive games, not including unit matches because he was still in the Army at the time. He just loved to play football, and could run all day and thrive on it.

The country was plunged into mourning when Duncan joined the seven other Busby Babes who lost their lives at Munich. As a young professional just starting out on my career I was engulfed by the misery of it all, and nearly 65 years later the memory still cuts deep.

He is buried with his sister Carol Anne, who died in 1947 at the age of 14 weeks. His tombstone reads simply, 'A Day of Memory Sad to recall Without Farewell He left us all'. In the nearby parish church of St Francis, in Duncan's home town of Dudley, there is a striking stained glass window showing him in action, a unique memorial to his brief life. And in the town centre stands a statue in memory of not only an extraordinary footballer but also a young man who made an enormous impact on everybody with whom he came into contact. As Billy Wright said, 'He was a smashing lad.'

He gets into my list simply because all the established pros I talked to when I joined the West Ham ground staff assured me he was the greatest footballer in the land. His tragic death at Munich turned him into a lasting legend. His memory lives on.

DUNCAN EDWARDS FOR THE RECORD:
- Born: 1 October 1936, Dudley, West Midlands (then Worcestershire)
- Manchester United: 177 games, 21 goals (1953–58)
- First Division: 1956, 1957
- England schoolboys: 9 games (1949–52)
- England under-23: 6 games 5 goals (1954–57)
- England B: 4 games (1953–54)
- England: 18 games 5 goals (1955–57)
- Died: 21 February 1958, Munich, aged 21

23

SIR GARETH EDWARDS

*'The coal miner's son who tried all the
time for Wales and the Lions'*

YOU MUST have seen it. THAT try, scored by Gareth Edwards for the Barbarians against the All Blacks in 1973 at Cardiff Arms Park. It was a moment of rugby brilliance that set in stone a place in sporting immortality for the coal miner's son from Wales. It is often referred to as 'the greatest try ever' and is continually replayed on the BBC.

It's not necessary to be a rugby fan to appreciate and applaud the sheer genius of the try. The move starts with a kick from the New Zealand winger Bryan Williams deep into the opposition half. Fly-half Phil Bennett collects the ball near his goal line, jinks and sidesteps and almost casually evades three tackles before passing the ball to master full-back J.P.R. Williams. It is next passed through the hands of Pullin, Dawes, David and Quinnell before Edwards, slipping between two team-mates, seems to appear from nowhere to take the final pass before diving over the line for a spectacular made-in-Wales try in the left-hand corner of the pitch. I can be this positive with my description because of the accompanying excited commentary from another Welsh rugby great, Cliff Morgan.

It was the pinnacle of the astonishing career of Gareth, who had a similar dilemma to me in his teenage years when he had to choose between two sports. Gareth had won a scholarship to the prestigious Millfield Public School in Somerset where he excelled at all sports, particularly gymnastics and athletics (he set a long-standing record at 220 yards hurdles and was a junior long jump champion).

But it was at two other sports that he was considered to have greatest potential: rugby and soccer. He was invited to join Swansea Town as it was then as a 16-year-old footballer but Cardiff Rugby Club intervened and persuaded him to concentrate on his first love of the oval-ball game.

In 1967, at the age of 19, he got his first call up for Wales and over the next 11 years established himself as a scrum-half of supreme skill and tenacity. He had two long-running partnerships with fly-halves Barry 'King' John and Phil 'The Sidestep' Bennett that lifted him into the land of rugby legend. Poetry in motion was a phrase often used to describe both pairings, each with the common denominator of Edwards as the instigator of their stunning running.

I had my head full of football matters, but it was a joy to relax away from the pressures of my game and watch a genius at work in his chosen field. Gareth played with speed, intelligence and a lot of cheek and invention as he gave the great Welsh team of those 1970s the spark to beat all comers. He shared in two Grand Slams and also made an impact with ten appearances for the British and Irish Lions.

He won all his 53 caps for Wales in succession, never missing a match through injury or loss of form. Gareth was Mr Consistency. The youngest ever Wales captain, he scored 20 tries and was a thinking-man's rugby player who was always coming up with winning tactics on the spot.

In a Five Nations international against Scotland in 1972 he raced virtually the length of the pitch for a try described as the best ever, until he topped it the following year for the Barbarians against the All Blacks.

Following retirement, the hugely charismatic Edwards was in demand as an after-dinner speaker and was a popular team captain opposite Emlyn Hughes in the BBC's *A Question of Sport*. In 2003 his rugby-playing peers voted him the greatest player of all time, and he was knighted in 2014.

One other statistic you might find a little fishy. In 1990 he set a British angling record when he landed a pike weighing 45lb 6oz in a reservoir near Pontypool. So this famous scrum-half could also hook a bit.

Not bad for the coal miner's son from Gwaun-Cae-Gurwen.

GARETH EDWARDS FOR THE RECORD:

- Born: 12 July 1947, Gwaun-Cae-Gurwen, Glamorgan
- Position: scrum-half
- Cardiff RFC: 1966–78
- Club games: 195, 67 tries
- Test career span: 1967–78
- Caps: 53 (20 tries)
- British and Irish Lions tours:
  - South Africa 1968 (2 Tests)
  - Australia and New Zealand 1971 (4 Tests)
  - South Africa 4 Tests (1974)
- Knighted: 2014
- Voted as the greatest player of all time in a 2003 poll by *Rugby World* magazine

24

HERB ELLIOTT

'The Mile Master who beat the sands of time'

THERE WAS an aura about the mile race that has all but disappeared in these metric times, but back in the 1950s and going into the 1960s it was the blue riband of the track and nobody could match the four-lap supremacy of Herb Elliott. Roger Bannister gave the race its romance, Elliott its refinement.

He was, without doubt, the Master of the Mile. Thirty-six times he went to the starting line and 36 times he was first through the finishing tape. Just a few years earlier the four-minute mile was considered impossible. He broke the barrier in 17 of his races.

Asked to explain his supremacy, Elliott – who had strong Irish ancestry on his father's side – said with what could have passed as Irish blarney, 'I do not have a will to win but a hatred of losing.' That was just the sort of thing my lovely old friend and West Ham team-mate Budgie Byrne was fond of saying.

I fancied myself as a bit of an all-round athlete at school, but could not get as involved as I would have liked because of my concentration on my summertime sport of cricket. My specialities were the field events, and in particular long jump, high jump and discus. I had little appetite for running long distances without a ball at my feet as I trained with Elliott-like fanaticism to become two-footed.

In the 1950s, there was an exceptional middle-distance runner at the time called Gordon Pirie, who was nicknamed 'Puff Puff' because of his habit of blowing out his cheeks as he ran. I often wonder if I subconsciously copied him, because I was always puffing out my cheeks when I was in full stride. Somebody said that it was if I was a glass blower, another that I was blowing West Ham bubbles.

There was none of that from Herb Elliott, who made running seem effortless, and I recall watching on television what were then known as the Empire Games from Cardiff in 1958 when he raced away to win the 880 yards and mile titles (for those not into the old distances, 880 yards is half a mile, which itself runs to 1,760 yards). In the same summer he lowered the world mile record to three minutes 54.5 seconds in Dublin and then nipped over to Gothenburg to break the metric mile (1500m) record. He was still only 21.

The race in Dublin, the first on the newly laid Santry track, was one of the most remarkable mile events in history. Elliott was up against Australian team-mates Merv Lincoln, Murray Halberg and Albie Thomas, along with Ireland's 1956 Olympic champion Ronnie Delaney. All five finished inside four minutes, and galloping Herb knocked a whopping two and a half seconds off Derek Ibbotson's recent record that had not yet been ratified.

What made the event even more memorable was that for much of the race the runners were accompanied by a black and white terrier dog racing with them on the infield. They were into the last lap when the dog elected to join them on the track but it was caught and pulled away before any of the runners could be impeded.

We watched film of it in England and could not believe what Elliott had achieved. Merv Lincoln, a crack Australian track star, told the TV interviewer: 'I can't fathom how I've beaten four minutes by four seconds and still only finished second. I swear that Herb feller is from another planet. I'm going to retire and take up tennis.'

Elliott, just shy of six foot and with long, loping strides, was a beautiful sight to behold when in full flow. He was nicknamed the 'Human Deer' and put his success down to a mixture of speed and the incredible stamina that he built up with exhausting runs through sand dunes on the beaches of his native Western Australia and at his Portsea training camp south of Melbourne. He was coached by the wildly eccentric Percy Cerutty, a man who many in athletics looked on as a crank because of his unorthodox training methods. He would not let Elliott train on a track between races, and encouraged him to study role models such as Leonardo da Vinci, Gandhi and Jesus for his motivation. 'Perfection, perfection, perfection,' was the mantra from his coach.

Cerutty would cajole Elliott into running to the edge of exhaustion and beyond and as he ploughed through the sand dunes, some more than 80 feet high, he would shout, 'Faster, faster. It's only pain.'

In the Olympic 1500m final in Rome in 1960, Cerutty sat quietly in the crowd with a white towel round his shoulders despite the heat of an Italian summer. With 600 metres still to run, he suddenly stood waving the towel above his head as a signal for Elliott to accelerate. 'Go, go, go,' he shouted.

The ambling Aussie reacted to the instruction by producing a kick finish a lap and a half from home that spreadeagled the field and left French silver medallist Michel Jazy 20 metres in his slipstream. It was considered one of the greatest last lap performances ever witnessed at an Olympics and he stopped the clock at a stunning world record three minutes 35.6 seconds.

He was continually being offered thousands of dollars to join the professional running circus in the United States in what was allegedly an era of amateurism, but soon after his Olympic triumph, Elliott – a maths genius – went to Cambridge University to continue his studies, virtually disappearing from the world athletics scene. He was just 22, and still well short of the age that athletes are considered to be at their peak.

His studying was as productive as his running and he later became chairman of one of the largest iron ore mining companies in the world and the driving force behind the Global Corporate Challenge Health initiative. He and his wife Anne had six children and were considered almost royalty Down Under.

A national treasure, he anchored the last leg of the torch relay for the opening ceremony to the Sydney Olympics in 2000.

He was miles ahead of the field.

HERB ELLIOTT FOR THE RECORD:

- Born: 25 February 1938, Subiaco, Western Australia
- Athletics career: 1956–62
- Coached by Percy Cerutty
- Competed in 36 miles races, won them all, 17 in under four minutes
- Empire Games half-mile and mile champion: 1958, Cardiff
- Olympic 1500m champion: 1960, Rome
- Fastest times, both world records:
  - Mile: 3m 54.5s, 1958, Dublin
  - 1500m: 3m 35.6s, 1960 Olympic Final, Rome

25

EUSÉBIO

'The Black Panther who pounced for Portugal and Benfica'

A SMILE automatically comes to my face just at the mention of the name of Eusébio, one of my all-time favourite footballers and somebody who enjoyed the 1966 World Cup almost as much as me. In the build-up to the finals he was already being talked of as Europe's answer to the phenomenon that was Pelé, and he lived up to the billing with a procession of scorching goals.

Eusébio wore the same number ten shirt, had a similar physique, and – without argument – a harder shot than the great man. He had the power, particularly in his right foot, to launch the ball like an Exocet missile. They had similar nicknames – 'The Black Pearl' and 'The Black Panther' – until Pelé became known simply as 'The King'.

Eusébio da Silva Ferreira – his full name – was Benfica's secret weapon in the early 1960s when they suddenly emerged as contenders for the European Cup, which had been monopolised by Real Madrid. He had joined them from Lourenço Marques in Mozambique, then under Portuguese rule. The major Brazilian clubs were given first refusal on signing the 19-year-old inside-forward, but passed because they thought they had plenty of players at home who were better. He then became the pawn in a fight to sign him between the leading sides in Lisbon.

Sporting Lisbon considered that Eusébio was already theirs because they used Lourenço as a nursery club. The story goes that Béla Guttman, Benfica's verbose, Hungarian-born manager, was sitting in his barber's chair in Lisbon when he overheard gossip about Sporting being interested in an exceptional prodigy with Lourenço.

Guttman went straight from the barber's shop and got the next flight out to Mozambique and came back with Eusébio safely locked in to a contract. Sporting cried 'foul' but the young African was bound for Benfica despite all the legal fisticuffs.

At the end of his first season with Benfica, Eusébio scored two memorable goals in the 5-3 European Cup Final victory over Real Madrid. The following year he scored in the final again, this time as Benfica were runners-up to AC Milan at Wembley.

Over the next 13 years he became a footballing legend, despite the handicap of a recurring knee injury that finally forced him into what were virtually walk-on parts with a cluster of clubs in Mexico, the United States and Canada.

Who will ever forget his impact on the 1966 World Cup, when his nine goals earned him the FIFA Golden Boot? I remember watching a full replay of his quarter-final performance against North Korea at Goodison Park on television with the rest of the England lads as Alf Ramsey worked on tactics for our semi-final battle. I had made my World Cup debut against Argentina on the same day that Eusébio became the talk of the tournament.

The tiny-tot Koreans had raced into an unbelievable 3-0 lead and then Eusébio took over. He scored four goals and won the match for Portugal virtually single-handedly, or, I guess, right-footed would be a more appropriate way of putting it.

As we watched a recording of the match at the England hotel headquarters in Hendon, one player was taking particular note – a short-sighted, toothless tiger called Norbert 'Nobby' Stiles. Alf Ramsey gave him the job of marking Eusébio in the semi-final at Wembley, and there was no better player on the planet for following orders than Our Nobby. The little feller told Alf, 'I'll stick closer to him than sh*t to a blanket.'

True to his word, Nobby hardly allowed the Portuguese man o' war a kick, and Eusébio's only real impact on the match was when he scored from the penalty spot, the first goal England had conceded throughout the finals. One of the most touching images of the 1966 finals was the sight of Eusébio using his shirt to wipe away tears that flowed after we had beaten Portugal 2-1.

When lists are drawn up of the world's greatest players, Eusébio often misses out in favour of Pelé, Maradona, Messi, Best, Cruyff, Di Stéfano, Puskás, Müller, Ronaldo and Zidane. Why? Because of that man Stiles.

In two of his biggest tests Eusébio failed to produce anything like his peak form because he could not shake off the pesky Stiles, who used to get almost inside his shirt with him. The second time that Nobby got the better of him was in the 1968 European Cup Final, when Manchester United beat Benfica on an emotion-charged night at Wembley.

Mind you, Eusébio very nearly won the match for Benfica in the closing moments of ordinary time when he at last managed to slip the Stiles shackles. He unleashed a signature shot – but with his left foot – that had goal written all over it. Everybody in the stadium thought Benfica were about to take a 2-1 lead until goalkeeper Alex Stepney produced a fantastic save to keep the ball out of the net.

I caught up with Eusébio a few years later when I went to Lisbon to play in a testimonial match for Portugal skipper Mário Coluna. 'I thought I was going to win us the match against United,' Eusébio told me. 'If only I could have hit the ball with my right rather than left foot. But Stepney was too good for me. As for Nobby Stiles, he was hard but fair. A good man.'

The picture that stays etched in my mind is of Eusébio pausing to applaud Stepney's save and shaking his hand. It was a moment that captured his sportsmanship and the spirit in which he always played the game.

Eusébio, arguably the greatest footballer ever to come out of Africa, had tremendous sprint speed to go with his natural power, and he topped the Portuguese league scoring list seven times. In 1965 he was voted European Footballer of the Year, and was European Golden Boot winner in 1968 and 1973 before his knee problems reduced both his pace and power.

In his retirement he became a roving ambassador for Portugal, just the sort of job the Football Association should have given to Bobby Moore. He worked as a spokesman against racism, representing the views of the world union of 57,500 professional footballers.

Yes, Portugal had a Special One long before José Mourinho surfaced.

I will never forget the day after we had won the World Cup in 1966, going with Eusebio to a casino in Knightsbridge where he was presented with a £2,000 cheque for being the tournament's top scorer. He told me that was the equivalent of six months' salary. I was presented with a 'Player of the Final' trophy.

Judith was with us, and she was completely won over by Eusebio's charm and charisma. On the way home and carrying the trophy, she said: 'I'd rather you'd been given the cheque.' She has always had a better head than me.

In all competitions and friendlies for Benfica, Eusébio scored 727 goals in 715 matches. That is a sensational output. How glad he must have been that a certain Nobby Stiles was not playing in the Portuguese league.

I don't mind admitting that I shed a tear when he succumbed to a heart attack in 2013, aged 71. He was a great part of my 1966 and just might have spoiled it for me but for our loveable rascal.

EUSÉBIO FOR THE RECORD:

- Born: 25 January 1942, Mozambique
- Career span: 1957–78
- Clubs:
  - Lourenço Marques 1957–60
  - Benfica 1961–75 (301 league games, 317 goals)
- Brief appearances with Rhode Island Oceaneers, Boston Minutemen, Monterrey, Beira-Mar, Toronto Metros, Las Vegas Quicksilver, Uniao Tomar 1975–78 (74 games in total, 26 goals)
- Portugal: 64 caps, 41 goals
- Club honours: ten Portuguese league championships, five Portuguese Cups, one European Cup
- European Footballer of the Year: 1965
- World Cup Golden Boot: 1966
- Died: 5 January 2014, Lisbon, aged 71

26

GODFREY EVANS

*'The batsman-wicketkeeper who
dived like Frank Swift'*

ONE OF my dreams as a sports-mad schoolboy was to become
an England batsman-wicketkeeper in the style of Godfrey Evans,
who was behind the stumps for England in 91 Tests. If I couldn't
be Denis Compton, then Godfrey was my man. He epitomised
how the game of cricket should be played, always with a smile
not far away and, just like Compo, providing entertainment to go
with his talent.

A former lightweight amateur boxer, he had a pugnacious face
and looked as if he had just stepped out of an illustration from a
Dickens novel. He was a real showman who would dive around
like the goalkeeper hero of his day, Frank Swift, to grab catches
that took the breath away and broke the hearts of batsmen who
thought they had hit a perfectly safe shot.

I used to study him every chance I got at the time when I
was trying to make up my mind whether to follow football or
cricket as a career. We had a wonderful batsman-wicketkeeper at
Essex in Brian Taylor, an ever-cheerful West Ham man nicknamed

'Tonker' because of the powerful style in which he could tonk the ball to the boundary. But like a procession of wicketkeepers in the immediate post-war years he had to play in the shadow of the untouchable Evans.

'Godders' spent all his county cricketing life with Kent, starting as a 16-year-old groundstaff boy and saying that the hardest he ever worked was as scoreboard operator in a famous game at Dover when Kent made 219 runs in 71 minutes to beat Gloucestershire.

He made his first-team debut in 1939, just before joining the Royal Army Service Corps for the duration of the war, winning promotion to the England Test team in 1946 against India. It was the start of a 12-year reign behind the stumps when he inspired a generation of young cricketers, including G.C. Hurst, which was the way my name appeared in the Essex Second XI as I tried to impersonate my hero.

It was during these cricketing days that I played for the first time with a beefy, blond schoolboy from Barking called R.F.C. Moore. Yes 'the' Bobby Moore before we became apprentice footballers together at West Ham. The first time we played in the same team was on the cricket field. He was an exceptional cricketer, but as I was later to find out an even better footballer.

Godfrey Evans was always the first name on the selectors' list after the captain, despite an unorthodox technique which was frowned on by 'old school' perfectionist and chief England selector, Plum Warner.

The statistics spoke for themselves about Godfrey's prowess. In his first-class career he held 811 catches and stumped 250 victims; with 173 catches and 46 stumpings in Test matches. He had a great mentor at Kent in Les Ames, and he himself inspired a young Alan Knott. Kent was the garden of England 'keepers!

Godfrey's belligerent batting was a bonus. He scored seven first-class centuries, and two in Tests. While he usually played with beef in his shots he could also put his head down when necessary as he proved in his debut overseas Test at Adelaide in 1947. He scored ten not out in 133 minutes, one of the slowest innings in Test history. With another of my idols, Denis Compton, at the other end he stubbornly anchored himself to the crease without scoring for 95 minutes while Compo completed his second century of the match to avert defeat. Always one for the quip, Godfrey later said, 'I took root to such an extent that I grew carrots on my boots. The Aussie fielders and spectators called me every name under the sun to try to put me off, but I was there for my country. Nothing beats doing a job for England.' You could almost see the flag of St George draped over his shoulders.

He was the first wicketkeeper to reach 200 Test dismissals, and the first Englishman to reach both 1,000 runs and 100 dismissals then 2,000 runs and 200 dismissals in Test cricket. No wonder *Wisden*, the bible of cricket, called him 'probably the greatest wicketkeeper in the history of the game'.

In retirement, this larger-than-life character cultivated mutton chop whiskers, had a spell as a publican, and for 20 years worked for Ladbrokes advising on cricketing odds.

I wonder what odds he would have given that I, rather than Greavsie, would score a World Cup final hat-trick.

GODFREY EVANS FOR THE RECORD:

- Born: 18 August 1920, Finchley, Middlesex
- County: Kent (1939–67)
- Tests: 91 (1946–59)
  - Runs: 2,439 (20.49), 2 centuries
  - Highest Test score: 104 v. India, 1952
  - Catches: 173
  - Stumpings: 46
- First-class career: 465 games (1950–78)
  - Runs: 14,882 (21.22), 7 centuries
  - Highest score: 144 v. Somerset, 1952
  - Kent catches: 816
  - Kent stumpings: 250
- Died: 3 May 1999, Northampton, aged 78

Muhammad Ali floated like a butterfly, stung like a bee and, in my book, was truly The Greatest ... even though he slept through the closing moments of the 1966 World Cup Final!

Gordon Banks: Golf day with my 1966 buddies Ron Flowers and Gordon Banks, who soared like Superman and could catch pigeons in goal for England. Gordon would get my vote as the greatest goalkeeper I ever played with or against.

Sir Roger Bannister broke the four-minute mile barrier and as a renowned neurologist saved lives. He used to say he wished he had spent less time on athletics and more on medical matters. A hero of heroes.

Franz Beckenbauer, known globally as Der Kaiser, ruled with regal splendour and was on the pitch for the highest and lowest points of my career in the World Cup finals of 1966 and 1970.

Serge Blanco emigrated from Venezuela to become the smoking gun of French rugby. A 40-fags-a-day man throughout his career.

George Best: What a pity George Best was not born ugly and able to go past the girls and the pubs the way he went past defenders. I would support those who describe George as the greatest British footballer of them all. A pity he could never escape his demons.

Usain Bolt, the Fastest Man on the Planet, would have loved my football World Cup medal. His unfulfilled ambition was to play the game professionally at the top-level.

Bjorn Borg, the 'IceBorg' who only melted at the sight of Charlton Athletic in action! The coolest sporting superstar I've ever seen.

Ian Botham, the cricketing great with bat and ball who now lords it over us all as Baron Botham of Ravensworth. A huntin', shootin' and fishin' man who has walked hundreds of miles for the smiles of underprivileged children. Nice one, Beefy.

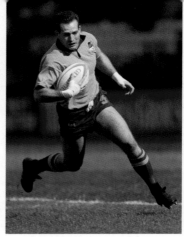

Don Bradman is remembered in stone at the Adelaide Oval. The Don was the nearest there has ever been to cricketing perfection. Nobody gets near his incredible batting average of 99.94. My County average was, uh, 0.

David Campese, the goose-stepping Aussie who was the Muhammad Ali of rugby ... and he always put action where his mouth was.

Wilt Chamberlain: There are lots of tall stories about Wilt the Stilt Chamberlain, the giant of the courts, including many bedroom adventures that remain secret.

John Charles was idolised at Leeds, Juventus and throughout Wales. Arguably the greatest all-round British footballer of any time, the Gentle Giant could score and stop goals with equal skill and effect.

Bobby Charlton and I tested the turf at Wembley as we campaigned together for England to get the 2006 World Cup Finals. Even the magical name of Sir Bobby could not help us there. It was a political stitch-up. Sir Bobby was simply a genius in football boots.

Jim Clark, the shy, retiring Scottish sheep farmer who roared to two world F1 titles in his Lotus before tragically dying in a crash at the Hockenheimring in Germany in 1968. He had won 25 F1 races before his horrific end. What a waste of a life.

Sebastian Coe, the elegant running pride of Great Britain who raced all the way to the House of Lords via Parliament. Here he beats Steve Cram to the line to retain his 1500m Olympic title in Los Angeles in 1984. His greatest triumph, overlording the 2012 London Games.

Denis Compton was one of the first sportsmen to cash in on his commercial value and it went nicely to his head. The Great Entertainer who inspired this all-rounder (I use the description loosely).

Sir Henry Cooper, who as Our 'Enery hooked first place in the popularity stakes with the British sports fans. Will always be remembered for putting the then Cassius Clay on the canvas at my favourite sporting venue, the old Wembley Stadium.

Colin Cowdrey was a cricketing artist who used his bat like Goya with a brush. Born to play for England, MCC was a formidable force at the wicket and as an administrator. He was the first cricketer to be awarded a peerage.

Johan Cruyff was the Dutch master who turned football into a total triumph. An inventive and incisive player, his style was imitated by players worldwide. I wonder how much better he would have been without his heavy smoking, including in the dressing-room at half-time?

Alfredo Di Stefano was a Nureyev on grass who pulled the strings for the magical Real Madrid team of the 1950s going into the 60s. His partnership with Ferenc Puskás was a thing of beauty.

Duncan Edwards: This Duncan Edwards statue stands in the town of Dudley in the West Midlands, remembering a fabulously gifted footballer who had so much more to give. Losing him in the 1958 Munich air crash was a terrible blow for the English game.

Sir Gareth Edwards is the Welsh miner's son who came to the surface as one of the all-time great rugby players. A charismatic character, he had to choose between football and rugby in his late teens. Rugby was the winner.

Herb Elliott, the Australian 'Running Deer', was miles ahead of the field. He broke the four-minute mile barrier 17 times and was never beaten over four laps in 36 races. He retired at 22.

Eusebio, the Black Panther of Benfica who so often pounced for Portugal. He and I had a 1966 World Cup to remember! One of the greatest footballers ever to emerge from Africa.

Godfrey Evans, my wicketkeeping hero who used to dive around like goalkeeper Frank Swift. He joined Les Ames and Alan Knott as the triumvirate of great wicketkeepers from Kent.

Juan Manuel Fangio: Two legends of motor racing, Juan Manuel Fangio and Stirling Moss, rivals on the F1 circuit and great friends off it. They drove their cars in the daredevil days before computers and proper attention to safety.

Roger Federer, the FedExpress from Switzerland, has always delivered the best possible service, and I've loved being at Wimbledon to see the master at work and play. He manages to be elegant and explosive at one and the same time.

Sir Tom Finney: Not a bad attack, lined up for a futile bid to get the 2006 World Cup finals for England, left to right: Tom Finney, young Gary Lineker, Prime Minister John Major, little old me, **Sir Stanley Matthews**, Nat Lofthouse and Sir Bobby Charlton. Finney, Matthews and Charlton made it into my Great Eighty.

Andrew Flintoff:
Freddie had us doubled up at his all-round exploits, and he could be ferocious whether batting or bowling. He has owned up to the mental pressures that can wear you down when in the public spotlight.

Jimmy Greaves:
Those balls Jimmy Greaves and I are carrying reminds me of how long it is since we were playing together for West Ham, gulp, more than 50 years. Greavsie was the greatest British goal scorer I've ever seen. It was not deliberate but I managed to steal his World Cup glory.

Sir Lewis Hamilton had made up his mind to become an F1 driver while still a ten-year-old primary schoolboy, and now gives all his rivals a schooling. Plenty consider him the greatest racing driver of them all.

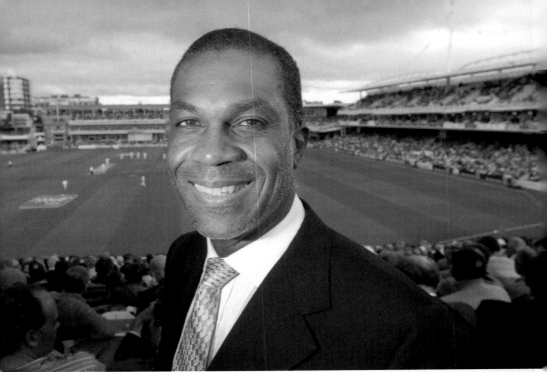

Michael Holding has the best nickname in sport ... Whispering Death. He bowled with speed and stealth for the all-conquering West Indies and is now a revered commentator on the game he played better than most.

Roger Hunt: THAT second goal in the 1966 World Cup Final and Roger Hunt had the best view of all, and he said the ball definitely crossed the line. Good enough for me! Roger was a magnificent player for Liverpool and England and it was my privilege to play as his striking partner. We were both Lancashire lads, you know!

Sir Len Hutton was the first professional to captain England, and inspired this young batsman to fall in love with cricket. He and Clitheroe-born Cyril Washbrook (my fellow Lancastrian) were a great white rose/red rose opening combination for England.

Pat Jennings, the Goliath of a goalkeeper with shovel hands that Liverpool manager Bill Shankly said should have disqualified him from playing in goal. He was joking, of course. I think. Big Pat was a marvellous last line of defence for Tottenham, Arsenal and Northern Ireland.

Michael Johnson was a golden hero of the athletics track who did it his way. He had a unique running style, and has educated many television viewers with his expert analysis of the technique of moving very quickly with least effort.

Michael Jordan featured in a television documentary series called The Last Dance, which I recommend for anybody who wants to know what made this king of the basketball court tick. A slam dunk of a watching experience.

27

JUAN MANUEL FANGIO

*'Man of mystery Fangio was El
Maestro of the F1 circuit'*

IF YOU'RE ever in Argentina and you want to impress locals of
a certain age, just mention Fangio to them and you will see faces
light up with smiles and acknowledgement that you are an amigo.
He is up there with footballing giants like Di Stéfano, Maradona
and Messi as a treasured all-time national hero.

When I was first taking notice of motor racing he was THE
god. He had been so successful on the South American racing
circuit that he was sponsored by the Juan Perón government to
go to Europe to continue his career after the end of the Second
World War. They saw him as an ambassador of all that was best
about Argentina. It was not until 1949, at the age of 37, that he
achieved regular success in Europe but established his credentials
when the Formula One World Championship was introduced in
1950, winning the title five times in the first decade. His record
stood for 46 years until overtaken by Michael Schumacher.

Fangio, nicknamed El Maestro, captured the Championship
with four different teams – Alfa Romeo, Ferrari, Mercedes-Benz and

Maserati. He held the highest winning percentage in Formula One – 46.15 per cent – and took the chequered flag in 24 of the 52 races he entered. A distinctive physical feature was that he had bowed legs through which you could have run a pig, and he answered to the affectionate name from rival drivers of 'the bandy legged one'.

He drove in an era when it was the man at the wheel who was totally in control, with no help from peripheral computers, and pit stops were leisurely compared with today's slick, lightning-quick operations. He was renowned for his generosity and always gave ten per cent of his winnings to his team of mechanics

Fangio's greatest race was the German Grand Prix at the Nürburgring circuit in 1957, when he was 45. He needed to win to clinch the title for a fifth time but was way behind his two young, British rivals Mike Hawthorn and Peter Collins after a disastrous pit stop. He started to set a succession of new lap records as he set off in almost reckless pursuit of the Brits, catching Collins on the penultimate lap and then overtaking Hawthorn to win by just three seconds.

His story reads like something out of an adventure book. In 1952 he broke his neck when crashing at Monza, cheated death and was back driving the following year. In 1958 he was kidnapped by pro-Castro supporters while in Havana for the unofficial Cuban Grand Prix, and was later released by his captors who brought down the Batista regime a few months later.

He lost his title to the suave Englishman Hawthorn in 1958. It typified the esteem in which everybody held Fangio that Hawthorn braked approaching the flag so that the Argentine could finish ahead of him. 'I did not want to lap my hero,' the cheerful, bow-tied Hawthorn said afterwards.

Fangio later became president of Mercedes-Benz and honorary life president in 1987.

Never married, he died in Buenos Aires in 1995 aged 84.

Judith and I once spent an entertaining afternoon in the stunning Mayfair home of the legend that was Sir Stirling Moss, as you do. Sir Stirling, one of Fangio's pall bearers, told us, 'He was The Teacher. Everything other drivers including me know about winning they learned from Fangio. He was simply the finest driver of racing cars there has ever been.'

There was a bizarre sequel to his life when his body was exhumed in 2015 to prove that he was the father of Rubén Vázquez, who then found out he had a half-brother, Oscar 'Cacho' Fangio. Together, they inherited the Fangio millions.

Man of mystery Fangio had taken his secrets with him to the grave. Olé!

JUAN MANUEL FANGIO FOR THE RECORD:
- Born: 24 June 1911 Balcarce, Argentina
- Grand Prix career span: 1950–58
- World F1 champion: 1951, 1954, 1955, 1956, 1957
- Teams: Alfa Romeo, Ferrari, Mercedes-Benz, Maserati
- Races entered: 52
- Wins: 24
- Podiums: 35
- Pole positions: 29
- Career points: 245
- Died 17 July 1995, Bueno Aires, aged 84

28

ROGER FEDERER

'Fed Express delivers the perfect
Wimbledon service'

TENNIS COMES hot on the heels of football and cricket in my list of favourite sports and there is no doubt in my mind that Roger Federer is the finest player I have seen in the flesh. My all-time hero was Rod 'The Rockhampton Rocket' Laver but I only saw him in the black-and-white television days.

Excuse me showing off, but I have been a regular spectator at Wimbledon since getting a useful calling card as an England World Cup winner.

Up until recent years the 1966 squad were often invited for special days during Wimbledon fortnight, and I have even been a guest – get me! – in the Royal Box. It was from that privileged position, with my oldest grandson Jack for company, that I watched Federer and then Novak Djokovic in back-to-back matches. I said at the time it was like seeing Pelé and then Maradona in successive games.

I have been an average tennis player but a fan of the sport for much of my life, and it is only when you see the superstars up close you realise the standard at which they perform. It is astonishing, and nobody does it better than Federer.

What a role model he is for tennis players worldwide, or for any sports competitor for that matter. He moves around the court with amazing agility and has almost balletic balance as he unleashes shots from forehand or backhand with power and accuracy, plus he seems to have so much time to play the game while his opponents appear to be at full throttle.

What puts him head and shoulders above so many of his contemporaries is the way he carries himself on court. He is a true gentleman of the game, always sporting and gracious and a wonderful ambassador for his homeland of Switzerland.

His record of triumphs is just unbelievable: as I write – and I am quoting Wikipedia now – he has won 20 Grand Slam men's singles titles, an all-time record shared with Rafa Nadal and Djokovic. He has been world number one in the ATP rankings for a total of 310 weeks – including a record 237 consecutive weeks – and has finished as the year-end number one five times. On top of that he has won 103 ATP singles titles, second only to Jimmy Connors and including a record end-of-season six ATP finals.

And he seems to have done it without breaking sweat. Talk about Mr Cool.

He is the man with the golden racket. He has picked up more than £100m in prize money, and much more than that from sponsorship and endorsement deals. He and his wife Mirka have produced identical twin girls and identical twin boys. I predict some formidable doubles partnerships in the years ahead!

How lucky we are as spectators to have the Fed Express, Rafa and Djoko at their peak at the same time. I could have picked any one of them to represent tennis in my list, but Roger got the nod simply because of the charisma he brings to the court to go with his talent.

Djokovic is arguably the more consistent player but lacks Roger's likability factor, while Rafa is the king of clay who is rarely seen at his scintillating best on the grass of Wimbledon.

Then there's Andy Murray, the great Scot who is definitely the best British player of my lifetime, and that takes in Fred Perry. Sir Andy has been so unfortunate to hit his peak at the time the Holy Trinity of Tennis are in command. He has performed miracles to get in among the Grand Slams while they are around. But the young guard are preparing to take over.

New balls, please.

ROGER FEDERER FOR THE RECORD:
- Born: 8 August 1981, Basel, Switzerland
- Career span: 1998–ongoing
- Career titles: 103
- Matches won: 1,251
- Matches lost: 275
- Prize money: $130,594,339
- Grand Slam titles: 20
- Wimbledon: 2003, 2004, 2005, 2006, 2007, 2009, 2012, 2017
- Australian Open: 2004, 2006, 2007, 2010, 2017, 2018
- US Open: 2004, 2005, 2006, 2007, 2008
- French Open: 2009
- Olympic Games: Silver medal, 2012, London

29

TOM FINNEY

'I literally followed in the footsteps
of the footballing plumber!'

IT'S TRUE to say that I almost followed in Tom Finney's footsteps into the world of professional football. I was the proud owner of a pair of Tom Finney boots that my dad bought me as I started to show potential as a schoolboy player. They were my most prized possession and I used to polish them after matches until I could see my face in the toecaps.

In those days you chose to be either Finney or Stanley Matthews in kick-abouts with your mates. I knew I was never going to be a Wizard of Dribble like Matthews, so in my head I was the Preston Plumber, Tom Finney. I prided myself on being two-footed like him, a versatile player who was capped by England in four forward positions.

Matthews and Finney were the two biggest names in British football at the time. Stanley, with all his now-you-see-me-now-you-don't dribbling tricks, was the people's favourite, but Finney is the one who could be described as the players' player.

Whenever I met an old pro who was a contemporary of the wing masters, they invariably made the point that while Matthews took the eye with his extraordinary dribbling, Finney gave something extra to the team effort and was the more productive all-round player.

All these years later I can point to Tom Finney as the man I hold up as an example of the perfect professional. He gave all he had to the game without asking for anything in return. He was modesty personified and a master of all the footballing skills.

Yet, astonishingly, Tom was never a full-time professional. Throughout his career he worked as an electrician and plumber, building up a nice little business in the trade he always insisted on having as a safety net in case he got kicked out of football. Imagine answering a knock at the front door today and finding Harry Kane standing there in a blue boiler suit with a bag of plumbing tools in his hand, saying, 'You want your pipes fixing, missus?' That was how it was with Tom. Every weekday after training he would go on his rounds as a plumber.

What you have to remember is that the most Tom ever earned in his career from football was £20 a week. He had hung up his boots by the time the maximum wage was kicked out in 1961. My career was just kicking off as his was closing and his name lives on as a giant of our game. I was on a special edition of *A Question of Sport* with him just before we left for Mexico and our World Cup defence in 1970, and it was such a pleasure to find him a lovely man without an ounce of arrogance. My team-mates were Bobby Moore and Alan Mullery, while Tom was answering questions alongside two other golden oldies, Stan Mortensen and Johnny Haynes. Know-alls Mooro, Mullers and I won comfortably, but with questions that were weighted in our favour.

Finney made a one-match comeback with Lisburn Distillery, doing a favour for their manager George Eastham Senior, and played in the 3-3 draw against Benfica in a European Cup tie in 1963/64. He did not play in the away leg because he could not afford the time off from his plumbing business. Distillery were hammered 5-0.

Tom's loyalty to Preston is legendary. He remained heavily involved with the club as president right up until his passing at the age of 91 in 2014, and there's a beautiful statue of him at Deepdale to remind future generations of the Finney legacy of class mixed with outstanding sportsmanship.

Amazingly, Preston turned him down when he first applied to join the club on leaving school in 1936. He was told he was too small and scrawny. At 14, he stood just 4ft 9in – as he said, 'A real Tom Thumb.' He began an apprenticeship with his father's electrical firm while in his spare time working out in the gymnasium.

Tom showed his determination to become a two-footed player by wearing a slipper on his strongest left foot to encourage himself to use the right. Preston suddenly realised they had a diamond in their midst, but Tom's dad refused to let him sign professional forms until he qualified as a plumber and electrician.

Then the little matter of the war intervened. He played for Preston in the 1940/41 Football League War Cup Final when Arsenal were beaten 2-1 in a replay at Ewood Park, but it was 1946 before his career really got under way.

He was such a versatile player that he won his 76 England caps in three different positions – outside-right (40), outside-left (33) and centre-forward (three) – and he also played much of one game as an emergency inside-forward. His 30 goals was then a record for an England player.

Injury cost Finney another dozen caps, and he would have won even more but for the selectors dithering over whether to play both him and Stanley Matthews in the same attack. When they finally played together in Portugal in 1947, England won 10-0! They scored a goal each, and between them laid on four each for Tommy Lawton and Stan Mortensen.

Gentleman Tom was never booked, and was respected throughout the game for his sportsmanship. When the lira-laden

Italians came hunting him in the late 1950s he was very tempted because it would have set him up financially for life, but the Preston chairman told them where to stick their offer. 'Tom Finney plays for no club but Preston,' he said. Tom wasn't even given the chance to talk to them. These were the 'soccer slave' days when players did what they were told by their clubs.

Tom experienced some downs as well as ups during his international career and was in the England team humbled by the United States at the 1950 World Cup finals. 'It was a complete freak result,' he said. 'We played them off the park for much of the game but it was one of those days when the ball just wouldn't go into the net.'

He sat in the Wembley press box nursing an injury when England were beaten 6-3 by Hungary in 1953. 'I remember the Hungarians coming out on to the pitch ten minutes earlier than usual, and doing all sorts of juggling tricks as they warmed up,' he recalled. 'My companion in the press box said, "It's easy to do that with nobody marking you." But we realised they were as good as they looked when they rattled into a 4-1 lead inside the first 20 minutes. That was as good an international team as I ever saw.'

Tom played in the second game against the Hungarians in Budapest the following year. England were thumped 7-1, the biggest defeat in their history.

'We all realised then that there was a different way to play the game,' he said. 'It was the start of a complete re-think. Suddenly it dawned on us that we were not as good as we thought we were.'

We met up again in the late 90s when sports-mad prime minister John Major put us in his ambassador's team to try to win the 2006 World Cup finals for England, along with Sir Stanley Matthews, Sir Bobby Charlton, Nat Lofthouse and Gary Lineker. That was when I got a close-up of world football politics and woke up to what a bent old business it is. The finals went to Germany.

The establishment suddenly realised Tom was missing from the honours list and awarded him a knighthood when he was 77! What a way to treat a hero.

The last word should come from his long-time Preston team-mate Bill Shankly, 'Tom was the most complete footballer ever to play the game. He could have worn an overcoat and still have run rings round any defence.'

Sir Tom Finney, master footballer who could fix your pipes.

TOM FINNEY FOR THE RECORD:

- Born: Preston, Lancashire, 5 April 1922
- Career span: 1946–59
- Club: Preston (473 games, 210 goals)
- Second Division: 1951
- FA Cup runner-up: 1954
- FWA Footballer of the Year: 1954, 1957
- Played one European Cup tie with Lisburn Distillery in 1963/64 (a 3-3 draw with Benfica)
- England: 76 caps, 30 goals
- Knighted: 1998
- Died: 14 February 2014, Preston, aged 91

FREDDIE FLINTOFF

'Freddie had us doubled up with bat and ball'

FEARLESS FREDDIE Flintoff, Tom Finney and I were born a few miles apart. While I lost my Lancashire accent pretty soon after moving to Essex to mix in with the locals, Freddie and Tom remained full-blown oop north Lancastrians and proud of it.

Freddie, of course, was really Andrew Flintoff but everybody latched on to the 'Fred Flintstone' nickname when he became the hero of the nation with his explosive all-round cricketing exploits for England.

You cannot help but make comparisons with that other great all-rounder, Ian Botham, of a generation before him. Both of them could be mighty match winners with bat or ball, both challenged the establishment with their off-field behaviour and both inspired the love of the people, even if they had only a fleeting interest in cricket.

Botham will go down in the cricket annals as the greater player; his stats see to that. But for a couple of seasons before injury interruptions Freddie was up there equal with the king. His career figures are fairly ordinary but what they don't show is how he motivated his team-mates and the crowd with bursts of absolute brilliance with both bat and ball and by holding blinding catches at slip. These were moments when he lifted a nation.

Standing 6ft 4in and weighing anywhere between 15 and 17 stone depending on his latest calorie intake, he could unleash 90mph deliveries that had batsmen ducking and dodging and wondering why he was described as only medium fast.

As a cricket fan, I loved watching him in his peak summers from 2003 to 2006. I remember his soaring six off South African express Makhaya Ntini that was still rising as it disappeared into the Bedser Stand at The Oval. In 2004 he hammered a spectacular Test-best 167 against West Indies at Edgbaston, when one of his seven sixes was memorably dropped by his father in the stands. And then there was the Everest of his career in 2005, when he dominated the Ashes series. Who can forget the photograph of him consoling Brett Lee after England narrowly beat Australia at Edgbaston? It underlined that he had great sportsmanship to go with his competitive nature.

Later, we saw the fun side of the big man when he and Kevin Pietersen were obviously three sheets to the wind as they staggered into 10 Downing Street to celebrate the Ashes victory. He played hard on and off the field and often had us doubled up with his antics, such as when he fell drunk off a pedalo in the West Indies. That made the splash headlines in all the papers. Everybody loved Freddie.

Sport is a great and often cruel leveller and when Freddie was promoted to captain he lost control of the ship and had to suffer through a 5-0 drubbing Down Under in Australia, and then his body started to rebel against the back-breaking pressures he put on it. Having had lower back problems for much of my later career, I sympathised with how he was suffering.

Finally his knees let him down and his all-too-brief career was over in 2009. It was great fun while it lasted, although a few years later he admitted much of his gung-ho attitude was an act to hide periods of dark depression. Pressures on modern sportsmen are growing because of the close scrutiny from the media and social networks, and I applaud the greater concentration on the mental health of our sports stars.

He was too big a personality to go quietly into the wings and, since his retirement, father-of-four Freddie has forged a new career for himself as an all-action television and radio celebrity and *Top Gear* presenter who is never anything less than entertaining, which was how he played his cricket.

Mind you, training to fight as a professional boxer was taking his all-round ability a bridge too far. Freddie is in a league of his own.

ANDREW FLINTOFF FOR THE RECORD:

- Born: 6 December 1977, Preston, Lancashire
- County: Lancashire (1995–2009)
- Tests: 79
  - Runs 3,845 (21.77)
  - Wickets 226 (32.78)
  - Top score: 167
  - Best bowling return: 5/58
- First-class career: 183 matches
  - Runs: 9,027 (33.80)
  - Top score: 185
  - Wickets: 350 (31.59)
- ODI matches: 141
  - Runs 3,394 (32.01)
  - Wickets 169 (24.38)
- *Wisden* Cricketer of the Year: 2005
- BBC Sports Personality of the Year: 2005

31

JIMMY GREAVES

'The greatest of all goal scorers, yet it was me who finished up the World Cup hero'

YOU NEEDED to be around where and when I was growing up to realise why Jimmy Greaves has always been gigantic in my personal rating of footballers. If there's been a greater British goalscorer then I've not seen him and, for Jimmy, it was cruel fate that he was not in England's 1966 World Cup-winning team.

I was a year younger than Jim and was in awe of him because of the way he monopolised matches in our local Essex school games. He once scored 11 goals in a 13-0 victory against the school where Martin Peters was a pupil. 'I watched from the sidelines,' the younger Martin later told me. 'I've never seen an individual performance to touch it.'

When I signed as an apprentice for West Ham in 1956 he was already a star in the making. That season, 1956/57, he scored the little matter of 114 goals for Chelsea, who presented him with an illuminated address to mark the feat. The following August, at the age of 17, he made his first-team debut for Chelsea against Spurs at White Hart Lane and scored a sensational solo goal that

Tottenham skipper Danny Blanchflower described as the greatest goal he had ever seen.

That was what it was like for Jimmy all the way through his career, stunning goals scored with natural ease and celebrated as casually as if he had picked an apple from a tree.

I personally thought he was at his most scintillating as a goalscorer when with Chelsea, his goals coming in fives, fours and plain ordinary threes. All of us other young pros looked on in wonder as he became a target for the super-rich Italian clubs and joined AC Milan for a record £80,000 in 1961. At the time the most you could earn in English football was £20 a week; he quadrupled his take-home pay by moving to Italy.

Then, after a series of threatened strikes by the Professional Footballers' Association, the Football League dramatically caved in to our demands and kicked out the maximum wage. Suddenly Jimmy could earn at home in England what he was picking up in Italy, where they were playing a miserly tight and physical defensive game. He was marked by two or three defenders everywhere he went – 'even to the bog', he said with a Cockney humour that was to become famous.

Tottenham manager Bill Nicholson brought him back to England for a then world-record £99,999, deliberately dropping below three figures to save Jim from carrying the burden of being the first £100,000 footballer. So he joined the team that in the previous season had been the first in the 20th century to win the First Division and FA Cup double – and he made them even better.

He became idolised at Spurs on his way to a club record 266 goals, FA Cup winners' medals in 1962 and 1967, a European Cup Winners' Cup medal in 1963 and legendary status.

Meantime, I had been converted by West Ham manager Ron Greenwood from a very average wing-half to a goal-seeking forward, not anywhere near the class of Greavsie but good enough to attract the attention of England boss Alf Ramsey. I wasn't a twinkle toes like Jim, but I brought more physicality and power to the game than the little genius.

I remember my first meeting with Jimmy away from football. Our daughter Claire was just a couple of months old and I was pushing her in a pram through our local supermarket in Essex when I came face to face with Jimmy. We both did a double take, laughed at the coincidence and then got involved in a conversation. I was so in awe of him that when I wandered back into the High Street I realised I had left Claire in the supermarket and rushed back and retrieved her. A year later, Greavsie and I were together in the England squad.

Jimmy had overcome an energy-sapping bout of hepatitis in the autumn of 1965 but got himself razor-sharp fit for the World Cup finals. He played in the first three matches while I looked on from the stands in those pre-substitute days, just glad to be part of the squad. In the third game against France he picked up a nasty gash on his shin that needed stitches and I – lucky boy – was the one who took his place, scored in my World Cup debut against Argentina (thanks, Martin) and had a pretty prominent part in our semi-final victory over Portugal.

The entire nation was debating whether Jimmy should be recalled for the final when he reported that he was fit again. Alf liked the way I moulded with my West Ham club-mates Bobby Moore and Martin Peters, so I was safe. Roger Hunt made the team tick with his tireless work rate, something Jimmy would never claim was his strongest suit. So Alf named an unchanged side, and it has now been a talking point for more than 55 years whether Jimmy should have played.

He later admitted that the hepatitis had robbed him of half a yard of speed, but he was still better than most strikers in the world and had a couple of years when he showed flashes of his old form before a miserable wind-down season at West Ham, where he seemed more interested in the social life with his best pal Bobby Moore than playing.

It was a sad day for football when he retired at the all-too-young age of 31.

Jimmy had a well-publicised battle with the bottle, but had the character to overcome it and reinvent himself as a television celebrity alongside Ian St John in the popular *Saint and Greavsie* show, and to produce loads of books with Norman Giller, the writing partner I have borrowed. He later become a stand-up comedian and after-dinner speaker, starring in roadshows compered by our agent Terry Baker. All of this came crashing down in 2015 when he suffered a paralysing stroke and and as I write the news has just broken of his passing after a long battle that wore him out. Rest in peace Jim. You were The King of goalscorers and a giant of a man.

The greatest British goalscorer of them all deserves better.

JIMMY GREAVES FOR THE RECORD:
- Born: 20 February 1940, East Ham
- Career span: 1957–72
- Club goals: 447, including a record 357 in the old First Division
- Clubs:
    - Chelsea (169 games, 132 goals)
    - AC Milan (14 games, 9 goals)
    - Tottenham (381 games, 266 goals)
    - West Ham United (40 games, 13 goals)
- Also played non-league football for Brentwood, Chelmsford, Barnet, Woodford Town
- England: 57 caps, 44 goals
- England under-23: 12 games, 13 goals
- FA Cup: 1962, 1967
- European Cup Winners' Cup: 1963
- World Cup: 1966

32

SIR LEWIS HAMILTON

'Who do you think you are, Lewis Hamilton?'

LEWIS HAMILTON is one of the few modern masters – along with the likes of Federer, Ronaldo and Messi – to make it on to my roll of honour. I have mostly confined my list to contemporaries and old heroes who have inspired and motivated me along the way. There are many exceptional sportsmen you will find missing, but this is a personal list and I suggest it's a good exercise to draw up your own hall of fame. You will be amazed how difficult it is to get all your favourites in.

Hamilton has driven me (another weak attempt at humour there) to include him with his phenomenal record on the track. He is making out a strong case to be considered the greatest motor racing driver of all time and when you think how many billions of people take to the wheel of their cars that is some weight to carry.

It is part of F1 folklore how, at the age of ten, Lewis approached the McLaren team boss Ron Dennis at the 1995 *Autosport* Awards ceremony and told him, 'I want to race for you one day.' He was signed up by McLaren and Mercedes-Benz to their Young Driver

Support Programme after the precocious youngster had proved himself an extraordinary prospect on the karting scene.

With his Grenada-descended father as a main influence, he won the British Formula Renault, European Formula Three and GP2 championship in 2006. He became a McLaren F1 driver for 2007, making his debut 12 years after that initial cheeky encounter with Dennis.

He then became the youngest F1 world champion when he captured the title in 2008 and at the time of writing has won seven championships to equal the all-time record of Michael Schumacher, the latest six triumphs coming since his switch to Mercedes in 2013. An intelligent young man, he understands all the intricacies of what goes on under the bonnet of a car, which, I admit, remains a mystery to me. I am to mechanics what Einstein was to ladies' hairdressing. He has taken over from Stirling Moss as the name on the lips of traffic cops asking speeding drivers, 'Who d'you think you are, Lewis Hamilton?'

Along the way, Hamilton has become a constant companion of controversy over questionable manoeuvres on the track or blistering remarks off it. Few sportsmen in the world are so often in the public spotlight and every word he says is closely scrutinised. He had headline-seeking MPs criticising him for becoming a tax exile, but I wonder how many of us in his position would have made a similar decision in his place? Last time I looked at the 'Rich List' he was reported to have a fortune in excess of £150m, so he has been well rewarded for his skill and speed.

The first black driver to win the world title, and knighted in 2021, he was the victim of racial abuse from Spanish supporters during his close rivalry with their hero Fernando Alonso and he later became a prominent spokesman for the Black Lives Matter movement. It was revealed that he had been 'scarred for life' by racial abuse in his childhood.

He is a professional-standard guitarist who often records under pseudonyms, an art lover and a fashion consultant, whose philanthropy is aimed mostly at under-privileged children. He puts back.

A vegan who has given up drinking, he is a man of strong principles and an iron discipline that you see in only the greatest competitors. I think I would fry under the sort of microscopic prying and surveillance he has to suffer. In fact it would drive me mad (there I go again).

I judge him by what he has achieved at the wheel and he is clearly a born racer and a master of his art. The best of British.

LEWIS HAMILTON FOR THE RECORD:

- Born: 7 January 1985, Stevenage, Hertfordshire
- Grand Prix career span: 2007–ongoing
- World champion: 2008, 2014, 2015, 2017, 2018, 2019, 2020
- Teams: McLaren, Mercedes-Benz
- Races entered: 276
- Wins: 99
- Podiums: 172
- Pole positions: 100
- Career points: 3,973 (as of August 2021)
- Knighted: 2021

33

MICHAEL HOLDING

'The Test in which England fell to Whispering Death'

WHISPERING DEATH! For me, the greatest of all sporting nicknames, and Michael Holding – the man who earned it – was one of the fastest and classiest bowlers ever to bowl in Test cricket. For a man who suffered from the curse of asthma early in his career, he arrived like a breath of fresh air for West Indies in their golden age.

He got his nickname because of his silent Rolls-Royce run-up that was so quiet the umpires could not hear him approaching. Holding was not only lightning quick, but also had such control of the ball that he could dominate batsmen with the trajectory of his deliveries. As a cricket lover, I used to be spellbound watching him in action, even when he was knocking over English wickets.

Michael, 6ft 3in tall and a perfectly sculpted 13st, was arguably the fastest but certainly the most accurate of the famed and feared West Indian pace attack which included Joel Garner, Andy Roberts, Sylvester Clarke, Colin Croft, Wayne Daniel and the menacing Malcolm Marshall.

He was virtually unknown except by cricket aficionados when he first toured England in 1976 but by the time the tour was over he was the talk of the sports world, with England left humbled and humiliated. That was the series when South African-born England skipper Tony Greig unwisely said, 'I'm not really sure these fellers are as good as everyone thinks. You must remember that the West Indians, these guys, if they get on top they are magnificent cricketers. But if they're down, they grovel, and I intend, with the help of Closey [Brian Close] and a few others, to make them grovel.'

The comments outraged the West Indians, who interpreted the word 'grovel' as the language of racism and apartheid. They responded by walloping England 3-0 and in the final Test at The Oval Holding took 8/92 and then 6/57 in one of the finest and fiercest bowling performances ever witnessed. These remained the best returns of Holding's career and his match figures of 14/149 have never been bettered by a West Indian in a Test match.

Holding's favourite and most productive new ball partner was Andy Roberts, and they opened the bowling together in 33 Tests, claiming 216 wickets at an average 25.27.

As a late-order batsman, Holding believed in the theory of 'hit out or get out'. He hammered 36 sixes in his Test career, which added up to a quarter of the runs he scored in total.

It was widely reported that on the BBC's *Test Match Special*, Brian Johnston said on commentary, 'The bowler's Holding, the batsman's Willey.' I was disappointed to find out that this was a story made up by Johnston for his after-dinner speeches, but it has gone down as having actually been broadcast.

A proud Jamaican, Holding – with a distinctive, lilting Caribbean voice and forthright views – went on to become a popular cricket commentator, always fighting the cause for purist five-day cricket and continually making disparaging remarks about the new and immensely popular short form of the game. The cricket world was saddened in the late summer of 2021 when he announced that he was hanging up his microphone. His good sense and balanced, authoritative views will be missed.

His biggest love, even greater than cricket, is horse racing and he admits to having had a life-long battle to try to get the better of the bookmakers.

Odds on you will never see a finer fast bowler than Michael Holding.

MICHAEL HOLDING FOR THE RECORD:
- Born: 16 February 1954, Jamaica
- Tests: 60
  - Wickets: 249 (23.68)
  - Five wickets in an innings: 13 times
  - Best figures: 8/92 (match 14 /149), v England, The Oval, 1976
- First-class games: 222
  - Wickets: 778 (23.43)
  - Five wickets in an innings: 39
  - Best figures: 8/92
- ODI matches: 102
  - Wickets 142 (21.36)

34

ROGER HUNT

'The stamina of a cheetah
but never ever a cheat'

I DON'T think anybody has ever cottoned on to the fact that Roger Hunt and I were born just a few miles apart and came together to spearhead England's 1966 World Cup triumph. Alan Ball and Nobby Stiles were also from roughly the same area, so as well as 'West Ham won the World Cup' – the common cry – there could be a counter claim that Lancashire won it. All this before the border changes, of course.

Roger, naturally, will always be associated with Liverpool, where to this day he is known as Sir Roger after plundering 286 goals in the famous red shirt – a club record until overtaken by Ian Rush. His combination with the silky-smooth Scot Ian St John was the stuff of fairytales.

Bill Shankly, dynamic manager of Liverpool in those swinging 60, once said of Roger, 'He will sweat buckets for the team. He's got the stamina of a cheetah ... but never ever cheats. You can trust him with your life.' That summed up Roger perfectly. He would run all day for the team and was totally honest with his contribution to every match he played. Under Shanks, Roger won two First Division titles and succeeded us at West Ham as an FA Cup winner in 1965. In many ways he was a contender for England's man of the tournament in 1966, playing in all six games and scoring three goals – one against Mexico and both against France.

People don't believe this, but I hardly knew Roger before we were thrown together in the quarter-final of the World Cup against Argentina. We had played in the same England team just twice before – the first time in my debut match in a friendly against West Germany at Wembley on 22 February 1966. Alf gave the number nine shirt to Nobby Stiles just to confuse the Germans, but Roger and I were twin strikers with Nobby consigned to his usual defensive duties. Purely by fluke, it was Nobby who scored the only goal of the match and many in the press were duped into calling him England's new secret weapon as a centre-forward!

The only other time we operated together was two months later when we beat Scotland 4-3 at Hampden Park. Roger scored twice and I got my first goal for England. That was duly noted by Alf. It was the game in which Celtic wing-wizard Jimmy Johnstone tried to play us on his own, scored two goals and continually had our defence tied in knots. If Alf could have picked him I don't think England would have become known as 'Wingless Wonders'.

In our three World Cup matches Roger and I went together like bacon and eggs, both of us working our socks off for the team and me being lucky enough to get those three goals in the final. He was delighted for me and has never once allowed envy to raise its ugly head. We were a team, and it was an honour to play with the Liverpool legend.

It's Roger I always quote when the arguments start over THAT second goal of mine in the 1966 World Cup final. As the ball bounced down off the bar, he was prowling just a few yards from the German net. He immediately raised his hand in celebration of a goal as the ball came down off the bar.

'I was convinced it was over the line,' he has told me a thousand times. 'If I'd had any doubts I would have dashed forward and challenged for the ball.'

There speaks an honest man. We Lancastrians stick together!

Roger had a wind-down period with Bolton Wanderers, for whom he banged in 24 goals in 76 matches before joining his family haulage business, often driving the lorries with the same concentration and dedication that he always revealed on the playing pitch.

I did not know Roger well when we first played alongside each other in the World Cup, but we were never passing strangers.

ROGER HUNT FOR THE RECORD:

- Born: 20 July 1938, Glazebury, Lancashire
- Career span: 1958–72
- Career goals: 289 (498 games)
- Clubs:
  - Liverpool (416 games, 261 goals)
  - Bolton Wanderers: (76 games, 24 goals)
  - Hellenic, Greece, loan (6 games, 4 goals)
- England: 34 caps, 18 goals
- First Division: 1964, 1966
- FA Cup: 1965
- World Cup: 1966

35

SIR LEN HUTTON

'364 reasons why this Pudsey bear
hugged the headlines'

LEN HUTTON, the first professional cricketer to captain England, played the game in an era that was like a foreign land compared with today's world of Big Bash and the new Hundred tournament. He was the picture of patience at the wicket, picking his runs as carefully as a miser counting his pennies, and trying to hit sixes would have been considered unacceptable showmanship.

I am tempted to call him the original Pudsey Bear because he comes from the same Yorkshire town as the creator of the Children in Need mascot, but Len was more a lion heart from his earliest days of arriving in the Test arena.

When I was first trying to interest Essex with my run-making and glovework behind the stumps, Hutton still held the individual Test world record of 364. Every schoolboy knew the story of how he carved out the record in what was only his sixth Test match and at the age of 22.

The previous high of 334 had been set by England's nemesis Don Bradman in 1930, and he was skippering the Aussies as

Hutton opened the fifth Test at The Oval on 20 August 1938. England needed to win the match to draw the series. Thirteen hours and 20 minutes and eight batting sessions later a close-to-exhaustion, stubborn Yorkshireman was still at the wicket, and he had lifted the record to 364 before finally being bowled by Aussie spinner Bill O'Reilly. England captain Wally Hammond declared at 903-7, and Len Hutton became a household name.

During the war, Hutton's arm was so badly injured while on a commando training course that he had to completely rebuild his batting technique to compensate for a lack of mobility. He batted on through 78 Test matches before retiring in 1955. His personal highlight apart from the history-making 364 was skippering the England team that won the Ashes for the first time in 19 years in 1953. This 12-year-old boy danced with his dad around the living room as Denis Compton swept the boundary that clinched the memorable triumph. Even all these years later I can hear the echo of commentator Brian Johnston's voice, 'And England have won the Ashes!'

Though by instinct a stroke maker, Hutton built his style on a bedrock of defence and caution because he was so aware that both Yorkshire and England depended on him. He averaged nearly 57, and remains statistically among the most dependable batsmen ever to have played Test cricket.

He lacked the charisma of a Compton, but was one of the most consistent and reliable batsmen to open the innings for England, and the balanced and authoritative *Wisden* described him as 'one of the greatest batsmen ever'. In many ways Joe Root reminds me of him, with his similar looks, the same cool, calculating Yorkshire temperament and even down to bowling useful spin deliveries when necessary. But it strikes me that Joe gets more enjoyment from his cricket, while too often Hutton looked as if he had the weight of the world on his shoulders. Anyway, that was how it looked to this cricket-daft kid.

Captaincy was a burden for Hutton and he suddenly retired from the game in 1955, completely worn out by the mental and physical stress of leading England and Yorkshire. In 23 Tests as captain, he won eight and lost four, with the others drawn. He was knighted a year after shouldering his bat, and became a respected Test selector and journalist, broadcaster and private businessman.

I've picked Sir Len because in those tough, immediate post-war years he played with a grit and determination that inspired the country to knuckle down and get the rebuilding job done. Not everybody could play with the joy and freedom of a Compton or an Evans. He carried the responsibility of captaincy with dignity and determination and Yorkshire recognised his service by making him their president, a post he held until his passing in 1990 at the age of 74. What an innings.

SIR LEN HUTTON FOR THE RECORD:
- Born: 23 June 1918, Pudsey, Yorkshire
- County: Yorkshire (1934–55)
- Tests: 79 (1937–55)
  - Runs: 6,971 (56.67), 19 centuries
  - Captaincy record: won 8, lost 4, drawn 11
  - Highest score: 364 v. Australia at the Oval, 1938
  - Catches: 57
- First-class career: 513 games (1934–55)
  - Runs: 40,140 (55.51), 129 centuries
  - Highest score: 364 v. Australia at the Oval
- Knighted: 1956
- Died: 6 September 1990, Kingston-upon-Thames, aged 74

36

PAT JENNINGS

'The man with bucket hands
who caught everything'

IF I had to name the most popular of all my selections in my hall of fame, Pat would come pretty close to the top. Everybody loves Big Pat, his former opponents as much as his old team-mates. Plenty put up the argument that he was an even better goalkeeper than Gordon Banks or Peter Shilton. Let's say the three of them were magnificent and leave it at that.

I remain pals with Pat because we are both ambassadors for the McDonald's grassroots football programme that gives young players help and encouragement, and on a recent visit to Belfast with the big man I witnessed how he is still an idol in the country whose jersey he wore a record 119 times.

The thing people always notice about Pat on a first meeting is the size of his hands. I used to marvel at the way he could catch the ball one-handed, a legacy of his days in Gaelic football. We played against each other in three internationals and I managed to put two goals past him in three victories, but at club level Spurs usually got the better of the Hammers in some ding-dong battles.

I never knew Pat to be anything other than modest in victory and sporting in defeat. A model footballer and man.

A little bit of trivia for you – he was brought up in the same Chapel Street in Newry where ten years before him Peter McParland had grown up. Peter collected an FA Cup winners' medal with Aston Villa in 1957, and a decade later Pat got the first of his two in the 1967 final against Chelsea. Not a bad record for one street.

Pat played more than 1,000 competitive games in all, and was voted FWA Footballer of the Year in 1973. The highlights of that season were two penalty saves for Tottenham against Liverpool at Anfield on the morning of the Grand National – one from Tommy Smith and then one from Kevin Keegan. Liverpool manager Bill Shankly was apoplectic. 'Have you seen the size of that man's hands?' he said to the press afterwards, only half joking. 'They are like bloody shovels. It shouldn't be allowed. He should be disqualified.'

Three seasons later he was voted the PFA Player of the Year, and is one of the few sportsmen who has been awarded both an MBE and an OBE. It all came as a surprise to Pat, whose next boast will be his first.

He once memorably scored a goal with a wind-assisted 100-yard kick in the 1967 Charity Shield against Manchester United at Old Trafford, which went first bounce into the net over the head of Alex Stepney. 'For a while there,' he said in his distinctive deep baritone voice, 'I was Tottenham's top goalscorer. You can imagine the stick I gave Alan Gilzean and Greavsie!'

I had finished my Football League career by the time, in 1977, Pat stunned the football world by moving to Tottenham's deadly rivals Arsenal at the age of 32. It was like Paul McCartney going from The Beatles to the Rolling Stones. Spurs thought he had little left to give. Pat was fuming with the Tottenham board at the time because they would not give him a financial loan to help him buy the house of his dreams. They just had no idea how to repay him for his great service to the club.

Pat answered Tottenham's lack of faith in him by playing on for another eight years at Arsenal, and he became as big a hero at Highbury as he had been at White Hart Lane.

He played a major part in getting the Gunners to three successive FA Cup finals, emerging as a winner in the middle one, 1979. 'I know a lot of Tottenham supporters were upset with me going to Arsenal,' Pat told me. 'But it suited my domestic life, because there was no need for the big upheaval of having to move to a new area. I was just happy to still be playing at the top level and I gave Arsenal the same 100 per cent commitment I had always given to Spurs. Of course, the fact that my old Northern Ireland captain Terry Neill was in charge at Highbury helped make it a smooth transition.'

All the games I played against Pat, at club and country level, I never knew him anything less than composed and looking huge between his posts. He was a master of positioning and had the reflexes of a panther. Under pressure, he never panicked and would quietly give positional orders to his defenders without barking at them.

I remember scoring one of my better goals against him for England with a scorching shot in a European championship qualifier at Wembley and as we were coming off after Northern Ireland's defeat he said, 'Great shot, Geoff. I'd have needed the Irish guards with me to save that one.' That typified his sportsmanship. A gentleman of the first order as well as one of the all-time great goalkeepers.

Pat semi-retired in 1986 to concentrate on golf, which he still loves, but he kept his eye in by returning to Tottenham in a coaching capacity while retaining his player registration. At the back of his mind was playing his last game in the 1986 World Cup finals, and he tuned up by going in goal for Spurs reserves.

His dream finale came true when Northern Ireland qualified for the World Cup in Mexico. All eyes were on him when he made his last competitive appearance with what was then a world record 119th international appearance, against Brazil. To add to the fairytale finish, it was his 41st birthday. Brazil won 3-0 but Pat was carried off at the end as an all-time hero of Irish football.

Pat had made his intentional debut against Wales in 1964 in the same match that a young winger called George Best was making his bow. They became good friends, although leading contrasting lifestyles. Pat settled down to a long and happy marriage with Hilton Irish Showband singer Eleanor Toner, while 'settled down' and 'George Best' never sat comfortably in the same sentence.

Pat was always a great advertisement for the Beautiful Game. You have to hand it to him.

PAT JENNINGS FOR THE RECORD:

- Born: 12 June 1945, Newry, County Down
- Career span: 1961–1986
- Clubs:
  - Newry Town 1961–63
  - Watford 1963–64 (48 league games)
  - Tottenham 1964–77 (472 league games, 1 goal)
  - Arsenal 1977–84 (237 league games)
- Northern Ireland: 119 caps
- FA Cup: 1967, 1979
- League Cup: 1971, 1973
- UEFA Cup: 1972
- FWA Footballer of the Year: 1973
- PFA Player of the Year: 1976

37

MICHAEL JOHNSON

'The Golden Man of the track
who did it HIS way'

BEFORE USAIN Bolt exploded onto the athletics scene, Michael Johnson was the sprinter who grabbed the headlines and my attention with his scorching performances on the track. I remember staring in astonishment at the television screen during the 1996 Atlanta Olympics when he was in full flow, wondering if I was watching somebody from another galaxy.

Johnson became the only male athlete in history to win both the 200m and 400m at the same Games. He had a running style all of his own, and reminded me of how my father used to encourage me to run, with short, chopping steps rather than the huge strides of a Bolt or a Bannister. Coaches always called for a high knee lift at peak pace, but he went against convention and kept a low centre of gravity while he held his torso stiff and upright, at times looking as if he was leaning backwards.

I had never seen anything like it, but the results his unorthodox technique produced proved he must have been doing something right. At various stages during his career he held the world and

Olympic records for 200m and 400m, the world indoor 400m record and also set the fastest time for the rarely-run 300m. When the United States set a 4x400m world record in the 1993 World Championships it was Johnson who ran the anchor leg.

Four years after his adventures in Atlanta, he became the only athlete to retain the Olympic 400m title in the Sydney Games, although his attempt at the double double was thwarted by injury. He ducked under 44 seconds for 400m 22 times, more than twice as often as any other athlete. He was a one-lap wonder, and faster than anybody over half a lap. He broke 20 seconds in the 200m 23 times.

Johnson was a master at turning his talent to commercial success. In 1997 he advertised a pair of Nike golden running spikes with the slogan 'Fastest Man in the World'. Donovan Bailey, the then world record holder and Olympic champion over 100m, protested that this 'title' belonged to him. The sharp mind of Johnson went to work and he and Ontario-based, Jamaican-born Bailey cooperated with promoters to put on a duel over 150 metres, with both men receiving appearance money of $500,000. The race, staged in Toronto, was given all the hype and ballyhoo of a world heavyweight title fight. There was a million-dollar prize for the winner, the money going to Bailey when, in an awful anticlimax, Johnson pulled up with a hamstring injury after 100 metres.

He was favourite to win the 400m gold medal in the 1992 Barcelona Olympics, but failed to make the final because of food poisoning. He recovered in time to anchor the USA 4x400 m team to victory.

At the final count when he hung up his golden running shoes after the Sydney Olympics, Johnson had eight World Championships golds and four Olympic golds. It would have been more but for two members of the 2000 4x400m relay squad in Sydney testing positive for drug use after Johnson had carried the baton first across the line in his usual anchor role.

Intelligent and articulate, Michael opened a string of performance centres around the world to help young athletes, and became a respected television analyst, particularly for the BBC. He suffered a severe stroke in 2018 but made a recovery by using what he described as 'my Olympic mindset'.

A footnote: Johnson's right foot is an inch longer than his left and he used to have running shoes specially crafted for him. Some feat.

MICHAEL JOHNSON FOR THE RECORD:

- Born: 13 September 1967, Dallas, Texas
- World Championship gold medals: 8
- Olympic Games gold medals: 4
- World records:
  - 200m (19.32s)
  - 300m (30.85s)
  - 400m (43.18s)
- USOC Sportsman of the Year: 1993, 1995, 1996

38

MICHAEL JORDAN

'Save the Last Dance for court king Jordan'

NO MATTER which way you measure Michael Jordan, you have a colossus not only of basketball, not only of sport but of humanity. There has never been anybody quite like him in the history of the world, amazing on the scale of Muhammad Ali and a giant of his sport who stands comparison with Pelé and Tiger Woods.

If you don't know his achievements and adventures, let me recommend that you catch up with the television documentary on him, *The Last Dance.* I watched it quite casually and was so amazed at what I saw that I immediately ran it back and watched the whole thing again. It is an intimate courtside portrait of Jordan the sensational basketball player and Jordan the man; in both cases he leaves you with your mouth gaping at his exploits.

I have been in or around sport most of my life, and have never seen anybody or anything to match what Jordan – 'His Airness' – has produced on and off court. Let's do some measuring.

He stands 6ft 6in tall, and at his peak weighed just over 15st. Jordan has amassed more than $1.6bn – yes, billion – from basketball earnings and prodigious business deals. He broke every basketball record in the book while winning six NBA championships with Chicago Bulls. Jordan played with a grace and power that you could liken to Superman as he flew through the air making astonishing slam dunks.

His scoring record over his 15-year career was never less than remarkable. He averaged 30.12 points per game and had a career play-off scoring average of 33.45. His highest scoring year was the 1986/87 season, when he averaged a mind-blowing 37.1 per game. In football speak that is like scoring a hat-trick in every match.

While famous for his scoring, he also won recognition as one of the greatest defensive players ever to step on to a basketball court, and he was the only player to win both the scoring title and the Defensive Player of the Year award in the same season.

Jordan's philanthropy is as amazing as his sporting accomplishments.He gives millions of dollars to charities, particularly those that help the under-privileged and fight racial inequality.

The world got a glimpse of Jordan away from the highly commercial American basketball circuit when he was a leading member of the USA 'Dream Team' squad that showed their skill and style in the 1992 Olympics. In 1999 he was named the 20th century's greatest North American athlete by ESPN.

His Nike Air Jordan sneakers, introduced in 1984, remain in demand today, and the Jordan brand continues to be one of the most sought after by investors and sponsors.

Anybody who has seen *The Last Dance*, will know that Jordan is not your average superstar. He has a mean temper, can put colleagues in their place with a brutally cutting tongue and is often mean and moody … but, on the court, always magnificent. And some of his generosity to charities and friends just take the breath away, such as giving a brand new $350,000 Ferrari to a team-mate 'because he liked it so much.'

There are whole websites on line devoted exclusively to anecdotes and gossip about MJ, and until the recent emergence of the wonderful Emma Raducanu was the most discussed sports celebrity on line. But then, Michael can't speak fluent Mandarin.

For all his fame and glory, Jordan has managed to be a perfect role model for how to handle celebrity, and his greatest triumph is that he has remained with his feet planted on the floor – except when making those astonishing gliding jumps on the court. He manages to keep his private life private, although it made worldwide headlines when his divorce from the first of his two wives cost him a world record $168m settlement. Don't tell Judith!

Michael leaps into my list and has transcended the world of basketball to become a truly global icon.

MICHAEL JORDAN FOR THE RECORD:
- Born: 17 February 1963, Brooklyn, USA
- Position: shooting guard
- Major teams: Chicago Bulls, Washington Wizards
- Career points: 32,292 (average 30.1 per game)
- Rebounds: 6,672
- Assists: 5,633
- NBA champion: 1991, 1992, 1993, 1996, 1997, 1998
- NBA Most Valuable Player: 1988, 1991, 1992, 1996, 1998
- NBA leading scorer: 1987, 1988, 1989, 1990, 1991, 1992, 1993, 1996, 1997, 1998
- Olympic gold medal: 1984, 1992

39

JASON KENNY

'Jason has the Midas touch on his bike'

I WAS spoiled for choice when it came to which rider to represent Britain's classic collection of cyclists. Sprint king Reg Harris was the top pedal pusher when I was young, but in recent years there have been a procession of outstanding British performers ranging from Sir Bradley Wiggins, Chris Froome and Geraint Thomas in the Tour de France to track titans Sir Chris Hoy, Ed Clancy and all-rounder Mark Cavendish. But my choice was made easy when Jason Kenny provided a golden finish to the Tokyo Olympics in August 2021.

Jason and I were born just a few miles apart, so I can claim him as a fellow Lancastrian along with Freddie Flintoff, Tom Finney and my 1966 team-mates Nobby Stiles, Roger Hunt and Alan Ball, who was from the same town. The red rose county has a proud sporting tradition and Jason, the cyclist with the Midas touch, is now one of its most famous sons.

His victory in the keirin in Tokyo was as explosive an individual performance as I've ever seen in the cycling world. He gambled on getting a jump on his rivals, and then to have the speed, strength and courage to cling on to his commanding lead made this old spectator jump out of his seat. The other five keirin finalists were left for dead as Jason pounded his pedals in a blur of speed. His 33-year-old legs must have been really feeling the pace but he remained in control right to the line.

Jason won his first Olympic gold, alongside then plain Chris Hoy, in the team sprint at the Beijing Games in 2008 and was one of the motivators of the hugely successful Team GB cycling squad at their home Olympics in London four years later. He lifted his career haul to three gold medals in the sprint and team sprint. But it was in Rio that Jason really wrote his name into British Olympic folklore, winning three more titles: in the team sprint, individual sprint and keirin. And then came his triumph in Tokyo to lift him to the top of Britain's all-time gold medal table.

I will be amazed if he now does not join me as a sporting knight. He truly deserves the tap of the sword on the shoulder, an experience I will never forget. Jason's latest triumph makes him the most decorated British Olympian in history with nine medals in total, and seven of them gold.

Watching his keirin smash-and-grab ride from the Tokyo pits was Jason's lovely, bubbly wife Laura, a north London girl with Tottenham Hotspur affiliations. Between them they have a glittering collection of 12 gold medals, and I wonder if they will be tempted to add to this haul when the next Olympics are held in Paris.

Laura revealed that Jason had quietly retired after the Rio 2016 Games but that he was inspired to make a comeback when watching his wife train. This unassuming, likeable man has been chasing the medals since the Beijing Games of 2008, and he admits that his body is beginning to tell him that he is no longer a youngster.

He had to compete in the keirin after watching Laura crash while defending her omnium crown. She picked herself up and gave all her support to her husband. Judith and I wonder what we will be seeing from their son, Albie, when he gets in the racing saddle. We must not put unnecessary pressure on him, but he comes from thoroughbred stock. Britain's golden couple have carved a special places in the hearts of the nation and this creaking old footballer urges them to carry on to the road to Paris. You are a long time retired.

Of course, cycling could always lose Jason to his other love – motor racing. He is a fanatical motorsport enthusiast and often takes the wheel in racing cars. He has experienced podium glory in a round of the Radical European Masters at the Nürburgring and admits that driving cars is easier on the legs than pedal pushing. Watch out Lewis Hamilton! But my bet is that he will not be able to resist the lure of Paris in 2024, particularly if Laura sets her sights on another Olympic challenge.

I want to take this opportunity to congratulate the members of Team GB and Paralympics GB on their magnificent showing in Tokyo, climbing above the perils of the pandemic to represent their country with pride and passion. The rowers, the throwers, the runners, the jumpers, riders, gymnasts (Max Whitlock!), hockey players, footballers, basketballers, volleyballers, ping pongers, divers (knitters), swimmers (Adam Peaty!), surfers, sailors, boxers, martial art experts, weightlifters, all those unbelievably committed paraplegic competitors, EVERYBODY.

As somebody who was for many years a professional sportsman, I know the sacrifices you have made, the time you have put in, the injuries you have had to battle through, the ups, the downs, the stresses and strains. You have every ounce of my admiration and support for the future.

It was particularly exciting and fascinating to see the stars emerging in the new sports such as wall climbing, BMX riding, mountain biking and skateboarding. The young generation get a lot of stick, but they made my chest swell and, as Judith said, 'Nothing wrong with today's kids. Give them the facilities and the encouragement and they are a wonderful advertisement for the country and themselves.'

Couldn't have put it better myself.

JASON KENNY FOR THE RECORD:

- Born: 23 March 1988, Farnworth, Bolton
- Major team: Team Sky+HD (2008–13)
- Medals collection:
  - Olympics: 7 gold, 2 silver
  - World Championships 3 gold, 5 silver, 2 bronze
  - European Games: 1 bronze
  - European Championships: 1 gold, 2 silver, 3 bronze
  - Commonwealth Games: 2 silver
- Olympic golds:
- Beijing 2008 (team sprint)
- London 2012 (team sprint, individual sprint)
- Rio de Janeiro 2016 (team sprint, individual sprint, keirin)
- Tokyo 2020 (keirin)
- World Championships golds:
  - Apeldoorn 2011 (individual sprint)
  - Minsk 2013 (keirin)
- European Championships:
  - Pruszkow 2010 (keirin)

40

JIM LAKER

'The day Australia got Lakered'

ISN'T IT great to be able to boast that you actually played with one of the finest bowlers ever to spin a ball in Test cricket. Prepare to be bored: I had the honour of being in the same team as the legendary Jim Laker in my one and only County Championship game for Essex.

Anybody who was around in 1956 will recall that Jim was the talk of the cricket world after wrecking the Australians with probably the greatest exhibition of spin bowling in history. His record of 19 wickets for 90 runs in the Old Trafford Test is unlikely to ever to be beaten. After claiming the final wicket, he took his sweater, dropped it over his shoulder and sauntered off the pitch as if on a walk through the park. Today there would have been leaping, screaming, air punching and fireworks. Another planet.

It was a spell-binding performance, made all the more incredible by the fact that his bowling partner at the opposite end, Tony Lock, could only take one wicket on a surface that the Aussies claimed had been doctored for England's spin twins.

There had been a warning of what was in store for the Aussies when Laker went through them like a dose of salts at The Oval for Surrey in May 1956, taking all ten wickets for 80 runs. Tony Lock at the other end was wicketless.

Laker and Lock operated in tandem for Surrey in their golden years, dominating the County Championship with seven consecutive title victories from 1952 to 1958. They were contrasting in style and personality; Jim a right-arm off-break bowler, mild mannered and often introspective, Tony a left-arm orthodox spinner with a fiery temperament to go with his red, thinning hair.

It was well known that Laker and Lock did not get on off the pitch, and that they were always trying to get the better of each other in matches. 'This worked for the team,' said their Surrey captain Stuart Surridge. 'If Laker took a wicket, you would see Lock exerting all his energy to match it. Once the game was over they went their separate ways. As different as chalk and cheese.'

Jim considered himself an 'accidental southerner'. He had been on Yorkshire's books and working at Barclays in Bradford as a £5-a-month clerk when war broke out, and it was while based in London on assignment to the War Office that he was approached by Surrey and signed a professional contract at £6 a week. Yes, another planet.

Throughout his career Laker battled against 'shamateurism', which was rife in cricket, and all sports with players claiming amateur status while taking backhanders to play their sport. 'You are either a professional or you are not,' he used to preach. 'You cannot be both.'

A big man with large hands, he could get vicious rotation on the ball and batsmen used to say they could actually hear the ball fizzing when he released it. He first took 100 wickets in 1948 and reached the milestone in 11 successive seasons to 1958. Playing in 450 first-class matches, he took a total of 1,944 wickets at a career average of 18.41, including ten-wicket match hauls 32 times and five-fors on an incredible 127 occasions. His most successful season in 1950 brought him 166 wickets at an average 15.32, including 8/2 against the Rest of England at Bradford.

In 46 Tests for England, he took 193 wickets at an average of 21.24. Jim could also bat a bit, using the long handle in his tail-end role and twice recording centuries while amassing 7,304 runs at an average of 16.60. He was a specialist fielder at gully and held 271 career catches.

I was recently asked at a question and answer session after a road show just how good a spinner Jim Laker was. I searched for the right words and then remembered a quote I had read by the king of commentators, John Arlott: 'Laker passed every test you could possibly apply to an off-spinner. His grip could be infinitely varied so that no batsman could read anything from it, and a procession of batsmen departed for the pavilion without ever solving the mystery of his deliveries. There have been few if any better exponents of the art of off-break bowling and disguising the grip on the ball.'

Towards the end of his career, I got a close-up view of the price Laker paid for the vicious tweak he used to give the ball. His right forefinger, infact all the fingers on his right hand were calloused, bent and looking arthritic. He used to spend hours massaging them with a special ointment. Big Jim would rarely shake hands with people because his right hand was so worn from thousands of overs, and he invariably had his hand covered in cream. The price we sportsmen pay for our glory.

Laker disliked the autocratic style of captaincy adopted by Peter May, Surridge's successor as Surrey skipper, and they had an earthquaking fall-out following a match against Kent when May accused Jim of not trying. They became less than friendly and when Jim attacked May's attitude in his autobiography, *Over to Me*, he had his honorary membership of Surrey and MCC withdrawn. He retired in 1959 but was talked back for a couple of wind-down seasons by Essex skipper Trevor Bailey.

That match with G.C. Hurst? Because of injuries to first-choice players I was on the same pitch as Laker for a 1962 game against Lancashire at Aigburth in Liverpool when I appeared on the scorecard with a 0 (bowled Hilton) and 0 (did not bat). Cue jokes about me never scoring at Liverpool.

Jim went on to become the voice of cricket for the BBC. I went on to to play football.

But I could always boast that I played with J.C. Laker, the king of spin.

JIM LAKER FOR THE RECORD:

- Born: 9 February 1922, Shipley, Yorkshire
- Counties and state teams: Surrey (1946–59), Auckland (1951–52), Essex (1962–64)
- Tests: 46 (1948–59)
  - Best bowling: 10/53 v. Australia, Old Trafford, 1956
  - Best match figures: 19/90 Australia, Old Trafford, 1956
- First-class matches: 450 (1946–59)
  - Wickets: 1,944 (18.41)
  - Career batting: 7,304 runs (16.60), two centuries
  - Highest score: 113 v. Gloucestershire, The Oval, 1954
  - Career catches: 270
- BBC Sports Personality of the Year: 1956
- Died: 23 April 1986, Wimbledon, aged 64

41

BRIAN LARA

'The batting Prince who scored
a Lara Lara runs'

AS SOMEBODY who fancied myself as a bit of a batsman, I used to get a tingle when watching Brian Lara at the wicket. He collected his runs – often, hundreds of them in the same innings – with a mastery that brought bowlers to their knees and applauding spectators to their feet. Am I allowed to say he took me into Lara Lara Land? Perhaps not.

There have been many exceptional batsmen from the West Indies but only a handful who could match Lara for all-round artistry. He did not have a single weakness and you got the impression he could have batted long after the groundsmen had shut the stadium gates and gone home. Left-handed, he used the bat more like a scalpel than a sledgehammer and reduced the best bowlers in the world to looking almost ordinary. What he had above all was tunnel vision and the ability to concentrate on each delivery bowled to him as if it were the most vital ball he would face.

I remember how astonished we all were when he stroked his way to 501 not out for Warwickshire against Durham at Edgbaston in the summer of 1994. It remains the only quintuple hundred in first-class cricket history. In all, he faced just 427 deliveries, and slammed 62 fours and ten sixes. On the final day he hammered 174 runs before lunch. As a wicketkeeper, I felt for Durham gloveman Chris Scott, who dropped Lara on 18 and said to first slip, 'Oh dear, he'll probably go on and get a hundred now.'

Earlier in that same summer the 'Prince of Port of Prince' had set a world Test record of 375, against England in Antigua, but he lost it to Australian Matthew Hayden, who lifted the target to 380 while destroying Zimbabwe at Perth in 2003. Lara's response was to become the only man to reclaim the world record by swiftly scoring 400 not out in April 2004, and again it was England's bowlers on the receiving end and again the slaughterhouse was the picturesque Antigua Recreation Ground at St John's.

He made his quadruple ton off 582 balls, hitting 43 fours and four sixes. Surrey batsman Graham Thorpe was the only man to play for England in both of Lara's record-breaking matches and must have had a sunburned tongue at the end of the run barrages.

Few have ever been able to match Lara's appetite for runs. Beautifully balanced and with footwork that a ballet master would have envied, the baby-faced, 5ft 8in tall Trinidadian scored nine double centuries, including five while carrying the responsibility of captaincy.

Yet for all his marathon knocks, the innings many pick out as his best is an unbeaten 153 against Australia in Bridgetown in 1998/99. He shielded a procession of late-order batsmen to steer West Indies to an unlikely victory. *Wisden* rated his innings the best in the history of post-war cricket. 'He played us on his own,' said Aussie skipper Steve Waugh. 'Hats off to him. I've never seen an innings to match it.'

While a cultured artist, he could use the bat like a cudgel as he showed when smashing a Test record 28 runs off a single over from South African left-arm spinner Robin Peterson in 2003.

Between 1990 and 2006, he scored 11,953 Test runs at an average 52.99. As Cilla would have said, 'That's a Lara Lara runs.' Perhaps I shouldn't say that.

BRIAN LARA FOR THE RECORD:

- Born: 2 May 1969, Santa Cruz, Trinidad and Tobago
- Teams: Trinidad and Tobago (1987–2008), Transvaal (1992–93),
- Warwickshire (1994–98), Southern Rocks (2010)
- Tests: 131
  - Runs: 11,953 (52.88), 34 centuries
  - Captaincy record: won 10, lost 26, drawn 11
  - Highest score: 400 not out v England at Antigua (2004)
  - Catches: 164
- First-class career: 261 games (1987–2006)
  - Runs: 22,156 (51.88), 65 centuries
  - Highest score: 501 for Warwickshire v Durham (1994)
- ODI matches: 299
  - Runs: 19,045 (40.48), 19 centuries
- BBC Overseas Sports Personality of the Year 1994

42

ROD LAVER

*'The Rockhampton Rocket was a
grand Grand Slammer'*

ROD LAVER was the biggest name in tennis when I was making
my World Cup debut for England, but he missed Wimbledon
in that eventful year of 1966 because he was touring America
with the professional circus. Two years later Wimbledon was
dragged kicking and screaming into the 20th century and the
Rockhampton Rocket returned to claim his title of king of the
courts as the era of Open tennis arrived.

It was Laver more than any other player who turned me into a
keen tennis fan in the early 1960s, and he remains in my view the
only one of the older generation who could live with today's Holy
Trinity of Federer, Nadal and Djokovic.

Remember, he played with a wooden racket that was like a
caveman's club compared with today's lightweight 'frying pans'.
Laver was an all-court player, a master whether patrolling the
baseline, rushing the net or playing a serve and volley game. Rod
could do it all. He had a perfect drop shot and his ground strokes
were precise as well as powerful.

The ginger-haired left-hander from the Queensland outback followed Donald Budge (1938) as only the second male player in the history of the game to win the four major singles championships – Australian Open, French Open, Wimbledon and US Open – in the same year. This was in the amateur days of 1962 and he was continually being offered huge incentives to join the outlawed American professional circuit along with giants of the game like Pancho Segura, Pancho González and his countryman Frank Sedgman.

He was considered too small to make an impact on the world's courts when he first started playing the game at which both his mother and father had been local champions. Australian Davis Cup captain Harry Hopman got to hear of his potential and took him under his wing at the age of 18 at the start of a golden period for Aussie tennis.

With Laver as the trailblazer, Australia started to dominate the Davis Cup, and the likes of Lew Hoad, Ashley Cooper, Neale Fraser, Roy Emerson and Ken Rosewall, and later John Newcombe and Tony Roche, became powerful performers around the world, all coached and cajoled by Hopman who demanded total commitment and discipline.

Laver finally gave in to the pressure to turn professional and he quickly became the dominant force in America. He won five US Pro Tennis championships before the doors of Wimbledon re-opened to him. In 1969 he again scooped up all four major titles, the first – and still only – male player to perform the ultimate Grand Slam twice.

Asked once if he had any regrets, Laver thought long and hard. 'Yes,' he finally replied. 'I once jumped over the net after beating Tony Roche instead of first shaking hands with him. I detest show-offs.'

In 1971 he became the first tennis player to surpass the million-dollar mark in career prize money and by the time of his retirement at the age of 38 he had won 198 titles.

Because they were forced by the tennis establishment to miss the conventional tournaments, Laver and his compatriot Ken Rosewall toured the world playing one of the longest-running duels in tennis history. They met each other a staggering 141 times, with Laver holding the edge at 75-66.

What I noticed about Laver was that he had a bulging left forearm like Popeye after spinach. He specialised so much in using heavy topspin that his left arm grew to an inch and a half larger than his right and twice as muscled. Always a fitness fanatic, his great physical shape helped him overcome a severe stroke in 1998 that hit him while being interviewed on ESPN on the subject of being one of the greatest sportsmen of the 20th century.

Laver always represented his sport with dignity and style and did more than anybody to make tennis a major sport for the masses. Not bad for the shy kid from the Australian outback.

ROD LAVER FOR THE RECORD:
- Born: 9 August 1938, Rockhampton, Queensland
- Career span: 1956–79
- Titles: 198 (72 in Open era)
- Matches won: 1,473
- Matches lost: 407
- Prize money: $1,565,413
- Grand Slam titles: 11
  - Australian Open: 1960, 1962, 1969
  - Wimbledon: 1961, 1962, 1968, 1969
  - French Open: 1962, 1969
  - US Open: 1962, 1969
- Doubles career titles: 26
- Doubles matches won: 235
- Doubles matches lost: 75
- Australian Sportsman of the Year: 1969

43

DENIS LAW

'The day I wrecked Denis 'The Menace'
Law's round of golf'

DENIS LAW blamed me for what he called one of the most miserable days of his life – when England beat West Germany in the 1966 World Cup Final. The fiercely proud Scot wanted anybody but England to win the Jules Rimet Trophy, and went out playing golf rather than watch the final.

Denis claimed his day was ruined as he came off the final green when somebody shouted that England were world champions. He famously reacted to the news by throwing his golf bag to the floor in disgust.

The following March he was a prominent member of the Scottish team that beat our eight fit men 3-2 at Wembley (Jack Charlton hobbling with a broken toe and Ray Wilson and Jimmy Greaves both limping) to end our long unbeaten run.

'England winning the World Cup meant that Bobby Charlton and Nobby Stiles had bragging rights for years,' Denis said. 'That's why winning at Wembley in 1967 was so important to us. It ended a run of 19 unbeaten matches by England, and from then on we could wind up our England club-mates by saying that we were the real world champions.'

A lot of it was tongue in cheek with the Lawman, one of my favourite footballers from the moment I saw him in action for Huddersfield in a 1960 FA Cup replay at Upton Park. I sat in the stands watching him tease and torment our defence – Huddersfield won 5-1 on an ice-crusted pitch – and knew I was watching a very special talent.

'Denis the Menace' was a true icon of the swinging 60s, the showman and the swordsman in the celebrated Best-Charlton-Law trio that dismantled defences in such stunning style. George Best was the genius, Bobby Charlton the commander and Law the executioner.

He would score with a rapier thrust, turning a half-chance into a goal in the blink of an eye. Then the showman would emerge, his right arm punched into the air and held there in a salute that inspired a procession of imitators. Allan Clarke and Rodney Marsh were just two who admitted copying their idol in the way they autographed goals.

Denis was the first and true 'King of Old Trafford', long before the emergence of Eric Cantona. He had come a long way from his roots in Aberdeen where his father was a trawlerman who could get work only in the good weather. Winters were so bad that Denis and his six brothers and sisters had hardly anything to eat. He did not have a new pair of shoes until he was 14, wearing cast-offs until then, and before he could start a professional football career with Huddersfield he had to have a badly squinted eye surgically corrected.

Bill Shankly, his manager at Huddersfield before moving to Liverpool, said, 'We didn't know who the hell he was looking at when he used to talk to us. Once he got the eye corrected, the defenders didn't know which way he was going!'

I have never seen a player before or since with quicker reflexes than Denis and he was always looking for opportunities to do the unexpected in the penalty area, be it a bicycle kick or a stunning header after appearing to hang motionless in mid-air.

Denis made his league debut with Huddersfield at the age of 16 in 1956, and two years later he became Scotland's youngest ever player at the age of 18 years 236 days. He marked his debut with a goal in a 3-0 victory against Wales at Ninian Park on 18 October 1958. That was the start of an international career that brought him a record 30 goals in 55 appearances. The first manager to pick him for Scotland was Matt Busby, who never made any secret of his belief that Denis was one of the finest players ever to come south of the border.

Manchester City snapped up Denis and then cashed in on him just a year later when – like Jimmy Greaves – he got dazzled by talk of all the money that could be earned in Italy at a time when there was a maximum £20-a-week wage in Britain. City bought him for £55,000 and doubled their money when selling him on to Torino just 12 months later. Huddersfield were sick.

Just like Greavsie, Denis struggled to settle in Italy where players – particularly forwards – were treated like prisoners, with little freedom for movement on or off the pitch.

He tried to get rid of his homesick blues by enjoying himself off the pitch in the company of his Torino team-mate Joe Baker, the Englishman from Hibernian who had a thicker Scottish accent than Aberdonian Denis. Their exploration of the Turin nightlife very nearly cost them their lives. Joe was at the wheel of a flash new Alfa Romeo with Denis beside him when the car tipped over going the wrong way around a roundabout. Both were lucky to escape with their lives.

It got to the point where Denis had to threaten to walk out of the game to get a move back to the Football League. He went home to Aberdeen and told Torino where to stuff their lira. They had been trying to sell him on to neighbours Juventus for a huge profit, but eventually they had to give in to his demands and allowed him to join Manchester United in 1962 for a British record £115,000.

This was after Tottenham had rescued Jimmy from AC Milan for £99,999.

His temper was as quick as his reflexes and he was often in trouble with referees for retaliating. He was once involved in a full-blooded fist fight with Arsenal centre-half Ian Ure at Old Trafford. Both got their marching orders, and long suspensions. What made it even more of a compelling spectacle is that they were good pals who roomed together when on Scottish international duty. Friend or foe, Denis refused to concede a penalty area inch to any opponent. A Red Devil, if ever there was one.

Over the next ten years, Denis ignited the United attack with his fire and flair. He was an FA Cup winner in 1963, European Footballer of the Year in 1964, and a league championship winner in 1965 and 1967. He remains the only Scot to have been elected European Footballer of the Year.

Sadly, because of a knee injury, he missed the ultimate prize of a European Cup winners' medal in 1968.

He scored 171 league goals for United in 309 matches, and took his FA Cup haul to what was then a record 40 goals. That total did not include the six he scored for Manchester City against Luton in a 1961 tie that was abandoned because of rain.

His Manchester United career ended in bitterness in 1973 when Tommy Docherty let him go on a free transfer. 'The first I knew about it was when I saw the news being announced on television,' a disgusted Denis said. 'I thought I would end my career at Old Trafford.'

Shrugging off his recurring knee problem, Denis returned to Manchester City and in the last game of the following season almost reluctantly back-heeled the goal that helped push United down into the Second Division. 'People wrongly say that my goal relegated United,' Denis said. 'But other results that day meant United were going down regardless of how many goals we scored against them.'

He had the satisfaction of making his World Cup finals debut in the last season of a magnificent career in which he inspired hundreds of youngsters to try to play the Lawman way. They could copy his style but few could get close to imitating his unique ability.

A good family man with five sons, Denis – like me – is now an 80-something granddad, and after beating cancer is a regular meeter and greeter at Manchester United and an amusing after-dinner speaker with scores of stories up those famous sleeves of his.

It has been quite a voyage of adventure for the trawlerman's son from Aberdeen. I was privileged to often be on the same pitch as him and always found him good, cheerful company off it, even if I did ruin his day on 30 July 1966!

Sadly, as I was preparing this tribute, Denis announced that he had become the prisoner of dementia, like so many of my treasured old colleagues. Nobody lucky enough to have seen him at the peak of his power will forget that he was, simply, the King.

DENIS LAW FOR THE RECORD:
- Born: 24 February 1940, Aberdeen
- Career span: 1956–1974
- Clubs:
  - Huddersfield Town 1946–60 (91 games, 19 goals)
  - Manchester City 1960–61 and 1973–74 (79 games, 37 goals)
  - Torino (28 games, 10 goals)
  - Manchester United 1962–73 (404 games, 237 goals)
- Scotland: 55 caps, 30 goals
- First Division: 1963, 1965
- European Cup: 1968
- FA Cup: 1963
- European Footballer of the Year 1964
- Voted Scotland's 'Golden Player' of the last 50 years in 2003

44

CARL LEWIS

'The Marmite Man becomes the
modern Jessie Owens'

I GREW UP with the legendary feats (or feet, if you prefer) of Jesse Owens as my bedtime stories but the rule for entry to my list was that sportsmen had to have operated at their peak in my lifetime. Carl Lewis was the obvious substitute, because in Los Angeles in 1984 he produced a carbon copy of the historic Owens performance in the 1936 Berlin Games.

Lewis became the first athlete since Owens to win four gold medals in track and field during the same Olympic Games: 100m and 200m, long jump and sprint relay. The public responses to those victories were very different. Owens returned to the United States in 1936 to a hero's welcome and retired from competition. Lewis, on the other hand, was jeered by many in the crowd at the 1984 Olympics and was shunned by major sponsors and fans alike. He came across as aloof and egotistical and his agent did not help by comparing him to eccentric pop star Michael Jackson.

The savage treatment Lewis received – a result he claimed of slanted press coverage against him – increased his resolve to continue competing. America's media reported that the Marmite Man of athletics had emerged from the 1984 Games less popular than before he scooped his four golds. The public found him arrogant and avaricious in his attempts to cash in on his victories in what was then a supposedly amateur sport.

We have to remember that this was immediately in the wake of the age of Ali. Lewis tried to go down the 'I am the greatest' road and it backfired on him. What went down as acceptable in the ballyhoo and hype of professional boxing did not wear well in the more genteel world of athletics.

Ed Moses, hugely respected king of the 400m hurdles, captured the mood when he said, 'Carl is a wonderful athlete but rubs it in too much. He needs to be taught a little humility.'

But slowly and by a procession of stunning performances, the beautifully chiselled, 6ft 2in, 13st Lewis won the public over and he got worldwide acclaim when, at the age of 31, he won Olympic golds in the long jump and relay at the 1992 Barcelona Games.

Sandwiched in between LA and Barcelona were the Olympics in Seoul and the sensational 100m final in which he crossed the line in second place. Ben Johnson, his eyes smouldering as if he was on fire, was first home but was disqualified for anabolic steroid abuse and the gold medal went to Lewis. I rather fancied myself as a long jumper but when I saw him on television soaring past 28 feet to retain his Olympic title I knew he had the jump on me.

The son of two star athletes, Lewis was born in Birmingham, Alabama, as race riots raged across the Deep South. While still at school, he moved to Willingboro, New Jersey, where his parents were prominent sports coaches. They encouraged Carl to concentrate on music because they rated him fourth in athletic potential of their four children.

Lewis started to make a name for himself while studying and competing at the University of Houston and then joined the crack Santa Monica Track Club in California. By 1992 Lewis had won eight World Championships golds and had dominated the long jump for ten years. 'I went through the Olympics and people tried to tear me down and force me to retire,' he said in a tell-all interview. 'For my own silly reasons I kept on running and ignored them, and now I've made it and I'm reaping the benefits of that perseverance. I'm publicly bigger than I've ever been, and it's a great thing to go through a career and be at this stage and everybody loves you the most.'

He achieved a remarkable 65 consecutive victories in the long jump over a span of ten years, one of the sport's longest undefeated streaks. Lewis broke ten seconds for the 100m 15 times and 20 seconds for the 200m ten times. But it was the long jump that was his speciality and he cleared 28 feet (8.53m) an astonishing 71 times.

For all his supremacy in the long jump, Lewis never had the satisfaction of setting the world record, although one prodigious jump over 30 feet was ruled a foul even though eyewitnesses swore it was a perfect leap.

His world championship head to head contest against fellow American Mike Powell in Tokyo in 1991 was considered the greatest long jump duel ever. Lewis set his lifetime personal best of 8.87m (29-1¼), but lost out to Powell, who with a leap of 8.95m (29-4), broke the legendary world record set by Bob Beamon in the high altitude of Mexico in the 1968 Olympics.

They had gone head to head fifteen times before, and Lewis had inched to victory in every one of the duels. 'He got me real mad,' Powell said after his triumph. 'I knew I had to jump out of the pit for a world record to beat him. He kinda gets you mad with his gamesmanship and I decided to take my anger out on the sandpit. Boy, at last I'd shut Lewis up. But he is one heck of a competitor. Only a world record could silence him.'

You would think I was quoting a boxer rather than a long jumper, but that's the effect Lewis used to have on his opponents with his mind games. But it was Mike Powell who had the last laugh, or should I say he had the jump on Lewis?

Eight of Lewis's Olympic gold medals are still in his possession. The ninth – his first, for the 100m – was buried with his father Bill in May 1988. 'My father was most proud of the 100,' Lewis revealed. 'More than anything, he wanted me to win that medal. Now he has it and he'll always have it.'

He became a leading coach and was voted Sportsman of the Century by the prestigious International Olympic Committee. This underlined that he was a superman of the track and a prodigious performer in the long jump pit. Every year was leap year for Carl the King.

CARL LEWIS FOR THE RECORD:
- Born: 1 July 1961, Birmingham, Alabama, USA
- Career span: 1979–1996
- Olympics: 9 gold medals, 1 silver medal
- World Championships: 8 gold medals, 1 silver medal, 1 bronze medal
- Best performances:
  - 100m: 9.86s (August 1991, Tokyo)
  - 200m: 19.75s (June 1983, Indianapolis)
  - Long jump: 8.87m (29ft 1in) 1991, wind-assisted 8.91m (29ft 2.75in) 1991 (both in Tokyo)
  - 4x100m relay: 37.40s (USA – Marsh, Burrell, Mitchell, Lewis; August 1992, Barcelona Olympics)
  - 4x200m relay: 1m 18.68s (Santa Monica – Marsh, Burrell, Heard; Lewis – 1994)
- IOC Sportsman of the Century: 1999

45

JONAH LOMU

'The All Blacks' colossus who used
England's defenders like doormats'

JONAH LOMU hit the rugby world like a tornado and then plunged it into mourning when he died far too early at the age of just 40. Even non-rugby followers were caught up in the Lomu legend, particularly the day he trampled over England in the 1995 World Cup semi-final in Cape Town.

Along with the rest of the millions tuned into the match on television, I could not believe what I was seeing as the 6ft 4in, 19st New Zealand wing went through a highly rated England defence like a huge black tank rolling over a field of white daisies. It was one of the most remarkable and destructive sights in sport, and England skipper Will Carling later admitted that Lomu had used him and his team-mates like doormats.

The All Blacks crushed England 45-29, and Lomu – then barely 20 years old – thundered to four tries that turned him into an overnight sporting legend. I found it hard to fathom how such a colossus of a man, just out of his teens, could be so rapid on his feet. Jonah was having a whale of a time.

Lomu went on to win 63 caps for the All Blacks and score 37 tries. He had played just over 200 first-class games when his rugby career was cut short not by injury but by a rare kidney complaint that meant that his playing days were effectively over before what became known as Jonny Wilkinson and England's World Cup in Australia in 2003.

His illness came at the time that Judith and I were dealing with a personal crisis of our own when our darling eldest daughter, Claire, was diagnosed with what was a terminal brain tumour. So we understood more than most what Lomu was going through as he had to dialyse five times a week.

He had a kidney transplant in July 2004 and less than a year later made a comeback of sorts with a try in a testimonial for England World Cup skipper Martin Johnson at Twickenham. But Lomu injured his shoulder in the game and needed surgery, torpedoing a playing return with North Harbour, where he coached. Still a massive draw, he then had a brief spell with Cardiff Blues. He scored his first try for the Blues in a man-of-the-match performance on 27 December 2006, but the following April broke his ankle playing against Border Reivers. There was a spell back in New Zealand with North Harbour and in France with the Marseille Vitrolles club, but the procession of injuries on top of his illness had robbed him of his enormous power and drive.

His death from a heart attack shocked the rugby world because it had looked as if he was getting everything back in order after a third marriage during what was generally a turmoil of a life. He was born into a broken family in Greenland, Auckland, but was brought up by an aunt in Tonga.

Lomu only seemed in total control of his life when on the rugby field and scoring some of the greatest tries ever witnessed. He was built like a back-row forward but had the speed of an Olympic sprinter.

He scored eight tries in the 1999 World Cup in England and Wales, including one against England, for whom he was always a nemesis. Another highlight was his dramatic late winning try in 2000 against Australia in an epic Tri Nations encounter in Sydney before a crowd of 109,874, the record for a rugby union game.

Away from rugby, Lomu was a gentle giant who came across as a modest, almost shy man. But once that whistle blew he was in charge like a raging bull. Here's one football man who was glad never to have got in his way. It must have been like facing Chopper Harris, Bites Yer Legs Hunter and Nobby Stiles rolled into one.

JONAH LOMU FOR THE RECORD:

- Born 12 May 1975, Auckland, New Zealand
- Position: wing
- Major club teams:
  - Counties Manukau (28 games, 95 points)
  - Blues (22/65)
  - Chiefs (8/10)
  - Hurricanes (29/55)
  - Wellington (21/65)
  - Cardiff Blues (10/5)
  - North Harbour (4/0)
  - Marseille Vitrolles (7/0)
- Test caps: 63
  - Points: 215
  - Tries: 37
- His 15 World Cup tries was a world record at the time
- BBC Overseas Sports Personality of the Year 1995

46

DIEGO MARADONA

'I was a stunned witness to
Diego's 'hand of God'

THE OFTEN-CONTROVERSIAL but always compelling Diego Maradona tried to be the number one at whatever he turned his hand to (particularly his left hand) – whether it was scoring goals, creating goals, drinking, taking drugs or just plain cheating. He was a law unto himself, a seriously flawed genius.

Let's start with Argentina's 1986 World Cup quarter-final against England in Mexico.

During this tournament Maradona confirmed that he was the greatest player on the planet. Unfortunately for followers of the Beautiful Game he was also confirmed as the greatest cheat.

To make it worse, the only footballer who could at the time look Pelé in the eye as the king of football was unrepentant, and boasted that his immoral moment was a divine intervention – 'the hand of God' he called the goal.

I had the perfect view of it. Judith and I were in Mexico City as part of a deal I had done with a travel company in return for hosting a party of travelling England supporters. Our seats in the

Estadio Azteca were in a direct eye line with where Maradona clearly and intentionally punched the ball into the net as leaping goalkeeper Peter Shilton caught thin air.

Everywhere around us and in a dozen different languages there were shouts of 'handball'. Judith was loudest of all. We all saw it – except the referee and his linesmen.

To put the match in context, Bobby Robson's England would have reached the semi-final if they could have overcome Argentina. We were in a crowd of 114,580, the game heavy with a tension that we could feel because of the overspill of animosity from the Falklands War. Squads of military police brandishing white batons patrolled the ground, but apart from a few isolated skirmishes the rival England and Argentine fans gave their attention to the game. And what a game it was!

All eyes were on Diego Maradona, who was in the form of his life and forcing good judges to reassess whether Pelé really was the greatest footballer of all time. Maradona might have been the shortest man on the field at just over 5ft 4in, but the chunky, wide-shouldered Argentine captain paraded across the pitch with the assured air of a giant among pygmies.

The two goals he scored early in the second half became the major talking point of the entire tournament and rivalled my second goal in the 1966 World Cup as a subject for debate. The first – punched into the net – showed Maradona at his worst; the second four minutes later at his scintillating best.

Judith and I looked on in a mixture of admiration and anxiety as he collected the ball in his own half and proceeded to run rings around England, drawing defenders to him like a spider luring its prey. Kenny Sansom, Terry Butcher and then Terry Fenwick all came into the Maradona web and were left in a tangle behind him as he accelerated past their attempted tackles.

Again, it was Maradona versus Shilton, this time on the ground. Maradona did not have to cheat his way past the England goalkeeper. He sold him an outrageous dummy that left Shilton scrambling for a shot that was never made, and then nonchalantly prodded the ball into the empty net for a goal of breathtaking beauty. We were still seething over the punched goal but reluctantly had to admit the second goal was astonishing. No wonder it was voted FIFA Goal of the Century in 2002.

I once palmed in one of the six goals I scored for West Ham in an 8-0 victory over Sunderland, but I owned up to it immediately afterwards and didn't come all that 'hand of God' nonsense. These things happen in football but it was Maradona's arrogance that angered us.

A funny story I must share about that match. I had to go into a TV studio in town before the match for a BBC interview. They laid on a taxi to take Judith and me to the Estadio Azteca and I arranged with the Mexican driver to pick us up after the game by the side of a huge, unmissable Camel Cigarettes advertising logo. It must have been 60 feet high and looked the perfect signpost. So we sat through the game watching Maradona at his worst and best and then made our way through the huge jam of spectators to our pick-up spot. Now, where the hell is that sign? It was a blow-up advertisement and had been taken down. Took us two hours to get back to our hotel!

Maradona's 'hand of God' was not there to rescue him as his private life became a horrendous mess later in his glittering career. From the early 1990s he was battling cocaine addiction, and he was banned for 15 months after failing a drug test in Italy, where he had almost single-handedly (no doubt his left) turned Napoli into a major force in Serie A.

He became involved in a controversy over an illegitimate son, alleged tax evasion, was criticised for having Mafia connections, had treatment for alcohol abuse, put on so much weight that this once super athlete waddled rather than ran, and was kicked out of the 1994 World Cup after failing another drug test.

FIFA conducted a poll on the internet in 2000 to find the people's choice as the Footballer of the Century. They stupidly forgot to take into account that most website surfers are under 30 and would not have seen Pelé in action. Maradona ran away with the vote but FIFA then decided that a 'football family of experts' would decide, and suddenly Pelé was announced in first place.

With a classic piece of compromise, FIFA decided to make two awards, one to Maradona for the website vote and one to Pelé. Maradona accepted his prize and arrogantly walked out before Pelé received his trophy. It was pathetic.

I have a stock answer when people ask, 'Who was the greatest out of Pelé and Maradona?' Not wishing to get involved in the never-ending argument, I tell people that you can only be the best of your generation. Pelé was the king of the 1950s and 60s, and Maradona the top man in the 80s.

Maradona was plagued by ill health as he approached middle age, much of it caused by his reckless lifestyle. Argentina was plunged into mourning when their favourite son died of a heart attack in 2020, aged just 60. He could not cheat death.

DIEGO MARADONA FOR THE RECORD:

- Born: 30 October 1960, Villa Fiorito, Argentina
- Career span: 1976–97
- Clubs:
  - Argentinos Juniors 1976–81 (166 games, 116 goals)
  - Boca Juniors 1981–82 and 1995–97 (71 games, 35 goals)
  - Barcelona 1982–84 (58 games, 38 goals)
  - Napoli 1984–91 (259 games, 115 goals)
  - Sevilla 1992–93 (30 games, 6 goals)
  - Newell's Old Boys 1993 (5 games, 0 goals)
- Argentina: 91 caps, 34 goals
- Argentine Primera División: 1981
- Copa del Rey 1983
- Serie A: 1987, 1990
- Coppa Italia: 1987
- UEFA Cup: 1989
- World Cup: 1986
- Golden Ball (World Cup Player of the Tournament): 1986
- Argentine Football Writers' Footballer of the Year: 1979, 1980, 1981, 1986
- South American Footballer of the Year: 1979, 1980
- FIFA Player of the Century (people's choice): 2000
- FIFA Goal of the Century: 2002
- Died: 25 November 2020, Dique Luján, Argentina, aged 60

47

ROCKY MARCIANO

'The REAL Rocky was the
Twentieth Century Caveman'

ASK PEOPLE who or what Rocky means to them, and most will conjure up an image of Rocky Balboa, the fictional film heavyweight boxer created by Hollywood actor Sylvester Stallone. The REAL Rocky – Marciano – was a flesh-and-blood hero of 49 fights and 49 wins, who carved an all-time place for himself in the record books as the only unbeaten world heavyweight champion.

His story is more compelling, more brutal and more unbelievable than anything that happened to the Rocky who lived only on the cinema screens. The *real* Rocky was not acting or pulling punches. Ask any of his pounded victims.

When I first took an interest in boxing, Marciano was the undisputed champion in the days when there were just eight world champions, one for each weight division. It was Rocky who grabbed the attention after demolishing old champion Joe Louis in eight rounds, a fight that earned him a crack at the title held by Jersey Joe Walcott. Like me, Rocky had more than one sport claiming his attention when he was a schoolboy known as

Rocco Marchegiano. Boxing did not figure on his radar and he had just one dream – to become a professional baseball catcher and batter. While at Brockton High School, he was also an outstanding footballer (the American kind) but he was obsessive about baseball.

His switch to boxing came with an unscheduled fight in Wales. He was drafted into the US Army after the Japanese attack on Pearl Harbor brought the United States into the war. Rocky was assigned to the 150th Combat Engineers and his initial posting was to a converted barracks on the outskirts of Swansea, which is where he had his first unrecorded, unofficial fist fight. Actually, it was a one-punch mismatch.

Under American law, Rocky at just 20 was not allowed to drink alcohol. He went to the bar and ordered a glass of milk, as he would have done in a milk bar in hometown Brockton. This brought a sneering response from an Aussie soldier, who was rewarded for his sarcasm with a one-punch swing to the jaw that reduced him to a heap on the saloon bar floor. Of all the gin joints in all the towns in all the world, the Aussie managed to pick out the one where the future world heavyweight king was ordering his milk.

The pub was the Adelphi in Wind Street, Swansea, and for several years it had a Marciano bar to mark the incident before a name change of the premises to The Bucket List.

Rocky's main sporting ambition remained wanting to become a baseball professional, but he switched to boxing on his return home and mowed down a succession of opponents with savage attacks that earned him the nickname Twentieth Century Caveman. He preferred to be known as the Brockton Blockbuster in honour of his hometown.

British bulldog Don Cockell was among Rocky's victims as he brutally defended his title six times without ever being on nodding terms with the Marquess of Queensberry rules. He clubbed all his opponents to defeat before surprisingly hanging up his gloves in 1955 at the relatively young age of 32. His speciality punch was known as his 'Suzie-Q', an overarm right that flattened a procession of opponents.

He had a perfect 49-0 record, with a record 87.75 knockout percentage. 'I am keeping a promise to my wife,' Rocky said. 'It's time I put my family first. I thought it was a mistake when Joe Louis tried a comeback. No man can say what he will do in the future, but barring poverty, the ring has seen the last of me. I am comfortably fixed, and I am not afraid of the future.'

Rocky became a businessman, television show presenter, boxing and wrestling referee and a money lender. He was only once tempted to make a comeback when he was offered $1m to fight Ingemar Johnasson after he had taken the world title from Rocky's successor, Floyd Patterson. But after a week of secret training he realised he did not have the necessary desire and determination.

The only time he got back into the ring was for a computer 'fight' with Muhammad Ali. Shortly after his death on 31 August 1969 the film of the pretend contest was released showing him stopping Ali in the 13th round. They had filmed four finishes, and Ali threatened to sue the producers for damaging his reputation.

Always conscious of his receding hairline, Rocky paid top dollar for several hairpieces from the same experts who hid the baldness of such stars as Frank Sinatra, Bing Crosby, Tony Bennett and Fred Astaire. It was not just vanity but a need to look as young as possible on the TV screen. He wore specially tailored jackets to hide his spreading waistline after quickly adding lots of pounds when he gave up his murderous training schedule.

He had started to give co-commentaries and then, much more ambitiously, presented a regular *Main Event* show in which he analysed major fights in the company of guests such as Nat 'King' Cole, Joe DiMaggio, George Raft, Sammy Davis Jnr, Jonathan Winters and his old foe, Jersey Joe Walcott. It's worth trawling the YouTube archives to find these collectors' items, and I think you will agree with me that Rocky – for a high school drop-out – was not half bad at TV anchor work.

Throughout his career he insisted on being paid for his fights and personal appearances in cash because he did not trust banks after the Wall Street crash when he was a boy. He hid his money behind false walls and in shoeboxes, and when he died in a plane crash on the eve of his 46th birthday more than $2m was unaccounted for. Nobody owned up to finding it!

ROCKY MARCIANO FOR THE RECORD:
- Born: 1 September 1923, Brockton, Massachusetts, USA
- Name at birth: Rocco Francis Marchegiano
- Career span: 1947–55
- Fights: 49
- Wins: 49
- Became world heavyweight champion on 23 September 1952 after knocking out Jersey Joe Walcott in the 13th round in Philadelphia
- Defences:
  - Jersey Joe Walcott, 15 May 1953, Chicago; won by knockout in first round
  - Roland LaStarza, 24 September 1953, New York; won by knockout in 11th round
  - Ezzard Charles, 19 June 1954, New York; won on points after 15 rounds
  - Ezzard Charles, 17 September 1954, New York; won by knockout in eighth round
  - Don Cockell, 16 May 1955, San Francisco; won by knockout in ninth round
  - Archie Moore, 21 September 1955, New York; won by knockout in ninth round
- Died: 31 August 1969, Iowa, aged 45

48

SIR STANLEY MATTHEWS

*'Wizard of Dribble who had defenders
and spectators spellbound'*

THEY SAY 'never meet your heroes' (Judith thinks people must be disappointed when they meet me!), so I was wary when I was invited to join a World Cup ambassadors team that included one of my boyhood idols, Stanley Matthews. He was everything you hope for in a hero – humble, modest, entertaining and knowledgeable.

You need to realise that I grew up in the bleak immediate post-war years of ration books, petrol coupons, no television and just the radio, Old Labour in power nationalising everything in sight, and my football gods earning a maximum 12 quid a week.

To us sports-mad kids of the 1940s, Stanley Matthews was the finest footballer who ever breathed; certainly the most famous Englishman to lace up a pair of boots. You could go anywhere in the world, from Argentina to Zanzibar, and they would have heard of the 'Wizard of the Dribble'.

Stanley's dad, Jack Matthews, was a professional featherweight boxer known as the 'Fighting Barber of Hanley'. In my days playing for Stoke, I learned that he was a very clever boxer, feinting with one hand and hitting with the other, and adopting now-you-see-me-now-you-don't tactics to avoid being hit by counter punches.

Well, that was also the way Stanley played the game, only he feinted with his feet rather than his fists, and he perfected a unique dropping-of-the-shoulder technique that confused and bemused a legion of full-backs. They used to say that when Stanley sold a dummy, half the spectators had to pay to get back into the ground.

I shared a theory with my old buddy Jimmy Greaves that the best forwards, those who can drift through defences as if they're not there Greavsie-style, are the best liars. They spend their careers 'conning' defenders into thinking they are going to do one thing while all the time having something else in mind.

Nobody was a better liar than Stanley. He told some whoppers to deceive defenders. He used to convince full-backs that he was going to go on their inside, and then, with a sudden shuffle and a subtle change of pace, he would dramatically nip past on the outside, leaving his marker to tackle his shadow.

His ball control was mesmerising. It was as if he had the ball on a piece of invisible elastic. He would shuffle towards the defender, tip-tapping it from one foot to the other; then, with the deftness of a juggler, he would flick the ball past the full-back and with jet-pace acceleration race to collect it and bring it back under his command.

Put Stanley in a 100 yards race and he would finish down the field, but over 20 yards with a ball to sniff he was whippet-quick.

Stanley loved proving the critics wrong. Time and again they predicted he would hang up his boots, but he kept playing and featured in a First Division match at the ridiculous age of 50 years and five days old.

I got out of the game at 34 because I was feeling aches and pains after 16 years of being clogged. Stanley played for another 17 years, and was still reluctant to retire when most people were looking forward to their old-age pension.

The reason he was able to play on and on is because of the lifestyle instilled into him by his dad. Almost as soon as he could walk, Stanley would follow exercises set for him by his father, a fitness fanatic who demanded that his three sons follow in his nimble footsteps.

When most fathers and sons were still thinking about getting out of bed, Stanley and his brothers would be early morning road running with their dad as he prepared for his next fight (he lost just a handful of more than 300 contests and was the 9st champion of the Potteries). I had a dad who was a professional sportsman and he passed on his discipline to me, and to this day as I reach the doorstep to my 80s I take a brisk 50-minute walk every day.

Stanley maintained this fitness regime throughout his life, and I remember him taking lots of vitamins and doing vigorous exercises when we used to keep company when he was into his 70s.

The game for which he is most remembered, of course, is the 1953 FA Cup Final at Wembley, which became known as the 'Matthews Final'. I watched it in black and white on a rented Ferguson television with a 9in screen, but could not have been more excited had it been in blazing colour on a panoramic cinema screen.

Blackpool, trailing 3-1 to Bolton with just 20 minutes to go, looked dead and buried. Enter stage right the Maestro, who was 37 years old and trying to win at Wembley after twice being a runner-up with the Seasiders in 1948 and 1951.

He turned the game – and Bolton's defence – inside out with a dazzling display of right-wing wizardry, inspiring a miraculous comeback and laying on a last-minute winner for South African outside-left Bill Perry.

This was the match in which the magnificent Stan Mortensen became the one and only player to score an FA Cup Final hat-trick at Wembley. In fairness, it should not be remembered as the Matthews Final and more the 'Stanleys Final'.

Stanley Matthews' value in today's transfer market? Let the bidding begin at £100m. When it looked as if Stoke were prepared to sell him for £10,000 in 1938, thousands of fans took to the streets in protest. He was finally allowed to move to Blackpool for £11,500 in 1947 because, at 32, Stoke felt he had little petrol left in the tank. He was still motoring down the wing 18 years later when back with his hometown Potteries club, where his journey had started in 1932!

England foolishly left him out of the 1950 World Cup finals match against the United States, and were beaten 1-0 in what remains one of the biggest shock results in the history of the game. He was left watching helplessly from the bench. It was like leaving Montgomery on the touchline at El Alamein.

Many years later, Stanley told me the background to the 1950 World Cup humiliation by the United States. 'The FA booked for me to play some exhibition matches in Canada, but I arrived in Chile in time to play against the USA,' he recalled. 'I was all ready to get stripped when the selector in charge, a fish monger from Grimsby, told me to save myself for the next match.

'"We won't need you against this lot," were his exact words. I sat kicking my heels on the touchline bench while watching a makeshift team of Americans, four of them from overseas, somehow fluking a 1-0 victory over an England team that must have had twenty goes at getting the ball into the net without any luck. It was the most miserable match I've ever had to watch. It was all so unprofessional, and we just seemed to take it for granted that we would beat the American part-timers. That's what happens when you let amateurs run the game. We should have approached the game as if we were playing against the favourites Brazil or Uruguay. I don't mind admitting I was close to tears with frustration when the final whistle blew.'

Stanley played in the 1954 World Cup finals at the age of 39, by which time he was losing some of his magic, but he rediscovered his Midas touch in a 1956 international against the soon-to-be-crowned world champions Brazil at Wembley. He was marked by Nílton Santos, one of the greatest ever left-backs. Stanley gave Santos such a run-around on the way to England's 4-2 victory that, when the Brazilian shook his hand at the end, he said, 'Mr Matthews, you are the king.'

He was the first footballer to be knighted. Sir Stanley Matthews, a shining knight and Wizard of Dribble. A hero who never disappointed.

SIR STANLEY MATTHEWS FOR THE RECORD:

- Born: 1 February, 1915, Hanley, Stoke-on-Trent
- Career span: 1932–65
- Clubs:
  - Stoke City 1932–47 (289 games, 57 goals)
  - Blackpool 1947–61 (428 games, 18 goals)
  - Toronto City 1961 (14 games, 0 goals)
  - Stoke City 1961–65 (66 games, 5 goals)
  - Toronto City 1965 (6 games, 0 goals)
- England: 54 caps, 11 goals
- Second Division: 1933, 1963
- FA Cup: 1953
- Oldest footballer to play First Division football, aged 50 years and five days
- FWA Footballer of the Year: 1948, 1963
- European Footballer of the Year: 1956 (first recipient of the award)
- First footballer knighted: 1965
- Died: 23 February 2000, Newcastle-under-Lyme, Staffordshire, aged 85

49

PETER MAY

'The classics master P.B.H. who made
much more than an initial impact'

IN THE days when I was playing more cricket than football, Peter Barker Howard May was the England batsman everybody looked up to, the supreme stylist setting the batting benchmark with a classical stance and strokes from the heavens. He was a committed amateur throughout his career and along with 'Lord Ted' Dexter and Michael Colin Cowdrey gave an elitist edge to the game.

Fully living up to his potential as a prodigiously talented Charterhouse schoolboy before going to Cambridge, he averaged an impressive 51 throughout his first-class career despite the pressures of captaincy with Surrey and England. Taking over from Len Hutton, he skippered England in a then record 41 Tests, winning 20 and losing only ten.

May will be remembered especially for his on-drive, a thing of power and beauty and unleashed with the timing of a Tchaikovsky concerto. In 66 Tests he scored 4,537 runs at 46.77; in first-class cricket he piled up 27,592 runs at 51 with 282 catches. He amassed 85 centuries, his early retirement at the age of 32 preventing him becoming the first amateur since W.G. Grace to score 100 hundreds. His skill with the bat was just sublime and all we 'minnow' batsmen used to look on in awe.

I can't stress enough that May and his contemporaries batted on indifferent, uncovered pitches and without helmets and grills to protect them, which brings me to a particularly painful memory.

It was trying to replicate the May on-drive that cost me a tooth. I stood tall in the style of P.B.H. when facing a rising ball playing for the Essex Second XI at Chelmsford. A crouch or a duck out of the way would have been a sensible course of action. I got a top edge and the ball flew up and smashed me in the mouth. My centre front tooth flew about 15 yards to point, and explained why I gave a gap-toothed smile to Her Majesty The Queen when I went up to collect my World Cup winners' medal seven years later.

I will now award myself another medal for bravery, because after having the blood mopped up I returned to the wicket and completed a half-century. I get no sympathy from Judith, who rated my batting as boring as watching paint dry. And to think we've lasted nearly 60 years together!

While I'm being candid about my cricket, I had better own up to the fact that I was more Edith Evans than Godfrey Evans as a wicketkeeper. I got to play behind the stumps because I was the only one silly enough to volunteer for the job. They were happy days with Essex, but at times it was as relaxed as Butlin's holiday camp. I was so lucky to have football as my safety net.

But back to a *proper* cricketer in Peter May, whose finest knock was his 285 not out in an unbeaten stand of 411 with Colin Cowdrey in the first Test against the West Indies at Edgbaston in 1957. The following season he averaged more than 63 while continuing the collection of County Championship titles in succession to Stuart Surridge as Surrey skipper.

He and his brother, J.W.H. May, were also unbeatable at Eton Fives, winning the national Kinnaird Cup three years running from 1951 and playing as a pair they were never ever defeated.

Peter was a serious-minded disciplinarian and perfectionist who fell out with team-mates if they failed to match his standards, an ideal that he later carried into administration as chairman of the selectors, with mixed results. You had to be extra special to meet the May demands.

His sudden retirement from cricket came soon after he had been bowled round his legs by Richie Benaud at Old Trafford in 1961, his dismissal virtually clinching the Ashes for the Aussies. He became a highly successful insurance broker and underwriter at Lloyd's and concentrated on his growing family: four girls, all of them sharing their mother Virginia's love of horses.

Benaud, one of May's most formidable opponents, later described him as not just the greatest English batsman to emerge since the war – which is the common judgement – but the *only* great one. He obviously did not see my brave 50 at Chelmsford!

Peter May: the complete master.

PETER MAY FOR THE RECORD:

- Born: 31 December 1929, Reading, Berkshire
- Teams: Cambridge University (1950–52), Surrey (1950–63)
- Tests: 66 (1951–1961)
  - Runs: 4,537 (46.77), 13 centuries
  - Captaincy record: won 20, lost 10, drawn 11
  - Highest score: 285 not out v. West Indies (Edgbaston, 1957)
  - Catches: 42
- First-class career: 388 games (1950–63)
  - Runs: 27,592 (51), 85 centuries
  - Highest score: 285 not out for England v. West Indies (Edgbaston, 1957)
  - Catches: 282
- Died 27 December 1994, Liphook, Hampshire, aged 64

50

JOHN McENROE

'Supermac's tennis talent trumped his tantrums'

EVERYTHING STOPS for tennis in the Hurst household, particularly Wimbledon. Judith shares my love of the sport and 'You cannot be serious' continues to be a catchphrase we use if we want to make a point. When John McEnroe first burst on the scene as the 'Superbrat' of the courts we all used to get annoyed at his obnoxious behaviour, which I thought scarred the traditions of one of the world's greatest sports tournaments.

But it was not long before he won us over with his talent rather than his temperament, and he eventually captured our affection and admiration for the way he could play the game with his inventive shot-making and volleying skills. We even began to look forward to his confrontations with umpires and line judges. When he was on court, anything could happen and you sat on the edge of your seat. His unexploded-bomb anger was a sign of his passion for the game and his flat-out will to win. But too often he went an insult too far against officials and opponents.

I just wonder how much duller games would have been back in the 1980s if Hawk-Eye had been around, instantly making obsolete his cries of, 'The ball was clearly in; chalk flew up.' Mac the Mouth would have been silenced.

The world became aware of McEnroe in 1977, when I was first trying my hand at football management with Telford United. He was just 18 years old and still an amateur when he battled through the qualifying rounds at Wimbledon and made it all the way to the semi-finals, where he lost in four sets to another quiet, modest American left-hander called Jimmy Connors.

One of my favourite trivia questions is, 'Who was the first German-born player to win the men's singles title in the 1980s?' The instinct is to say Boris Becker but the answer is John McEnroe, who was born in Wiesbaden in West Germany, where his father was then serving with the US Airforce.

My ears pricked up when he said in a television interview that he was a soccer lover. He had played the game for four years at Trinity School, the prestigious Ivy League preparatory establishment in New York, where his father was a lawyer. I tried and failed to imagine him calling Bites Yer Legs Hunter 'the pits'. He later studied at Stanford University before becoming one of the most successful professional tennis players of his generation.

Because so much attention centred on his tantrums and rows with officials, it tends to be forgotten just how skilled a player McEnroe was at peak power. He was even ranked number one in the world in both singles and doubles at the same time.

He finished his stellar career with 77 singles and 78 doubles titles, which remains the highest men's combined total of the Open era. He won seven Grand Slam singles titles – four US Opens and three Wimbledons – nine men's Grand Slam doubles championships and one mixed doubles crown, the French Open with American Mary Carillo.

Aside from his domination of the singles court, many good judges rated him the best doubles player of all time and he and his partner Peter Fleming won 52 doubles titles, including four at Wimbledon (1979, 1981, 1983, 1984) and three at the US Open

(1979, 1981, 1983). He also had a formidable partnership with his younger brother, Patrick.

He was a major force on the veterans' circuit for many seasons while establishing himself as one of the most authoritative of all television pundits. A professional-class rock guitarist, McEnroe is also an art connoisseur and opened a popular gallery in Manhattan in the 1990s.

McEnroe was always an artist of a tennis player. What a pity he so often allowed his tantrums to rule his talent. It's like finding scratches on a masterpiece.

JOHN McENROE FOR THE RECORD:

- Born: 16 February 1959, Wiesbaden, West Germany
- Career span: 1976–2006
- Titles: 77
- Matches won: 883
- Matches lost: 198
- Prize money: $12,552,132
- Grand Slam singles titles: 7
  - Wimbledon: 1981, 1983, 1984
  - US Open: 1979, 1980, 1981, 1984
- Doubles career titles: 78
- Doubles matches won: 530
- Doubles matches lost: 103
- Grand Slam doubles titles:
  - Wimbledon: 1979, 1981, 1983, 1984, 1992
  - US Open: 1979, 1981, 1983, 1989
- Grand Slam mixed doubles titles:
  - French Open: 1977 (with Mary Carillo)
- Davis Cup: 1978, 1979, 1981, 1982, 1992
- ATP Player of the Year: 1981, 1983, 1984
- ITF World Champion: 1981, 1983, 1984

51

COLIN MEADS

'Pinetree packed awesome power'

WHEN I was hitting the headlines in the summer of 1966, Colin Meads – at least physically – was making a bigger impact 11,000 miles away. He was the powerhouse in the All Blacks pack, helping them to a clean sweep of winning all four Tests against the British and Irish Lions in New Zealand while the football World Cup was being staged in England.

Famously nicknamed Pinetree, he was a legend in his sport long before I made a bit of a name for myself. Colin the Colossus was the driving force for the All Blacks in 55 Tests between 1957 and 1971 – 48 at lock and seven in the number eight position. He went 20 matches from 1965 with only one defeat. As we entered the new millennium, Meads was voted the greatest New Zealand player of all time, which illustrates just how special he was in that rugby-mad nation.

He won 11 of his caps alongside his younger brother, Stan, and they used to toughen up for their rugby challenges by carrying sheep under their arms on their father's farm in King Country. At 6ft 4in and 16st, he was not a giant by modern standards, but seemed much bigger to opponents as he dominated matches with his ferociously competitive spirit and fantastic strength.

Meads was a friendly giant off the pitch, but famed and feared for his merciless and often brutal aggression when the whistle blew. It was part of his legend that he once played through a match against South Africa with a broken arm, and he was sensationally sent off against Scotland at Murrayfield in 1967 for trampling on a rival forward.

I've been advised by rugby-playing friends that I should mention Colin's All Black contemporaries to put into context his status as the greatest player of his generation. He was part of one of New Zealand rugby's most productive eras and his peers included players such as Ken Gray, Brian Lochore, Wilson Whineray, Waka Nathan, Don Clarke and Kel Tremain, every one of them a Hall of Famer in rugby.

The undefeated 1967 team with which Meads toured Britain was recently voted the best New Zealand has ever fielded. I remember watching that team in action the year after we won the World Cup and thanking the heavens that they were rugby rather than association footballers. They were physically the toughest team I've ever watched in any sporting arena, but along with their might and muscle they also had method, and their three-quarter line had pace and invention. When Meads was sent off in Scotland it was seismic news in his homeland. It was as if the king of rugby had been pushed off his throne.

Mervyn 'Merv The Swerve' Davies, the idolised Wales number eight, summed up the status of Meads when he wrote, 'No player encapsulates a nation's attitude to sport like Colin Meads does for New Zealand. In a land of rugby giants, he still reigns supreme and is regarded by many as the greatest ever All Black. He was the flag-bearer of New Zealand manhood.'

As if he had not done enough to cement himself into folklore, Meads added to his incredible story in 1971 when he broke his back in a motoring accident after skippering the All Blacks 11 times. He was written off as finished but had the character to recover enough to continue playing for King Country for two more years before retiring, amassing a total of 361 first-class matches, a record that stood for 42 years.

The 'Pinetree' finally fell in 2017 aged 81, brought down by pancreatic cancer. An American newspaper trying to convey Colin's standing to its readers described him as the 'Babe Ruth of rugby.' He was one of the Great Untouchables. His name will live on in the rugby world for ever.

COLIN MEADS FOR THE RECORD:

- Born 3 June 1936, Cambridge, New Zealand
- Position: lock
- Test caps: 55 (only five missed in 15-year international career)
- Tries: 7
- Provincial rugby:
- King Country, 155 matches (1955–73)
- Bledisloe Cup: 12 times
- Voted greatest All Black of all time: 1999
- Knighted in New Zealand honours list: 2009
- Died: 20 August 2017, Te Kuiti, Waikato, New Zealand, aged 81

52

LIONEL MESSI

'The day I met the baby-faced 'new' Maradona'

IT WAS 2005 when I first met Lionel Messi, a baby-faced teenager little known outside Barcelona. I was introduced to him as 'Leo', which is the name he prefers. We were in Leipzig for the 2006 World Cup finals draw, and I was among the representatives of the Football Association while Leo was out there making a film for sponsors.

I watched as he performed some juggling tricks for the cameraman. After 20 minutes of keeping the ball up in the air with astonishing ease and control, he went off for a photo shoot leaving me open-mouthed at his completely natural skill. When I got home I told Judith that I had seen the next Maradona.

Now, 16 years on, he is established as the greatest footballer of his generation and a player who can be mentioned in the same breath as Pelé and his countrymen Maradona and Alfredo Di Stéfano. His latest stage is in France with Paris Saint-Germain after a shock split with Barcelona in the summer of 2021 because they could no longer afford his sky-high salary. Just a mere £1m a week. Sacre bleu!

He had been with Barcelona since the age of 12 after being spotted playing in youth football with Newell's Old Boys in Argentina. Since he was five, Messi was coached by his father, Jorge, but there was concern that his career could be over before it had even started because he had been diagnosed with a growth hormone deficiency. At 12 years old he had the physique of an eight-year-old.

Yet as slight as he was, he could run rings around seasoned defenders. River Plate, one of the major clubs in Argentina, were keen to sign him but because of an economic crash they could not afford the medical bills to cure his problems.

Barcelona sporting director Carles Rexach spotted Messi's potential and persuaded his father to bring the entire family to Barcelona while his son was receiving growth therapy in a Spanish hospital. He was so keen to seal the deal that he got Jorge Messi to sign an agreement scrawled on a table napkin.

As he gradually grew in inches, so Messi's talent grew. He started playing for Barcelona's B team and in his first full season scored 35 goals in 30 matches.

It was October 2004, the year before I met him, that Leo made his official debut for the Barcelona first team against Espanyol, and he scored his first senior goal the following May against Albacete. He was just 17 and had grown more than a foot to 5ft 6in.

His first goal was scored from a pass by the established master Ronaldinho, who said prophetically, 'This will be the first of many. Leo is a natural.'

He quickly became a favourite at the Camp Nou as Frank Rijkaard guided Barcelona to back-to-back La Liga titles. Messi was prominent in driving them to the first Champions League triumph since 1992 but missed the 2-1 victory over Arsenal in the final because of a torn hamstring.

Messi won his first Ballon d'Or at the age of 22, and was described by one Spanish newspaper as, 'Maradona, Cruyff and Best all rolled into one.' So my prediction to Judith that I had seen the 'new' Maradona was on the ball. It was when Pep Guardiola took over the reins at Barcelona that he stepped up a gear to become a true superstar. Pep built his team around the little man and the results were stunning. He became a goal machine, with 38 in 2008/09, 47 in 2009/10, 53 in 2010/11 and then in 2011/12 an absolutely mind-blowing 73 goals, the most in a single season by a player in the history of European club football. In the calendar year of 2012 he netted a staggering 91 goals.

The nearest I have seen to Messi is our own Jimmy Greaves. He has the same low centre of gravity, the ability to control the ball in crowded penalty areas and the sudden acceleration and changes of direction that made Greavsie so difficult to mark. The difference is that he has a work rate that would not have appealed to Jim, who liked to play at his own pace and take breathers when it suited him. Messi is perpetual motion.

Diego Maradona – Messi's hero – said, 'Messi has the ability to become Argentina's greatest ever player. His potential is limitless. He is a genius.'

Never was his ability better showcased than his performance in the 2014-15 Champions League semi-final first leg against Bayern Munich. The match was shown live on television from the Neu Camp and this old pro jumped out of his seat in wild appreciation of a goal that he conjured out of nothing.

He skipped past the formidable Jerome Boateng as if he was an extra in a film about to be shot, leaving him on the floor as he accelerated into the penalty area. Then he teased and tricked one of the great goalkeepers, Manuel Neuer, before coolly lifting the ball over him with his 'weaker' right foot for a dream of a goal.

'Remember,' I boasted to Judith, 'I spotted him when he was an unknown 16 year old.'

That magnificent solo goal would have been good enough in isolation, but it was just one of the thrusting inroads made by Messi during a startling 25-minute period when he scored twice and made an assist for a third goal. This was sheer brilliance, and I began to wonder if perhaps he is the greatest of all time after all.

Barcelona went on to lose the second leg 3-2 in Germany, but progressed to the final on aggregate and then beat Juventus to lift the trophy. I have rarely seen magic to match the football that Messi produced in that first leg of the semi-final, and it sits large in my memory as I put together my Eighty at Eighty.

People query whether he could have done it with a Norman 'Bites Yer Legs' Hunter, a Nobby 'Toothless Tiger' Stiles or a Ron 'Chopper' Harris booting him from behind which was the sort of minefield Jimmy had to operate in back in the days when brutal tackling from behind was allowed (I've got the scars to prove it).

My firm belief is that Messi would have been a star in any era. He has bravery to go with his exceptional talent, and I knew from his teenage years that he was going to be something very special. But let's be honest, a blind man could have seen his potential.

And there's more to come in the autumn of his career in his new home in France. He was born to score goals.

LIONEL MESSI FOR THE RECORD:
- Born: 24 June 1987, Rosario, Argentina
- Career span: 2003–ongoing
- Clubs:
  - Barcelona (778 games, 672 goals)
  - Paris Saint-Germain (yet to make debut as of August 2021)
- Team trophies with Barcelona: 34
- Argentina: 151 caps, 76 goals and counting (as of August 2021)
- Olympic gold medal: Beijing 2008, two goals in five games
- Ballon d'Or: 2009, 2010, 2011, 2012, 2015, 2019
- European Golden Boot: 2010, 2012, 2013, 2017, 2018, 2019
- FIFA World Player of the Year: 2009
- Best FIFA Men's Player: 2019

53

BOBBY MOORE

*'Everybody but nobody knew
the REAL Bobby Moore'*

I HAD absolutely no hesitation in putting Bobby Moore's name down on my list. He is simply one of the finest defenders ever to emerge on the playing fields of England, and I felt privileged to have been his team-mate for both club and country. How can I ever forget those last moments of the 1966 World Cup Final when, as casually as if in a practice match, he dribbled forward and stroked the 30-yard pass for me to complete my hat-trick? That perfectly captured Bobby's coolness and class.

I am continually asked, 'What was Bobby Moore like away from football?' I defy anybody to give a definitive answer. I was as close as anybody could get to Bobby, but would never claim that I really knew him. Everybody yet nobody knew the real Bobby Moore.

He built an impenetrable wall around himself; there were lots of acquaintances who followed him like disciples but never pierced his defence. He enjoyed a good drink after a match and found the perfect partner in Jimmy Greaves, but that was never my scene and

I was just happy to be part of Bobby's football world. He was only eight months older than me, but I always felt I was playing with a big, much older, more worldly brother.

Bobby, Tina – his first wife – Judith and I used to socialise, and to be around him you could actually feel the magnetic field of celebrity. But still he managed to stay somewhat aloof and to protect his privacy. The public Bobby Moore, just like the footballing Bobby Moore, was always in control.

Bobby had a wonderful sunset to his glorious playing career when, after his magnificent service to West Ham, he held a passing out parade at friendly Fulham, with our old mate Alan Mullery as a side-kick. They went beyond the bounds of expectations by steering the Cottagers all the way to the 1975 FA Cup final at Wembley. Waiting for them, of all teams: West Ham.

I had departed for Stoke by then and so I did not feel guilty when willing Bobby to make one last climb up those Wembley steps to collect a winners' medal. But it was not to be and little did we know it but that was his last match on the big-time stage that he had dominated and decorated for so long.

From there on, apart from some fun and games at Fulham with the double act of George Best and Rodney Marsh, it was downhill all the way. Football no longer wanted to know Bobby Moore, the greatest English defender of my long life time.

I was fairly recently alongside excellent England manager Gareth Southgate at a fundraising dinner when somebody in the audience asked him, 'Who do you think was man of the match in the 1966 World Cup Final?' Gareth did not pause for a second – even with the 'hat-trick hero' next to him – as he responded, 'Bobby Moore.' For me, Bobby was the man of a lifetime.

It continues to be my view that Bobby was let down by the sport's powerbrokers, who just did not know how to utilise his achievements and aura for the benefit of the game. He would have made the perfect ambassador for our football and our country if he had been used in the way Franz Beckenbauer has represented

Germany. I always feel that the knighthood that was kindly bestowed upon me should have gone to Bobby for his performances on the football field.

Since he was claimed by cancer at the age of 51, statues of him have been erected at Wembley and West Ham, a stand has been named after him, television documentaries have lauded him and people who barely knew him have compiled books and websites galore about the master.

But they turned their backs on him when he was alive after he had captained his country 90 times in 108 appearances, and played a key role in winning the World Cup in 1966. I was proudly behind him when he climbed the 39 steps at the old Wembley for three successive years to collect major trophies for West Ham and then England, and later he had to climb down and almost beg for jobs in the game he had served so well.

It beggars belief that Bobby told me that when he applied for the England manager's job, he didn't even get the courtesy of a reply.

One of the greatest defenders the world has ever seen was forced to scratch a living on the periphery of the game after a few business projects had gone belly-up. He went to Denmark, Hong Kong and those soccer hotspots of Oxford and Southend to earn his bread and butter. He then became sports editor of a daily paper that peddled soft porn before winding up as a pundit on London radio station Capital Gold, giving his opinions on football in between the pop songs.

He had become a sideshow. What a way to treat one of England's finest sportsmen – ignored when alive, acclaimed and applauded in death.

Bobby was outwardly so cool and dignified in the way he handled himself going into the 1970 World Cup after his crazy arrest on a trumped-up jewel theft charge in Bogotá. The way he carried himself typified how he could be commanding and in control in situations that would have crushed most people. He came out of the tournament with the stature and recognition he deserved as one of the absolute masters of football.

But after retirement he found doors closed to him at home. The hypocrisy was sickening.

There will only ever be one Bobby Moore, and I considered myself so lucky to be in his orbit.

BOBBY MOORE FOR THE RECORD:

- Born: 12 April 1941, Barking, Essex
- Career span: 1957–78
- Clubs:
  - West Ham 1957–74 (647 games, 27 goals)
  - Fulham 1974–77 (148 games, 1 goal)
  - San Antonio Thunder 1977 (24 games, 1 goal)
  - Seattle Sounders 1978 (7 games)
- England: 108 caps, 2 goals
- FA Cup: 1964
- European Cup Winners' Cup: 1965
- World Cup: 1966
- Defender of the Tournament: 1970 World Cup
- FWA Footballer of the Year: 1964
- BBC Sports Personality of the Year: 1966
- Died: 24 February 1993, Putney, London, aged 51

54

GERD Müller

'Der Bomber, the German with the
unquenchable thirst for goals'

A PSYCHIATRIST could have a ball with goalscorers, trying to discover why so many of them seem to turn to the bottle after the shooting and the shouting is over. Is it that their thirst for goals has to be replaced by a substitute? The question is prompted by the fact that Gerd Müller, who was arguably the greatest of all marksmen, is yet another who had serious alcohol problems when he stopped hunting goals for a living.

Thank goodness I never got a taste for the demon drink on a major scale, but Müller was in good company with his craving. George Best, my mate Greavsie, Garrincha, Ferenc Puskás, Jim Baxter, Paul Gascoigne and Diego Maradona – although cocaine was a bigger problem for him – were among those who had an alcohol dependency after hanging up their shooting boots.

Müller was one of those who thought opening a bar was a good idea when he retired and – like Jim Baxter before him – did his best to drink his premises dry. I also dabbled in the pub landlord business but had the discipline to keep the hard stuff out of reach.

Stocky and seeming to be almost as wide as he was tall, Müller had to watch his weight throughout all his years plundering goals. Once all restrictions were lifted, though, he dived into the life of an alcoholic until rescued by his old friends in football.

Bayern Munich, the club where he spent 15 mostly glorious years, brought him back into their family, helped him get straightened out, and he spent several contended years happily helping coach the next generation of Bayern football stars until he sadly became a victim of the footballers' curse of Alzheimer's and passed on in the summer or 2021.

I have nagging memories of Müller scoring the winning goal during our nightmare in León in the 1970 World Cup quarter-final, and then two years later he gave a repeat performance in a European Championship quarter-final against us at Wembley. These were peak years for the brooding, brilliant Bavarian and he was the main strike force for the West German team that won the World Cup in 1974.

This is the same man who back in the early 1960s was told by Bayern that he was too fat and slow to make the grade. They changed their minds when he started grabbing goals galore for his local youth team in his Bavarian birthplace of Nördlingen. He earned the nickname 'Der Bomber' as he blitzed defences with more explosive results than any other striker in European and World Cup history.

Including qualifying matches, Müller scored 19 goals in the 1970 campaign with his then record of ten earning the Golden Boot in the finals – one of his haul was that heartbreaking winner in León. His contribution to West Germany's World Cup triumph in 1974 was four goals, including the all-important clincher against Holland in the final on his favourite hunting ground in Munich.

He was just as prolific in club football with Bayern, scoring more than 560 competitive goals. His 36 goals in European Cup football made a nonsense of the early predictions that he would be too weighed down with muscle and fat to make an impact at the top level.

At just 5ft 9in tall, Müller was squat almost to the point of squashed in build. His short, tree-trunk legs gave him a low centre of gravity and as well as his finishing accuracy with either foot, his secret was stunning acceleration. Like so many goalscorers, he was carthorse-slow over 100 metres, yet like a flash of lightning in the space of a hall room carpet.

For a short man, he was a nuisance in the air and was brave enough to challenge the tall, strong central defenders in aerial combat. His ability to shoot on the turn made him as dangerous in the penalty area as a Wild West gunman in a bar duel.

His speciality was to swivel and shoot all in one rapid movement. His golden goal that beat Holland in 1974 was a typical example of this technique, which caught out dozens of defenders.

Very few players matched his scoring ratio at international level. His 68 goals in just 62 matches is mind-blowing stuff.

Asked about his gift for goals, Müller said, 'I have this instinct for knowing when a defence is going to relax, or when a defender is going to make a mistake. Something inside me says, "Gerd, go this way; Gerd, go that way." I don't know what it is.'

Müller was at the forefront of all the great German successes of the late 1960s and into the 1970s. He helped the Bayern Munich 'dream team' to an unprecedented run of success in the Bundesliga as they dominated at domestic and then European level.

Who could have guessed that his 1974 World Cup winner against Holland would be the last international goal Müller would score, and indeed the last international game he would play? He was just 28 and at the peak of his powers, but everything ended in tears because of a huge bust-up at the after-match victory banquet.

The spirit in the German camp had been fragile throughout the tournament following a bitter dispute over win bonuses. When the players arrived at the hotel for the celebrations, they found loads of German officials but no wives or girlfriends. They had been banned from attending. Just like the English FA, the German association was full of old farts who thought they were more important than the players. Our wives and girlfriends got the same shabby treatment in the aftermath of the 1966 final. If my gorgeous Judith was writing this page it would have to be printed on asbestos.

Uli Hoeness led a mass walk-out in protest, and Müller not only joined in but announced instantly that he would never play for Germany again. He made his statement in a downtown bar, where most of the players had headed after the banquet fiasco. Wolfgang Overath, Jürgen Grabowski and Paul Breitner were equally angry, and they too declared that their international careers were over. The World Cup-winning side had broken up overnight.

This all came in the middle of a run of three successive European Cup Final victories for Bayern Munich from 1974 to 1976. It was domination on a Real Madrid scale.

Then came the downhill run as Müller started to feel the effects of his dynamic action. Like me, he started to have back problems and – like me – he wound down his career playing with the United States circus, teaming up with George Best at Fort Lauderdale. I'm surprised there was elbow room for them both.

He returned to the Fatherland and got lost in a sea of alcohol until helped back to the shores of sobriety by his old Bayern Munich chums, who paid for his clinic treatment.

The football world mourned Gerd's passing in August 2021, and when contacted by German newspapers for my comments I told them we had lost one of the all-time great goal scorers. He hardly looked athletic with his short torso and thighs like Chris Hoy but he had the spring of a gymnast and the strength of a bull.

I told the German reporters how he had given me one of my most disappointing moments on a football field when he scored the winner against England in extra-time in the 1970 World Cup quarter-final in Léon. It was a typical Müller goal, volleying from close range after Jürgen Grabowski had crossed from the right. He scored these sort of goals by the dozen throughout his career and he broke our hearts that day in Léon. He was his own man on and off the pitch, and played hard home and away, never following conventional ways of behaviour and he was a law to himself in the penalty area. Give him a sniff of a chance and – bang! – the ball was in the back of the net. A light has gone out on German football.

During his playing career Der Bomber built a mountain of goals that will guarantee him a place in football history. You could say that he had an unquenchable thirst for goals.

GERD MÜLLER FOR THE RECORD:
- Born: 3 November 1945, Nördlingen, Germany
- Career span: 1964–81
- Clubs:
  - Bayern Munich 1964–79 (605 games, 563 goals)
  - Fort Lauderdale Strikers 1979–81 (80 games, 40 goals)
- West Germany: 62 caps, 68 goals
- Bundesliga: 1969, 1972, 1973, 1974
- German Cup: 1966, 1967, 1969, 1971
- European Cup: 1974, 1975, 1976
- European Cup Winners' Cup: 1967
- World Cup: 1970, 1974
- Scored a then record 14 World Cup finals goals
- World Cup Golden Boot: 1970
- European Championship: 1972
- European Footballer of the Year: 1970
- Died: 15 August 2021, Munich, aged 75

55

RAFAEL NADAL

'Tennis wins as King of Clay Rafa
turns his back on a football career'

IF THE world was made of clay, Rafael Nadal would be unchallenged as the greatest tennis player ever to have swung a racket. No fewer than 62 of his 88 titles have been won on clay, a surface on which he plays with a power and precision that to my layman's eyes puts him in the Superman class.

I have to bow the knee to Judith for having the best knowledge of tennis in the Hurst family, and she insists he is the finest of all the present-generation players. There would be arguments put forward for Roger Federer and Novak Djokovic, but if it was going to be decided purely on clay performances there is no doubt that Rafa would come out top.

It could easily have been the case that I was including Rafa as a footballer. In his early teens he was being tipped to become a Spanish international, following his uncle, Miguel Ángel Nadal, who played in three World Cups and was a notoriously tough defender with Barcelona. Surprisingly, Rafa supports Real Madrid rather than Barça. 'It causes controversy in the family,' he reveals. 'But my father and I have always preferred Los Blancos.'

Rafa was persuaded by his other paternal uncle Toni – Miguel's brother – that the tennis path was the one to follow, and he coached him for much of his career and played a vital part in making him a king of the courts.

'Football is my favourite sport to play,' said Rafa. 'But it's tennis for serious business. I had to make the choice between the two sports when I became a teenager and I knew in my heart that tennis was the one on which I should concentrate, but football will always be very special to me.'

Twenty Grand Slams later, we know he made the right choice. He has been ranked number one in the ATP ranking for a combined 209 weeks and has finished top at year end five times. As we went to press with this book, he shared the all-time record of 20 Grand Slams with Federer and Djokovic in what has been a golden era for tennis.

His remarkable tally of 13 French Open titles takes the eye, and 26 of his 36 ATP Masters championships have been on clay. His 81 consecutive wins on clay is the longest single-surface streak in the Open era. The left-handed artist from Majorca was the most successful teenager in the history of the ATP tour, and when he became number one for the first time in 2008 he also won the Olympic singles final in Beijing that year. He collected a gold medal in the Olympic men's doubles in the 2016 Rio Games to complete the Career Golden Slam.

While master of the clay, Nadal is a formidable force on the grass and his two Wimbledon titles include what many good judges have described as the greatest match of all time. In the 2008 final he and Federer were locked in a titanic tussle, with the Spaniard winning the title after a 9-7 victory in the fifth set fought in semi-darkness in the pre-roof days.

Djokovic came through as Nadal's main rival in the following decade and they battled each other through a modern record 58 matches, nine of them major finals. The Serbian leads 30-28, a serial interrupted by a series of injuries to Nadal.

The always totally committed and sporting Nadal has the perfect big-occasion temperament. Never throughout his career has he broken a racket in a show of temper. 'My family would not approve,' he says. 'I was always taught to control my emotions.'

Rafael Nadal, the perfect champion.

RAFEL NADAL FOR THE RECORD:

- Born 3 June 1986, Manacor, Mallorca
- Career span: 2001–ongoing
- Prize money: $124,937,195
- Career highlights:
- Won an ATP Tour title in record 18 straight seasons (2004–21)
- Ranked in top ten for record 822 consecutive weeks (2005–21), including 209 total weeks as number one
- Record title victories on clay, 62, including 13 Roland Garros, 11 Monte Carlo and 10 Rome titles
- Record 81-match win streak (2005–07)
- Tied with Djokovic and Federer for most Grand Slam titles (20)
- Tied with Djokovic for most ATP Masters titles (36)
- Joined Agassi as second man to complete career Grand Slam and win Olympic gold medal in singles (2008 Beijing), then added gold medal in doubles (2016 Rio)
- Led Spain to five Davis Cup titles
- ITF World Champion four times
- ATP Player of the Year five times

56

JACK NICKLAUS

*'The Golden Bear finished a
fair way ahead of the field'*

I WAS first drawn to golf by the exploits of the great trio of the
fairways in the early 1960s – Arnold Palmer, Jack Nicklaus and
Gary Player. They more than anybody turned golf from an elitist
recreation into a hugely popular and commercialised game across
the world.

Palmer, an amazingly aggressive and charismatic competitor,
was the trailblazer, followed around every course by huge galleries
known as Arnie's Army. He was rivalled in the title hunt by South
African fitness fanatic Player, and the player who was to take his
crown as the king of golf, Nicklaus.

It's Jack – the Golden Bear – I have picked to represent these
three jolly green giants in my list of heroes simply because he set
records that are unlikely ever to be surpassed, as hard as Tiger
Woods has tried. He won 117 out of 164 professional tournaments
in his career, including an all-time record 18 major championships.
His record of 73 PGA Tour victories was surpassed only by Sam
Snead (82) and Woods (82).

Nicklaus had signalled that he was going to be a golfing powerhouse when he won the United States Amateur Championship in 1959 and 1961, and in 1960 finished second in the US Open, two shots behind Palmer, the world number one.

In his first full year on the pro circuit, Nicklaus defeated Palmer by three shots in an 18-hole play-off to decide the 1962 US Open. He was just 22 and already established as a force on the fairways.

He won back-to-back US Masters titles and – just two days before the 1966 World Cup finals kicked off on Monday, 11 July – he captured his first Open Championship at Muirfield. It was the sixth of his major titles and completed the first of his three career grand slams.

Nicklaus overtook the Bobby Jones record of 13 majors, and won his 18th major when taking the 1986 Masters in his final championship at the age of 46, the oldest winner of the Green Jacket.

In 1990 he joined the Senior PGA Tour and won eight majors before officially retiring in 2005. He continued his involvement with golf as one of the world's most in-demand course designers. Golf not only owes him a debt for putting the game on the world map, but he also set new standards of dignity and decency. His behaviour has been impeccable. What a great role model.

Nicklaus is quite the philosopher, and two quotes of his have stuck with me because they can apply to any sport, including in my football world. 'Sometimes,' he said, 'the biggest problems are in your head. You've got to concentrate and believe you can make the next shot, rather than waste time on wondering and worrying about that last bad shot.'

So true, and how about this for good sense: 'Confidence is the most important single factor in golf – or any sport – and no matter how great your natural talent, there is only one way to obtain and sustain it ... work at it. Work at it.'

Plenty to chew on there for anybody who wants to improve themselves, and so topical when you think how many major sports stars seem to be having mind and confidence problems. Think about the next shot, the next game, the next challenge. And work at it. I've never found a substitute for hard work.

As somebody who spent 30 years of my life in the world of motor insurance, I played surprisingly little golf because I simply could not find the time even to charm clients on the course. When I finally went into semi-retirement – looking forward to bringing down my rabbit handicap – I had to have a hip replacement and decided there and then to put my golf clubs away rather than risk causing any more physical damage.

I have played in dozens of celebrity and charity tournaments over the years, but never with the low-handicap skill of an Alan Hansen, Alan Shearer, Gareth Bale or Harry Kane. And Jack Nicklaus could have beaten me with one hand tied behind his back.

One of my last games was in Brisbane, to where my dear friend Terry Hopley – once an Essex journalist and then highly successful entrepreneur – had emigrated. He had shares in the beautiful Glades club in Queensland and he invited me to play a round one Christmas when Judith and I were staying with him at his home.

We teed off one short in a foursome, and I was ankle deep in rough when I was aware of being closely watched by a stranger. I swished and missed, swished and missed. Finally the stranger introduced himself as Tim Jacobs, an Englishman on holiday from Portsmouth who could not believe he had found one of his footballing heroes – me – on an Australian golf course. He had been sent from the clubhouse to make up our foursome. Terry then introduced him to Ian Baker-Finch, the Aussie who won the 1991 Open. Tim was in a daze and said, 'This is the greatest day of my life!'

Another laugh I had on a golf course was when I was playing with Roger Hunt, Alan Ball and Martin Peters at a charity event at Stoke Poges in the 1990s. We were halfway through our round when we came to a tee that gave no indication of which way to drive. Ballie knew the course and pointed the way to where Roger should drive, as it was his honour. He smacked the ball 200 yards down the fairway and then Ballie teed up and drove in completely the opposite direction. We fell about laughing, because Alan had deliberately given wrong directions. The look on Roger's face was priceless as Ballie drove off the other way.

Jack Nicklaus always knew where he was on a golf course, and played throughout his career with sublime power and skill. There will never be another like the Golden Bear.

JACK NICKLAUS FOR THE RECORD:

- Born 21 January 1940, Columbus, Ohio
- Career span: 1961–2005 (including Senior Tour)
- Prize money: $9,100,000
- US Amateur champion: 1959, 1961
- PGA Tour titles: 73
- Major titles:
  - US Masters: 1963, 1965, 1966, 1972, 1975, 1986
  - US PGA Championship: 1963, 1971, 1973, 1975, 1980
  - US Open: 1962, 1967, 1972, 1980
  - Open Championship: 1966, 1970, 1978
- European Tour victories: 9
- Senior Tour victories: 10
- PGA Player of the Year: 1967, 1972, 1973, 1975, 1976
- Presidential Medal of Freedom: 2005
- Congressional Gold Medal: 2015

57

PELÉ

'The King of football has built
a monument of goals'

WITH A gun to my head I would have to select one Edson Arantes do Nascimento as the greatest footballer ever to grace a football pitch, better known across the world, of course, as Pelé. I played against him twice, and have seen enough footage of him as a younger player to know that he was sent here from the gods.

My first up-close view of him came in Rio in 1969 in front of a roaring 160,000 crowd in the vast Maracanã Stadium. It was a warm-up match to get us prepared for the 1970 World Cup in Mexico, and Alan Mullery did a superb marking job on Pelé before two late goals gave the Brazilians a flattering 2-1 victory. A year later we met in the midday heat in Guadalajara, the famous match in which Gordon Banks made THAT save from a Pelé header. Brazil won 1-0 and went on to win the Jules Rimet Trophy outright after their third World Cup triumph.

Pelé did not stand out in either game because of Mullery's disciplined defensive work, but there was an aura about him in both matches that made me realise I was in the presence of football genius.

I would have Pelé top of my all-time list of great footballers, certainly from my era. Just look at his goalscoring record: 1,216 goals in 1,254 matches from his debut at the age of 15 until his first retirement on 2 October 1974, 21 days short of his 34th birthday.

His peak year for goals was 1958 when he scored the little matter of 139 times, including two classic goals in the World Cup Final, when we first became aware of the developing legend that was Pelé. He went on to collect 12 goals in four finals, and he remains the only player to have been a member of three World Cup-winning teams (1958, 1962 and 1970), although he missed the latter stages in 1962 because of a pulled muscle. European clubs queued to try to buy him but the Brazilian government, fearing street riots, declared him an 'official national treasure' so that he could not be taken abroad.

Born on the poverty line in Três Corações, 14 months ahead of me in 1940, he came under the influence of former Brazilian World Cup player Waldemar de Brito while playing for his local team Noroeste. De Brito, realising he had unearthed a diamond, whisked him off to Santos in Sao Paulo, where he made a scoring first-team debut at the age of 15.

A year later Pelé was in the Brazilian international team and in 1958 became, at 17, the then youngest ever World Cup debutant. It was the launch of one of the great sporting journeys.

Averaging almost a goal per game throughout his career, Pelé had power and accuracy in both feet and, while essentially a striker, he often dropped deep to play a scheming role, providing assists with his vision and passing precision. He made nearly as many goals as he scored by clever positioning and the natural ability to read situations more quickly than his opponents.

What surprised me when I played against him is that he stood only 5ft 8in tall, and was three inches shorter than me. Yet he managed to out-jump far taller defenders to score with spectacular headers. He had the dribbling skill to evade his markers, and was as brave as a lion. When tackled in what was a physically challenging era he would often retaliate and give as good as he got.

Pelé, sadly for the spectators, was mercilessly kicked out of the 1966 World Cup, but he got his old appetite back in time to steer the greatest of all the Brazilian teams to the 1970 triumph. I speak from painful experience of being twice on the losing side against the yellow-shirted maestros. 'The King' played on for four more years before announcing that his fantastic reign was over.

In 1975 former *Daily Express* football writer Clive Toye, then general manager of New York Cosmos, persuaded Pelé to make a comeback in the North American Soccer League. He made a final farewell appearance against his old club Santos in New Jersey before a sell-out 60,000 crowd on 1 October 1977. It was Pelé's 1,363rd match and he naturally marked it with a goal to bring his career total to 1,281.

He built a monument to himself. It was made of goals.

PELÉ FOR THE RECORD:
- Born: 23 October 1940, Três Corações, Brazil
- Career span: 1955–77
- Clubs:
  - Santos 1955–74 (605 league games, 589 goals)
  - New York Cosmos 1975–77 (64 games, 37 goals)
- Brazil: 92 caps, 77 goals
- Club honours: 13 Brazilian league titles
- World Cup: 1958, 1962, 1970
- Competitive games, 840, goals 775
- Voted Athlete of the Century by the International Olympic Association: 1999
- FIFA Player of the Century: 2000

58

MARTIN PETERS

'The Ghost who could haunt
defenders from any position'

THIS IS a tough one for me to discuss. Martin was not only a respected team-mate at club and country level but a treasured friend whose passing from Alzheimer's in 2019 still cuts deep. We were like brothers on the pitch, then business partners in the motor insurance world and always – for more than 50 years – close pals.

I am trying not to be biased as I describe Martin as one of the most versatile footballers the British game has ever produced. Alf Ramsey famously described him as 'ten years ahead of his time'. He would have fitted into today's game with ease and elegance, and any team would have benefited from his radar-like ability to be in the right place at the right time. Not for nothing was he known as 'The Ghost' because of his uncanny ability to find space where others without his vision could only see defenders.

A couple of memories from those 1966 World Cup finals that were the making of both of us. It was a made-in-West Ham goal that gave us a quarter-final victory over Argentina, my debut match in the tournament. Martin knew exactly where to find me with a cross from the left and I headed the winner. It was the sort of move we had perfected under the expert coaching of Ron Greenwood since we were teenagers together at Upton Park.

Martin and I were sharing a room at the Hendon hotel headquarters and on the eve of the final we also shared a secret. Alf had told each of us in confidence that we were in the team to face West Germany. Like a pair of excited schoolboys, we blurted out to each other that we had been selected for the game of our lives.

It looked as if Martin had scored the winning goal for England when he coolly slotted the ball home after I'd had a shot saved; then came the last-minute German equaliser and my hat-trick (that I may have mentioned before).

That final tied the knot between Martin and I, along with our Hammers club-mate and captain Bobby Moore, of course. For ever after we were known as the West Ham Three.

If anything, Martin was a victim of his versatility. He wore every West Ham shirt, including playing in goal in an emergency, and it took time for him to establish his favourite position – as an 'invisible' left-sided midfielder, coming through to score some fabulous goals.

After West Ham, he served Tottenham, Norwich City and Sheffield United with distinction. He was far too nice to cut it as a manager and became an industrious and respected man of the insurance world. I never once heard him boast about his achievements on the football pitch: 882 club appearances and 220 goals, 67 England caps and 20 goals. He was football's first £200,000 player but never shouted about it.

Off the pitch, he was never the life and soul of the party, preferring privacy to public showboating. But when you got through his shyness barrier you found a warm, likeable and gently humorous person who was always surprising with his little nuggets of knowledge. Judith and his wonderful wife Kathy remain the closest of friends, and we all still feel bruised at the suddenness of his illness that took away a footballer of renown and a human being of dignity and untold kindness.

Ironically, he left us ten years ahead of his time and will always be remembered as a thoroughbred footballer who was like a brilliant multi-instrumentalist in an orchestra. He could do it all.

MARTIN PETERS FOR THE RECORD:

- Born: 8 November 1943, Plaistow, West Ham
- Career span: 1959–83
- Clubs:
  - West Ham 1959–70 (302 league games, 81 goals)
  - Tottenham Hotspur 1970–75 (189/46)
  - Norwich City 1975–80 (207/44)
  - Frankston City, Australia 1979 (5/3)
  - Sheffield United 1980–81 (24/4)
  - Gorleston 1982–83 (no stats available)
- Total league games: 727
- Total league goals: 178
- Total career games: 882
- Total career goals: 220 goals
- European Cup Winners' Cup: 1965
- League Cup: 1971, 1973
- UEFA Cup: 1972
- England: 67 caps, 20 goals
- World Cup: 1966
- Died: 21 December 2019, Essex, aged 76

59

LESTER PIGGOTT

'The Long Fellow provides fireworks all his life'

THERE ARE 5,300 reasons why Lester Piggott makes it into my list – the total number of winners he rode as arguably the greatest of all flat race jockeys, and for making a huge impression on me when I was a sports-silly schoolboy. He rode a record nine Epsom Derby winners and his first, in 1954, was on a horse that gave the nation a slogan in those tough immediate post-war days, Never Say Die.

I doubt there has been a more disciplined champion in any sport. For years he kept himself 30lb under his natural weight and followed a spartan diet to keep fit for a punishing racing schedule that took him all over the world. He rode winners in more than 30 countries during his 47 years in the saddle. Actually, he rarely sat in it and adopted a unique 'bottoms-up' style that was imitated by many of his rival jockeys.

At 5ft 8in, he was tall for a flat race jockey and was known throughout racing as 'The Long Fellow', and for most of his career he rode at 8st 6lb. This was the sort of sacrifice that enabled him to become champion jockey 11 times.

He took over from Sir Gordon Richards as the housewives' favourite, and bookmakers automatically slashed the odds the moment he chose a mount. I have selected him ahead of Sir Gordon because fabulously successful Richards rode most of his races before I got the kick of life in 1941.

Lester was born to ride. His Cheshire farming family could trace its roots as jockeys and trainers back to the 18th century. His grandfather Ernie Piggott owned a racehorse stable at The Old Manor in Letcombe Regis and his father Keith Piggott was a successful National Hunt jockey and trainer, who encouraged Lester to ride over hurdles early in his career. He won his first race in 1948, when just 12 years old and on a horse called The Chase at Haydock Park. It was the start of one of the longest winning streaks in history, and he was still going first past the post in the 1990s.

Quiet and introverted away from the race course and with a speech impediment, Lester appeared to get on with horses much better than humans. He suffered from a deafness that he used to his advantage when telling stewards that he could not hear when rival jockeys complained that he would not let them through in tight finishes.

He rode 30 Classic winners and was renowned for his competitive nature, and was often in trouble for using the whip too liberally. For those tuned into his ultra-nasal speech, he could come up with some cutting remarks. When he won the prestigious 1969 Washington DC International on Karabas he was asked by a reporter just when he thought he had the race won. The taciturn Piggott – once described as having a face like a well-kept grave – replied dryly, 'About two weeks ago when I was booked for the ride.'

A journalist asked him why he was so stony faced when his many followers used to applaud him. 'Why should I smile?' he responded. 'They'd be throwing things at me if I lost.'

Alan Ball was Lester's biggest fan and used to go on about him non-stop. Alan bought a racehorse in the 1970s called Go

Go Gunner, and he persuaded his trainer to hire freelance Lester to ride it. After Lester had been beaten, Ballie – who had a broken leg in plaster at the time – described how he hobbled after Piggott for a comment as he dismounted. Lester was infamous for giving brief, brutal summaries to owners on their horses. Ballie chased him to the changing room as best he could in the plaster cast. 'What d'you think of the horse, Lester?' The great man mumbled over his shoulder, 'Sell him.' That was all Ballie got, and his horse never won another race.

Lester was notorious for being careful with his money, and his miserly ways caught up with him in 1987 when he was given a three-year prison sentence and stripped of his OBE for tax evasion on a colossal scale. He was found guilty of a £3m tax fraud.

Everybody thought that would be the last they saw of Lester in the saddle, but on his release from prison he came out of retirement to notch a famous victory in the Breeders' Cup Mile in America aboard Royal Academy. Then, aged 56, he won the 2000 Guineas in 1992 on Rodrigo de Triano to claim his 30th British Classic win. He eventually hung up his riding boots and became a trainer in 1995, although he took part in a special tribute race at the Melbourne Cup meeting in 2001, aged 65.

Racing's equivalent of the Oscars are known as The Lesters (idea: wouldn't it be fitting if the PFA called their awards The Bobbys, after Moore and Charlton?).

Lester was born on 5 November 1935. He has certainly provided fireworks for most of his life.

LESTER PIGGOTT FOR THE RECORD:

- Born: 5 November 1935, Wantage, Berkshire
- Career span: 1948–95
- Total wins: 5,300 (4,493 in UK)
- British Classic wins: 30
  - 2000 Guineas: Crepello (1957), Sir Ivor (1968), Nijinsky (1970), Shadeed (1985), Rodrigo de Triano (1992)
  - 1000 Guineas: Humble Duty (1970), Fairy Footsteps (1981)
  - Derby: Never Say Die (1954), Crepello (1957), St Paddy (1960), Sir Ivor (1968), Nijinsky (1970), Roberto (1972), Empery (1976), The Minstrel (1977), Teenoso (1983)
  - Oaks: Carrozza (1957), Petite Etoile (1959), Valoris (1966), Juliette Marny (1975), Blue Wind (1981), Circus Plume (1984)
  - St Leger Stakes: St Paddy (1960), Aurelius (1961), Ribocco (1967), Ribero (1968), Nijinsky (1970), Athens Wood (1971), Boucher (1972), Commanche Run (1984)
- British Flat Racing Champion Jockey: 1960, 1964, 1965, 1966, 1967, 1968, 1969, 1970, 1971, 1981, 1982
- Triple Crown (2000 Guineas, Derby and St Leger): Nijinsky (1970).
- Ascot Gold Cup: Zarathustra (1957), Gladness (1958), Pandofell (1961), Twilight Alley (1963), Fighting Charlie (1965), Sagaro (1975, 1976, 1977), Le Moss (1979), Ardross (1981, 1982)
- Prix De L'arc De Triomphe: Rheingold (1973), Alleged (1977, 1978)
- Washington DC International: Sir Ivor (1968), Karabas (1969), Argument (1980)
- Breeders' Cup Mile: Royal Academy (1990)
- British Champions Hall of Fame: 2021 (first person to be elected)

60

FERENC PUSKÁS

*'The left foot of Puskás was all
right for Real Madrid'*

I FIRST saw the most famous left foot in football through 12-year-old eyes on black and white television when it was used to destroy England at Wembley in 1953. It belonged, of course, to Ferenc Puskás, one of the Magical Magyars who were monopolising football with their football from the future.

His left foot was a magic wand of a weapon with which he took apart the best defences in the world. We first became aware of it in England when Puskás led Hungary's waltz to a 6-3 victory at Wembley, a night that changed the way we thought about and played football.

This was all in the first phase of a Puskás career that fell into two distinct halves. In part one he was the captain and chief executioner of the club side Honvéd and of the Hungarian national team, which were almost one and the same thing.

Honvéd were originally known as Kispest, a Budapest-based club for which Ferenc's father had been an outstanding player. He followed his dad into the team and had just established himself as

248

the star striker when the government decided they wanted the club to be represented by the Hungarian Army.

Kispest was merged with another club, and the best footballers in the country were transferred to what was now the Army team. All the players were given a rank, and Puskás, as skipper, became a major. Forever after he was known as the 'Galloping Major', yet funnily enough he never ever galloped on a football pitch. He used to glide over the turf, always extremely light on his feet for – how can I say this politely – a rotund gentleman.

The Hungarian team he led was sensational, first coming to world prominence when they won the Olympic title in 1952. Amateurs? Shamateurs more like. They didn't do a day's work in their lives and were full-time footballers. It made a mockery of what was then an amateur competition before the word was rightly scrubbed from the sporting vocabulary.

On the way to the 1954 World Cup, Hungary put together a sequence of 29 unbeaten matches over four years, including the 6-3 and then 7-1 victories over the 'Old Masters' of England. They eventually fell at the heartbreak hurdle of the final.

Puskás went into the game carrying an injury picked up during an 8-3 first-round victory over a deliberately under-strength West Germany. It was the German first team they met in the final, and Puskás scored the opening goal as Hungary went into a 2-0 lead inside ten minutes.

But the gamble of playing a half-fit Puskás failed and Germany hit back to win 3-2. Puskás started to celebrate what he considered a late equaliser until English referee Bill Ling controversially ruled it offside after consulting Welsh linesman Mervyn Griffiths.

Puskás later said, 'The Germans deliberately kicked me in the first match so that I would not be fit for the final. It was the most miserable time of my life, because I knew in my heart we were the best team in the finals.'

The second part of Ferenc's two-pronged career followed the Hungarian Revolution against Russian occupancy in 1956 when

Moscow ordered tanks to roll through Budapest. Honvéd were on a football tour at the time, and most of the players decided to seek exile rather than go back to live under the Red thumb.

Puskás settled in Spain after Italian clubs had decided he was past it and overweight, and he became a key member of the Real Madrid team from 1958 until 1966. His prolific partnership with Alfredo Di Stéfano got off to a dodgy start. The suspicious Di Stéfano – a complete contrast as a character to the always joking, heavy-drinking Puskás – was clearly jealous that his empire was being invaded by what he first thought was a fat clown.

They were neck-and-neck in the first season at the top of the Spanish goalscoring charts, and in the last game Puskás had the chance to become the outright leader as he raced towards an empty goal. But instead of shooting he unselfishly squared a pass for Di Stéfano to score, and from then on they were the best of mates.

The dynamic duo reached their peak together with that 7-3 drubbing of Eintracht Frankfurt in the 1960 European Cup Final. 'The greatest night of my life,' was how four-goal Puskás summed it up. But the game very nearly didn't take place. Eintracht were going to be pulled out of the game by the German FA just hours before the kick-off until Puskás agreed to issue an apology for saying the 1954 German World Cup winners had used drugs to increase their energy, a charge that was later proved to be true.

It's remarkable to think that Puskás was 31 before he joined Real. His goals output for Hungary had been nothing short of astonishing – 84 in 85 games – and he scored another 357 in 349 Hungarian league fixtures. This was better than a goal a game, almost unheard of at any level of football.

The old left foot was still working its magic in Spain, and he netted 155 times in just 179 La Liga appearances.

Football remained his life after Ferenc hung up his shooting boots. He coached in Spain and Canada before taking the reins of Greek club Panathinaikos. Against all odds he inspired them to reach the final of the European Cup in 1971, where they lost 2-0 to Johan Cruyff's Ajax.

Two Greek championships followed before Puskás – by then as big as a baby hippo and an alcoholic – took to travelling the world. He coached in Chile, Saudi Arabia, Spain, Greece, Egypt, Paraguay and Australia, improving teams wherever he went and winning the Australian championship with Hellas in 1990/91. He feared returning to his homeland because of the poison spread against him by the Communist regime when he defected after the 1956 uprising. Messages were sent to him making it clear that as a major in the Hungarian Army he was being treated as a deserter; his punishment would have been execution by firing squad.

He was granted a full pardon by the Magyar government after the Berlin Wall came tumbling down, and arguably the most famous of all Hungarians returned home to spend his declining years in Budapest. He put in a spell as caretaker coach of the national team in 1992 before accepting a role in youth development.

Puskás had been so poor when he was a kid that he and his brother shared the same clothes and shoes. Tragically, he finished up where he had begun, with so little money that FIFA and Real Madrid were persuaded to pay for his health care when he became another victim of Alzheimer's. There was a scandal over a sell-out testimonial match arranged to raise money for him when only a small percentage of the profits found their way into the Puskás pocket.

Following his death in 2006 at the age of 79, his former partner Alfredo Di Stéfano made a rare public statement. 'Ferenc was first and foremost a wonderful human being, who loved life,' he said. 'He was also the best of footballers, who loved playing. I considered it a privilege to have him as a friend and as a partner on the football pitch.'

The Hungarian Football Association named its national stadium after him. Ferenc had definitely come home.

FERENC PUSKÁS FOR THE RECORD:

- Born: 2 April 1927, Budapest
- Career span: 1943–1967
- Clubs:
  - Kispest/Honvéd 1943–56 (349 league games, 357 goals)
  - Espanyol (guest player, 1957)
  - Real Madrid 1958–67 (179 league games, 155 goals)
- International caps:
  - Hungary: 85 games, 84 goals
  - Spain: 4 games, no goals
- Hungarian championship: 1950, 1951, 1952, 1954, 1955
- La Liga: 1961, 1962, 1963, 1964, 1965
- European Cup: 1959, 1960, 1966
- Olympic gold medal: 1952, Helsinki
- World Cup runner-up 1954
- Died: 17 November 2006, Budapest, aged 79

61

SIR STEVEN REDGRAVE

'Olympian giant Steve is the hero of heroes'

SIR STEVEN Redgrave is a hero of heroes, not only as one of the greatest Olympians of all time but also a role model for anybody who seeks success despite medical hurdles. He conquered the hugely competitive rowing world while battling with the double whammy of ulcerative colitis and type 2 diabetes. The 6ft 5in giant is a walking – or rather sitting-down – miracle man. He travelled backwards but was always thinking forwards.

His boyhood dream growing up by the Thames in Marlow was to follow his idol Peter Bonetti as Chelsea and England goalkeeper, but he answered the inevitable call of the water at the age of 16 to launch a career paved with gold. His record is just fantastic: gold medals at five consecutive Olympic Games from 1984 to 2000, three Commonwealth Games titles and nine World Rowing Championship golds.

We all remember Steven saying while exhausted at the end of his winning row in the Atlanta Olympics of 1996, 'If anyone sees me going anywhere near a boat again, they have my permission to shoot me.' Four years later he teamed up again with his rowing mate Matthew Pinsent in the coxless fours to complete his golden sweep in the Sydney Games of 2000.

He is simply the most successful rower in Olympic history, and to do it with his burden of medical complications is just beyond belief. Steven was very wise in his choice of wife, Dr Ann Callaway (now Lady Redgrave), who was an accomplished champion rower in her own right before becoming chief medical officer to the GB rowing team.

Steven's priceless collection started with the coxed fours in Los Angeles in 1984 and was followed by gold with Andy Holmes in the coxless pairs at Seoul in 1988. He then doubled up with fellow giant Matthew Pinsent for gold in the coxless pairs at Barcelona in 1992 and then at Atlanta in 1996.

Just to underline his supremacy, he went four seasons unbeaten from 1993 to 1996 and then captured his ninth World Championship gold in Canada in 1999. Finally, he was back on Golden Pond in the 2000 Sydney Olympics, sharing his title with Pinsent, James Cracknell and Tim Foster.

Steve and I were brought together to defend ourselves when a property developer in Spain tarnished our good names with false claims, but there is nothing false about this great man. He is big in every way, physically, in heart and spirit, in willpower and in commitment. There has rarely been a competitor to match his determination and desire to succeed.

A non-stop action man, he does love a challenge. He dominated at Henley for 20 years before becoming chairman of the Henley Regatta, is a mid-handicap golfer, played rugby to a high level, attempted kayaking, is a skier and in 1989 joined the British bobsleigh team. As a London Marathon runner he has raised record amounts for the Steven Redgrave Charitable Trust. But he still regrets not following Peter Bonetti into goal at Chelsea and remains a frequent visitor to Stamford Bridge. He carried the GB flag at two Games and the Olympic Torch into the stadium at London 2012. He carries British pride for ever.

SIR STEVEN REDGRAVE FOR THE RECORD:

- Born: 23 March 1962, Marlow, Buckinghamshire
- Career span: 1978–2000
- Olympic gold medals:
    - 1984, Los Angeles: coxed fours with Martin Cross, Adrian Ellison, Andy Holmes and Richard Budgett
    - 1988, Seoul: coxed pairs with Andy Holmes and Patrick Sweeney
    - 1992, Barcelona: coxless pairs with Matthew Pinsent
    - 1996, Atlanta: coxless pairs with Pinsent
    - 2000, Sydney: coxless fours with Pinsent, James Cracknell and Tim Foster
- World Championship gold medals: 1986, 1987, 1991, 1993, 1994, 1995, 1997, 1998, 1999
- Commonwealth Games gold medals: 1986 – single sculls, coxless pairs, coxed fours
- Henley Diamond Challenge Sculls: 1983, 1985
- Knighted: 2001
- BBC Sports Personality of the Year Lifetime Achievement Award: 2011

62

SIR VIVIAN RICHARDS

*'Master Blaster who savagely
brought bowlers to their knees'*

SPEAKING AS a proud member of the batting community (remember my 0 and 0 not out for Essex), I have no hesitation in naming Viv Richards as the most exciting cricketer ever to wield the willow. I should not mention my name in the same breath or even the same millennium as the great man.

I think it a fair description to say that King Viv used to prowl at the wicket with an animal-like rhythm, thumping the best of bowlers to all points of the compass with a controlled aggression that fielders feared and spectators feasted on. When Viv was in the mood, he fancied himself to score runs on any surface, in any conditions, and particularly with the sun on his back in his native Antigua.

He was equally destructive on the playing fields of Somerset where he and his multi-talented cricketing brother Ian Botham produced some of the most entertaining county moments of all time.

You can tell the impressive Richards story in figures. He scored 8,540 runs in 121 Test matches for the West Indies at an average of

50.23, including 24 centuries. As a captain, he won 27 of 50 Test matches and lost only eight. He also scored nearly 7,000 runs in one-day internationals and more than 36,000 in first-class cricket.

But what the statistics don't reveal is that Viv amassed his runs with a style and savagery that had even bowlers he had annihilated applauding the sheer brilliance of his batting. Many of his shots were unorthodox and could not be found in the MCC coaching manuals that I studied at Essex. He made it up as he went along and was a master of invention.

Did I tell you I'd played cricket with the Master Blaster? Well sort of. When I was manager (briefly) at Chelsea, the West Indies team visited Stamford Bridge for a look round while waiting for a Test match against England at the Oval. We had a short knockabout game of cricket on the football pitch for the photographers. Viv told me he had aways been a keen footballer, played for his Antiguan national side but could not give the time he needed to the game because of his cricket commitments. I tried to summon up the courage to tell him I had played County cricket for Essex, but was stopped from mentioning it by a sudden attack of good sense. We kept the subject on football and he informed me he was a Liverpool supporter. So we found ourselves discussing the merits of Roger Hunt, but he preferred the later teams with Kevin Keegan and then Kenny Dalglish. I managed to embar-rass him by telling him he was one of my heroes ... and here, to prove it, he is in my Great Eighty selection.

Expert judges bracket Richards with Don Bradman, Brian Lara and Sachin Tendulkar as the greatest batsmen ever to take their guard at the wicket, but if you measure their impact purely on the pleasure they gave to the eyes then Master Blaster Richards takes the prize as the number one.

He was a regally proud cricketer and notoriously punishing on bowlers who did not treat him with respect. I love the story about his verbal clash with Glamorgan fast bowler Greg Thomas. After Viv had uncharacteristically played at and missed a succession of balls from the Welshman, Thomas unwisely tried to wind him up by saying, 'Just to remind you that the ball is red, round and weighs about five ounces.' Viv said nothing in reply but waited for the next delivery and smashed it out of the ground and into a nearby river. Viv looked in the direction of Thomas and responded, 'You know what it looks like, now go and find it.'

When he was growing up in Antigua, Viv was rated one of the best footballers on the treasure island and it is claimed (though unsubstantiated by the record books) that he is the only sportsman to have played in both the cricket and football World Cups, including an appearance in a qualifying match in the soccer version for Antigua.

But it was cricket's gain that he chose to concentrate on the small-ball game, and anybody who saw a Richards knock felt privileged to have been a witness. Nobody will ever forget his majestic innings against England in an ODI at Old Trafford in 1984. He scorched to 189 not out from just 170 balls, including 21 fours and five sixes. His last 58 balls produced 86 runs, which included nine fours and five sixes. It is still rated the greatest ODI innings ever played.

Viv is also the scorer of the equal second-fastest Test century and again England were on the receiving end. He rushed to a ton from just 56 balls on his home ground at Antigua in 1986. He was a graceful and magnificent fielder and could be a deadly off-spinner when conditions were right. But it was his brutally brilliant batting that lifted him into the land of the gods.

I think of my 0 and 0 not out in my one county appearance and I bow the knee to Viv. He was the Pelé, the Marciano and the Jonah Lomu of cricket. A perfect machine. The King.

SIR VIVIAN RICHARDS FOR THE RECORD:

- Born: 7 March 1952, St John's, Antigua
- Career span: 1971–93
- Teams:
  - Combined Islands (1971–81)
  - Leeward Islands (1971–91)
  - Somerset (1974–86)
  - Queensland (1976–77)
  - Glamorgan (1990–93)
- Tests: 121 (1974–1991)
  - Runs: 8,540 (50.23), 24 centuries
  - Captaincy record: won 27, lost 8, drawn 15
  - Highest score: 291 v. England (The Oval, 1976)
  - Catches: 122
- First-class career: 507 games (1971–93)
  - Runs: 36,212 (49.40), 114 centuries
  - Highest score: 291 for West Indies v England (The Oval, 1976)
  - Catches: 464
- ODI matches: 187
- ODI runs: 6,721 (average 47), 11 centuries
- Top score: 189 not out v. England (Old Trafford, 1984)
- Voted in *Wisden* as the greatest ODI Batsman of all time: 2002
- Voted one of the five *Wisden* Cricketers of the Century (along with Don Bradman, Garfield Sobers, Jack Hobbs and Shane Warne): 2000
- Knighted: 1999

63

SUGAR RAY ROBINSON

'Sugar Ray tasted the sweet and
sour of the fight game'

BOXING BUFFS always assure me that Sugar Ray Robinson –
the *original* Sugar Ray – was the rightful wearer of the crown that
Muhammad Ali claimed as The Greatest. Bobby Moore was well
informed on the fight game and used to sing the praises of Sugar
Ray when we often had discussions about who were the greatest
boxers.

Another ex-Hammer always worth listening to on boxing
was Dave Sexton, whose father Archie challenged for the British
middleweight title before the war.

Robinson's story was fascinating. For a start, it was not his real
name. He was born Walker Smith in Georgia, and when he entered
his first boxing tournament at 16 after moving to New York via
Detroit, the organisers told him the American Athletic Union rules
demanded that he be 18. He borrowed a birth certificate from a
friend called Ray Robinson, and from then on that was how he
was billed. A lady sitting ringside watching him box shouted, 'Ray
Robinson, you're sweet as sugar.' The name stuck.

Just a summary of his career gives you an idea of his talent and longevity. He boxed professionally for 25 years from 1940 and was world welterweight champion for four years before abdicating when he won the middleweight crown, a title he captured five times. Sugar Ray was on the brink of winning the world light-heavyweight championship until overcome by heat exhaustion when in sight of victory against Joey Maxim.

During his career he contested 25 world-title fights, fought 19 world champions, never took the ten-second count and was beaten only 19 times in 202 contests.

When he was a kid known as Walker Smith he used to tap dance on the streets of Harlem to earn money to give to his divorced mother, who had brought him and his two sisters to New York City. He moved like a dancer in the ring while going unbeaten through an exceptional amateur career during which he won all of his 85 contests, 69 of them inside the distance and an amazing 40 in the first round.

Sugar Ray turned professional in 1940 after winning the Golden Gloves title first at featherweight and then as lightweight. A charismatic character outside as well as inside the ring, Robinson won 40 successive fights before dropping a decision to the 'Bronx Bull' Jake LaMotta. It was their second of five meetings and the only one in which Ray came off second best.

The Robinson/La Motta fights featured in the popular film 'Raging Bull', in which Robert de Niro played La Motta. The real Jake said of his nemesis in his Bronx drawl: 'The three toughest fights I've had were against Sugar Ray Robinson, Sugar Ray Robinson and Sug-ar Robinson. The guy's a fantastic fighter, the best there's ever been. We knock the hell out of each other in the ring, but once the final bell goes – if I'm around to hear it – we lay down our weapons and make the peace. We're soldiers and only fight when there's a war on. In fact Ray's such a good pal, he's agreed to be best man when I get married for a sixth time. My toughest opponents have been my wives.

Why d'you think I'm still fighting. Those broads have taken every cent.'

Robinson, managed by the gregarious George Gainford, went unbeaten for the next eight years and 91 fights, and on 20 December 1946 he won the vacant world welterweight title by outpointing Tommy Bell in his adopted home town of New York City.

Sugar Ray made five successful defences before reluctantly agreeing to relinquish the title after ripping away the 11st 6lb middleweight championship from his old rival LaMotta with a savage 13th-round victory in Chicago on Valentine's Day 1951.

Travelling with an entourage that included his personal hairdresser, a French tutor, a trumpeter and a dwarf, this born entertainer took things too easily on a tour of Europe. He completely underestimated British champion Randolph Turpin, who relieved him of his title with a brilliantly executed 15-rounds points victory at Earls Court on 10 July 1951.

Robinson whipped himself into magnificent shape for the return in front of 61,370 spectators at the Polo Grounds in New York just 64 days later. He regained his crown with a tenth-round stoppage after dropping Turpin with a thunderous right after sustaining a badly cut right eye.

Mixing his boxing with a nightclub song-and-dance act, he won and lost in fight serials with Gene 'The Mormon Mauler' Fullmer, Carl 'Bobo' Olsen, the tough-as-granite Carmen Basilio and had two wars with the 'Fighting Fireman' Paul Pender. He announced his retirement several times but continually returned to the ring because of crushing debts, particularly to the Inland Revenue. His famous Sugar nickname was later copied by Ray Leonard, who was in the Robinson class as a boxer but did not make the mistake of fighting on long after his peak years.

It all ended sadly for the original Sugar Ray, who was a victim of pugilistic dementia when he passed on in 1989 aged 68. Boxing mourned a champion who could genuinely claim at the peak of his power to have been The Greatest.

SUGAR RAY ROBINSON FOR THE RECORD:

- Born: 3 May 1921, Alley, Georgia, USA
- Name at birth: Walker Smith
- Amateur career: 1937–40
  - Fights 85
  - Wins: 85
  - Golden Gloves champion, featherweight: 1939
  - Golden Gloves champion, lightweight: 1940
- Professional career: 1940–65
  - Fights: 202
  - Wins: 175 (110 inside the distance)
  - Defeats: 19 (1 stoppage)
  - Draws: 6
  - No-contests: 2
- World welterweight champion: 1946–51
- World middleweight champion five times: 1951–60
- Died: 12 April 1989, Los Angeles, aged 68

64

CRISTIANO RONALDO

'A slice of Madeira cake for
football's first billionaire'

THIS OLD pro has watched with open mouth the rise and rise of Cristiano Ronaldo, the miracle man from the tiny mid-Atlantic treasure island of Madeira. He has established himself as arguably the greatest winger ever to play on the world stage. I never thought I would see a better wide player than George Best but here he is, a bit too much of a showboater for my taste but that's the modern way.

Ronaldo – Cristiano Ronaldo dos Santos Aveiro to give him his glorious full name – always brings me to the edge of my seat whenever he is in possession. His achievements throughout his career have been just mind-blowing: five Ballon d'Or awards, four European Golden Boots, 32 major trophies including seven domestic league titles in three different countries, five UEFA Champions Leagues and one UEFA European Championship with Portugal. He holds the records for most Champions League goals (134 at the last count), most assists (42), most goals in the European Championship and as we go to press he is tied for most international goals (109). Simply the 'mostest'.

I played around 700 games in total, so it makes my old bones creak when I take on board that Ronaldo has made more than 1,100 professional appearances and has registered 780 goals, and there's still mileage in his legs and ambition in his head and heart. The boy's done good!

He had to grow up fast from the teenager who, at Sporting Lisbon, was banished from a youth tournament for throwing a chair at a teacher. Emotional outbursts were common in a sensitive boy who left his family in Madeira at the age of just 11 for the Portuguese capital. 'He rang me many times crying and telling me he wanted to give it all up,' recalled his mother, Maria Dolores.

By the time Ronaldo arrived at Old Trafford, Sir Alex Ferguson was torn between treating him with kid gloves and boxing gloves.

In modern language that I struggle to understand, the tall (6ft 1in), handsome Ronaldo, with his dark Latin looks and flashy ear diamond, is described in celebrity magazines as 'a babe magnet'. There was a heart-stopping moment for the United management in October 2005 when he was arrested and questioned about an alleged rape in the penthouse of a five-star London hotel. The whoosh of relief when all charges were dropped could be heard the length of the M6.

But less than a year later he was engulfed in a controversy that led to him becoming English public enemy number one, and lumbered with a nickname that he struggled to lose – 'The Winker'.

Ronaldo was seen stirring it up for his Manchester United teammate Wayne Rooney when Rooney was red-carded for appearing to stamp on Ricardo Carvalho's family jewellery during the 2006 England v Portugal World Cup quarter-final in Germany.

The television cameras picked up Ronaldo clearly winking at Portugal's coaching staff as Rooney made his sad exit. It was a gesture that seemed to say 'Gotcha!' and confirmed that the plan had been to wind up the temperamental English boy.

The rage of the country at England's dismissal from the World Cup was turned on Ronaldo, who was hardly at fault for Rooney's sending-off or for England's missed penalties in the shoot-out that meant Portugal progressed after a goalless draw.

By the end of the following season Ronaldo had made such an impact with his fellow professionals that he was voted both the PFA Young Player of the Year and PFA Player of the Year, a double achieved only once before by Andy Gray back in the 1970s.

He took his box of tricks to Real Madrid where he won two La Liga titles, two Copa del Rey crowns and four Champions Leagues and became the club's all-time leading scorer. Then in 2018 he was off on his golden bike to Juventus, winning two Serie A titles, two Supercoppa Italianas and a Coppa Italia in his first three seasons with the 'Old Lady' of Italian football, before surprising everybody by taking his shooting boots back to Old Trafford for the 2021/22 season.

Ronaldo never seems far away from controversy, and in 2017 received a $22m fine and a two-year suspended jail sentence for alleged tax fraud. This old pro thinks back to his £7 a week apprentice days at West Ham and winces.

His rewards apart from cups and medals have been substantial. He has a popular range of CR7 sports and fashion wear and officially became football's first billionaire – but am I allowed to say he has not got a World Cup winners' medal? I've been told to shut up. Cristiano Ronaldo is a footballing king of kings.

CRISTIANO RONALDO FOR THE RECORD:

- Born: 5 February 1985, Funchal, Madeira
- Career span: 1999–ongoing
- Clubs:
  - Sporting Lisbon 1999–2003 (31 games, 5 goals)
  - Manchester United 2003–2009 (292 games, 118 goals)
  - Real Madrid 2009–2018 (438 games, 450 goals)
  - Juventus 2018–2021 (134 games, 101 goals)
  - Manchester United 2021–present
- Portugal: 179 caps, 109 goals
- UEFA European Championship: 2016
- Champions League: 2008, 2014, 2016, 2017, 2018
- FIFA Club World Cup: 2008, 2014, 2016, 2017
- UEFA Super Cup: 2014, 2017
- Premier League: 2007, 2008, 2009
- FA Cup: 2004
- League Cup: 2006, 2009
- La Liga: 2012, 2017
- Copa del Rey: 2011, 2014
- Serie A: 2019, 2020
- Ballon d'Or: 2008, 2013, 2014, 2016, 2017
- UEFA Club Footballer of the Year: 2008
- FIFA World Player of the Year: 2008
- UEFA Best Player in Europe: 2014, 2016, 2017

65

IAN RUSH

'The Welsh warrior who found
scoring goals gave him a rush'

IF I had to name a player whose style and attitude most mirrored mine, I would select Ian Rush. We had the same approach to the game: no fuss, no frills, just do your best for the team and be in the right place at the right time to bang the ball into the net. We were both lucky to have partners who made us better players by their support play. I could always count on Martin Peters to pop up to create chances for me; Rush was blessed with having the mighty Kenny Dalglish as his sidekick for many years.

Rush was never a fancy Dan. He just got on with the job of scoring with the coldness of an assassin and would continually baffle his markers with his subtle positioning, sudden acceleration and deadly accurate finishing. He would then run back to the centre circle ready to start hunting the next goal. The way they celebrate goals today, the players are like consenting adults. Rushie never mixed arrogance with his artistry.

Rush and Dalglish followed two legendary Liverpool double acts, Roger Hunt and Ian St John and then Kevin Keegan and John

Toshack. All were dynamic together and too much of a combined handful for most defences.

Dalglish and Rush – sounding like a television detective duo – were equal partners. If Kenny didn't get you then Ian would. They brought the best out of each other, with Rush collecting 229 First Division goals in his two spells at Anfield, with a further 20 in Europe during Bob Paisley's golden days in charge at Liverpool.

Rush's honours haul included five league championship medals, and a record five League Cups. He also picked up three FA Cups, scoring a record five FA Cup Final goals. But you never heard him boasting about his deeds. He shared with his predecessor Roger Hunt the common trait of being modest unassuming men, despite having plenty to shout about.

Rush also had a European Cup medal to show off at the end of the 1983/84 season, in which he was in unstoppable form. He plundered 49 goals as Liverpool completed what was the 'Impossible Treble' of league championship, League Cup and European Cup.

In that memorable 1984 season Rush pulled off the individual hat-trick of winning the Football Writers' Association Footballer of the Year award, the Professional Footballers' Association Player of the Year trophy and the Golden Boot as Europe's top marksman.

But it all might have been a different story if wise old Bob Paisley had not given Rush some sound advice after he had joined Liverpool from Fourth Division Chester City at the age of 18.

Rush got impatient playing for Liverpool's reserves. He was talking about finding a club where he could get first-team football when 'Uncle Bob' sat him down and explained, 'We're playing you in the reserves so that you get used to the Liverpool style of play. I promise it will pay dividends when you get into the first team. You're developing just the way we want, and if you show just a little more selfishness when you get the ball in the penalty area, I think you'll soon be the perfect Liverpool player.'

That's the way they did it at Anfield, bringing players off a conveyor belt, doing it the Liverpool way. In the following season

Rush scored 30 goals in 49 appearances, and proved that he was already the finished article.

He once had a remarkable run of 145 successive games with Liverpool without being on the losing side having scored. Rush didn't just decorate matches. He *decided* them. His total league and cup haul was a club record 346 goals.

His career went pear-shaped when he fell for that old feeling that the grass was greener on the Italian side of the football fence and he joined Juventus for £3m in the summer of 1986. Like Jimmy Greaves before him, Ian soon found out that Italy was a sterile place to be after the excitement and adventure of the Football League.

It was a nightmare for Rush as Juventus suffered through their worst season for 20 years. He had been hailed as the 'new John Charles' on his arrival in Turin, a link strengthened by the fact that both were sons of Wales. But I know of no player who could live up to that billing. The Italian press nicknamed him 'The Eagle' when he kicked off with Juventus, and the cartoonists had great fun giving him the eagle image. But they soon realised that this was one eagle that had not landed. A man of simple tastes, he said that he was missing his pints in the pub at home with his pals.

The goals dried up – just seven in 29 Serie A games – and his brain also seemed to freeze. Asked what was wrong with Italy he reportedly replied, 'It's like being in a foreign country,' although it's an exchange he has always denied happened.

Rush got back to Anfield as quickly as possible and had to battle for his place against a formidable challenge from John Aldridge, who scored an impressive 329 goals in his travels with Newport, Oxford, Liverpool and Tranmere.

Ian added another 89 goals to his league collection before a less than successful final flurry to his career with Leeds, Newcastle, Sheffield United, Wrexham and – a long way to go for two games – Sydney Olympic.

Idolised in his native Wales, Rush scored a then national record of 28 goals in his 73 international appearances without ever reaching the finals of a major tournament. The highlight for him was scoring the winning goal against world champions Germany in a Euro 92 qualifier.

In 2006, Rush came third in a Liverpool poll titled 100 Players Who Shook the Kop. The two ahead of him were Kenny Dalglish and Steven Gerrard. Ian and I are still linked in the record books by both of us scoring a record 49 League Cup goals. Far be it from me to point out that it took me 60 games to reach the target, while Ian played in 81 ties.

The ninth of ten children, Rush was fittingly born in Flintshire in North Wales. There was a touch of flint in his competitive spirit, and I am proud that we are locked together in the record books. His career was quite a Rush.

IAN RUSH FOR THE RECORD:
- Born: 20 October 1961, St Asaph, Flintshire, Wales
- Career span: 1979–2000
- Clubs:
    - Chester City 1979–80 (39 games, 18 goals)
    - Liverpool 1980–87 and 1988–96 (660 games, 346 goals)
    - Juventus 1987–88 (40 games, 13 goals)
    - Leeds United 1996–97 (42 games, 3 goals)
    - Newcastle United 1997–98 (14 games, 2 goals)
    - Sheffield United 1998 (4 games, 0 goals)
    - Wrexham 1998–99 (24 games, no goals)
    - Sydney Olympic 1999–2000 (2 games, 1 goal)
- Wales: 73 caps, 28 goals
- First Division: 1982, 1983, 1984, 1986, 1990
- FA Cup: 1986, 1989, 1992:
- League Cup: 1981, 1982, 1983, 1984, 1995
- European Cup: 1984
- Record 49 League Cup goals (shared with Geoff Hurst)
- European Golden Boot: 1984
- FWA Footballer of the Year: 1984
- PFA Player of the Year: 1984

66

PETER SNELL

'Nothing snail-like about Olympic legend Snell'

PETER SNELL was a middle-distance runner who seemed to have wings on his feet, and was on top of the world at the same time as I was starting to make my way as a professional footballer and hoovering up all knowledge of sporting feats. Built like an All Blacks forward, the Kiwi grabbed unexpected glory at the Rome Olympics of 1960 and then performed a rare golden double in Tokyo four years later.

He was an almost unknown 21-year-old when winning the 800m in Italy, overtaking Belgian world record holder Roger Moens on the inside lane and barreling his way to a shock victory. Those who dismissed it as a freak performance were forced to reassess their opinions when Snell went on to set world records for the mile and 800m on a grass track in New Zealand in 1962.

His mile record was reported around the world by an agency news flash that read, 'Snell broke the record despite the handicap of a rabbit impeding him on the final lap.' On closer investigation, it was found that a hare – an athlete setting the record pace – had been overtaken by Snell as he sprinted for the finishing line!

Snell's sporting ambitions changed when he came under the intoxicating influence of demanding coach Arthur Lydiard, a former marathon runner who persuaded him to switch from a promising tennis career to specialise in athletics. Lydiard concentrated on building Snell's stamina with long-distance running rather than the traditional middle-distance work. 'Endurance leads to excellence,' was one of his sayings.

A national idol at home, Snell was given the honour of carrying the flag at the opening ceremony in Tokyo and then stole the show with a devastating double in the 800m and 1500m. It had not been achieved since Great Britain's Albert Hill performed the feat at the Antwerp Olympics 44 years earlier and has not been done since, despite the efforts of outstanding athletes such as Sebastian Coe.

For four years he never lost in global competition, and he would still have been a medal contender in Tokyo 2020 with the sort of times and runs he was producing in 1964. Incredibly, the world record 800m time he set in 1962 of one minute 44.3 seconds would have won him the gold at the Beijing Olympics of 2008.

Snell disappeared from the world athletics scene as quickly as he arrived. He suddenly retired in 1965, and took a controversial job as a spokesman for the Rothmans tobacco company – just as the world was waking up to the health dangers of smoking. He was never comfortable in the role and after the break-up of his marriage changed direction to become an academic.

In 1973 he moved to the USA, where he gained a science degree at the University of California and a PhD in exercise physiology at Washington State University before moving to Dallas in 1981. He became director of the Human Performance Center at the University of Texas Medical Center, concentrating mostly on sports fitness and establishing himself as one of the most authoritative experts in his field.

He satisfied his competitive spirit by becoming the US over-65s orienteering champion before switching to table tennis and – with his second wife Miki – won a silver medal in the World Masters mixed doubles at Auckland, aged 78.

Following Snell's passing from a heart attack in 2019, Sebastian Coe said, 'Peter's performances were a huge inspiration to me and a whole generation of athletes. He changed the way middle-distance runners prepared for their events, both physically and mentally. Peter was unbelievably fit and would think nothing of a 20-mile training run. His 800/1500 double in Tokyo was something I dreamed of emulating but it was beyond me. Peter Snell is a legend.'

I was at the peak of my speed and stamina when Peter was conquering the world. He would have left me, uh, a mile behind. There was never anything snail-like about Snell.

PETER SNELL FOR THE RECORD:
- Born 17 December 1938, Opunake, New Zealand
- Career span: 1957–65
- Olympic gold medals:
  - 800m: 1960, 1964
  - 1500m: 1964
- Commonwealth Games gold medals:
  - 880 yards: 1962
  - Mile: 1962
- Fastest times, then all world records:
  - 800m: 1m 44.3s
  - 880 yards: 1m 45.1s
  - 1000m: 2m 16.6s
  - 1500m: 3m 37.6s
  - Mile: 3m 54.1s
  - 4x1 mile relay: 16m 23.8s (with Murray Halberg, Gary Philpott, Barry Magee)
- New Zealand Sports Champion of the Century: 2000
- Knighted in New Zealand honours list 2002
- Died: 12 December 2019, Dallas, USA, aged 80

67

SIR GARFIELD SOBERS

'Twelve fingers, hundreds of wickets
and thousands of runs'

TREVOR BAILEY, our captain at Essex when I was torn between making cricket or football my career, used to say of Garfield – Garry – Sobers, 'He has been sent to us from the heavens and I feel privileged to walk on the same hallowed turf as him.' He later became Sir Garry's biographer and his book was an anthem of acclaim to arguably the greatest all-rounder ever to hit and bowl a ball.

In those days I respectfully called Trevor 'Mr Bailey', or 'Sir'. I say this because I clearly remember our two senior players, Trevor and Doug Insole, refering to Sobers almost in hushed, reverential terms as 'King Garry' long before he got his knighthood in 1975. That showed his standing among fellow cricketers. He was simply a god of the game.

Even as a boy growing up on the sunshine island of Barbados, he was thought of as being a chosen one. He was born with 12 fingers, and locals saw that as a sign he was something special. His two extra digits eventually fell off, but they would have been useful to help count the runs he collected by the busload.

The world sat up and took notice of Sobers when he scored his maiden Test century against Pakistan in 1958. You can imagine the way I reacted as an impressionable 17-year-old batsman as he went on to convert that ton into a then world record 365, overtaking the Len Hutton total that had for so long been part of cricket folklore.

Sobers was just 21 and with the cricket world at his feet, but tragedy struck in 1959 when his closest friend and exceptional cricketer Collie Smith died in a car crash while Garry was at the wheel. He never ever forgave himself, and said that throughout the rest of his career he was two players at the wicket. 'Collie was always with me,' Garry later revealed after retiring from a 20-year career in which he was not only an outstanding left-hand batsman and blinding fielder, but also a bowler who was equally destructive delivering seam or spin.

Competitive but always sporting, across his 93 Tests for the West Indies, Sobers scored 8,032 runs at an average of 57.78, and also took 235 wickets at 34.03. His 383 first-class matches realised over 28,000 runs and more than 1,000 wickets.

Sobers was an elegant yet belligerent batsman, and when fielding moved around with the grace of a ballet dancer and made catching look easy. He became a cricketing nomad in the second half of his career, featuring with South Australia and Nottinghamshire.

It was while captain of Notts in 1968 that he savagely set a world record of six successive sixes off one over from Glamorgan spinner Malcolm Nash, the final ball disappearing out of the Cardiff ground and last seen on the way to Swansea. Sobers and Nash became good friends and the Welshman always insisted that his part in the six-fest should be celebrated. 'Garry could not have done it without me,' he said. 'I was honoured to be hammered by the greatest cricketer that ever lived.'

Sobers was a gambling man on and off the pitch, always ready to make sporting declarations and a frequent visitor to bookmakers, casinos and racecourses. 'Life is there to be enjoyed,' was his philosophy.

His captaincy was often criticised because of his carefree spirit, particularly when a declaration against England in a Test in Trinidad handed victory to the tourists after they had seemed down and out. 'But we gave the spectators great entertainment,' an unrepentant Sobers said.

When South Africa were banned from international cricket because of the country's apartheid policy, he was made captain of a Rest of the World team in 1970 that played England in place of the cancelled Springbok tour. On the opening June day of the first unofficial Test at Lord's, Sobers, bowling with blistering pace, took 6/21. On the second day he blasted 183 with his bat.

I remember it well because Bobby Moore and I were keeping up to date with the scores while sunning ourselves on the beach at Acapulco after England's elimination from the World Cup in Mexico. Judith was with us along with Bobby's then wife, Tina.

'Here we are in paradise and all you two can talk about is bloody cricket,' complained Judith, who thinks the game is like watching paint dry.

How could I tell her that 'King Garry' transcended cricket. He was a god.

Sir Garry never tried to hide the fact that he enjoyed late nights and gambling. He often told the story of ignoring advice when he was starting out in the game he graced for more than 20 years. 'I'll never forget when I first started playing for the West Indies,' he recalled 'They told me to get a good night's sleep before a match. Well, I tried. But going to bed early was no good to me. It affected my form. I'd just lie there worrying, thinking about Freddie Trueman or Alec Bedser bowling and working out how I could get the better of them. I couldn't handle that discipline stuff. It just wasn't my style. I was a beach boy and used to playing until the sun went down and then going and enjoying myself in the beachside bars. So rather than lie there not sleeping I went back to my old ways, did what I'd been doing since I was 14 years of age, stay out all night and come home when I was tired.'

Once at a function where we were guests of honour, I asked Sir Garry if all the stories of him staying up all night drinking and gambling before and even during matches were true.

He smiled the rascal's smile I used to see on the face of George Best as he responded: 'It's all ridiculously exaggerated. I only stayed up every other night during matches.'

If ever there was a misnomer, it has to be Sobers! But what a cricketer. Genius personified.

SIR GARFIELD SOBERS FOR THE RECORD:

- Born: 28 July 1938, Bridgetown, Barbados
- Career span: 1953–74
- Teams:
  - Barbados (1953–74)
  - South Australia (1961–64)
  - Nottinghamshire (1968–74)
- Tests: 93 (1954–1974)
- Runs: 8,032 (57.78), 26 centuries
  - Captaincy record: won 9, lost 10, drawn 20
  - Highest score: 365 not out v. Pakistan (Kingston, 1958)
  - Catches: 109
  - Wickets: 235 (34.03)
  - Best figures: 6/73
- First-class career: 383 games (1954–74)
  - Runs: 28,314 (54.87), 86 centuries
  - Highest score: 365 not out for West Indies v. Pakistan (Kingston, 1958)
  - Catches: 407
  - Wickets: 1,043 (27.74)
  - Best figures: 9/49
- Knighted: 1975
- Voted one of the five *Wisden* Cricketers of the Century (along with Don Bradman, Vic Richards, Jack Hobbs and Shane Warne)

68

MARK SPITZ

'The Spitz Blitz tarnished by terrorism'

I DREW up a shortlist of swimmers, with Ian 'Thorpedo' Thorpe and Michael Phelps challenging for a place until I remembered the 'Mark Spitz Blitz' in the Munich Olympic pool in 1972. Swimming has never been a compelling sport for me, but that Spitz golden splash grabbed my attention at what was a crucial time in my career.

Spitz's feat coincided with my move from West Ham United to Stoke City, and Stoke's warm, personable manager Tony Waddington and I found ourselves talking swimming as the American took all the headlines in the week that I switched from east London to the Potteries.

Every time he went into the water in search of an incredible seven gold medals he broke a world record. There has never been record-smashing to beat it. This was Olympic supremacy of unparalleled proportions. And remarkably, all the records that 'Mark the Pool Shark' broke were those he himself had set.

Spitz, from Modesto, California, was not the most modest of champions. After winning five gold medals in the 1967 Pan

American Games, the brash 18-year-old had boldly predicted he would win six in the 1968 Olympics in Mexico City. The fact that he managed just two – both in relay races – left him feeling deflated and unfulfilled.

He was determined to make up for his disappointment in the 1972 Games and this time put action where his mouth was in spectacular style. He set a new world record in each of the seven events – 100m freestyle (51.22s), 200m freestyle (1m 52.78s), 100m butterfly (54.27s), 200m butterfly (2m 0.7s), 4x100m freestyle relay (3m 26.42s), 4x200m freestyle relay (7m 35.78s), and 4x100m medley relay (3m 48.16s).

There was unexpected drama when Spitz said he was ready to pull out of the 100m freestyle because he felt he would be beaten by team-mate Jerry Heidenreich. 'Six golds would be a triumph,' he reasoned, 'but six golds and one defeat would constitute failure.' He was persuaded to 'go for it' by his former coach Sherm Chavoor, who was in Munich coaching the US women's team. Spitz went ahead with the race and in a thrilling finish beat Heidenreich by half a stroke.

Soon after his seventh gold, the Spitz Blitz was tragically overshadowed by the brutal killing of 11 Israeli athletes and coaches by Arab terrorists. The siege at the Olympic Village began hours after Spitz's last race. As he was Jewish, the golden hero was hustled out of Munich immediately, unable to bask in the glory of one of the greatest performances in Olympic history.

Back home in California, Spitz turned his swimming success into a commercial coup and became the self-promoted Olympic poster boy for sponsors and advertisers as he cashed in on having set 23 world records and 35 United States records.

He later went into real estate and worked as a motivational speaker. Then, aged 41 and as the theme for a TV documentary, he attempted to qualify for the 1992 Olympics in his favourite event, the butterfly. But time had caught up with him and he failed to make the Olympic qualifying requirement by more than two seconds.

Nobody could ever take away his golden splash of 1972. 'These Olympic Games will go down in history as a triumph and tragedy' he said on a return to Munich as a spectator. 'We all came away, I think, smarter and wiser, too. So did the Olympic movement. It lives on stronger than ever.'

A magnificent seven gold medals that I thought would never be matched. And then along came Michael Phelps with his EIGHT golds in the 2008 Beijing Games.

Records are there to be broken and one day – one day – somebody will beat my 1966 World Cup Final hat-trick. Meantime, I will bask in the glory.

The Spitz Blitz. How about The Hurst Burst? I shall shut up.

MARK SPITZ FOR THE RECORD:

- Born: 10 February 1950, Modesto, California
- Career span: 1965–72
- Set 23 world and 35 US swimming records
- Maccabiah Games gold medals: 4 in 1965, 6 in 1969
- Pan American Games gold medals: 5 in 1967
- Amateur Athletic Union championships: 24 titles
- Olympic medals:
    - Mexico 1968: 4x100 m freestyle relay gold, 4x200 m freestyle relay gold, 100m butterfly silver, 100m freestyle bronze
    - Munich 1972: golds in 200m butterfly, 4x100m freestyle relay, 200m freestyle, 100m butterfly, 4x200m freestyle relay, 100m freestyle, 4x100m medley relay
- Individual world records:
    - 100m freestyle: 51.22s
    - 200m freestyle: 1m 52.78s
    - 100m butterfly: 54.27s
    - 200m butterfly: 2m 0.7s
- International Swimming Hall of Fame: 1977
- United States Olympic Hall of Fame: 1983

69

SIR JACKIE STEWART

'The Flying Scot who thought outside the box'

ALPHABETICALLY, I should be featuring here motor racing legends Michael Schumacher and Ayrton Senna, but both are such sad stories that I settled for a master from my generation, the Flying Scot Jackie Stewart. Aficionados assure me that Senna was potentially the greatest of all time until his tragic death while leading the 1994 San Marino Grand Prix. Schumacher came safely through his career with a then record seven F1 titles and then in a freak skiing accident suffered the sort of brain injuries that are so often a risk at the wheel.

Stewart not only survived his racing adventure but went on to become the most respected voice in his sport as a TV commentator and campaigner for improved safety for drivers. Between 1965 and 1973 he won three world championships, and twice finished as runner-up over those nine seasons when every F1 competitor took his life in his hands just by taking part.

Racing was in Jackie's blood. His father, a successful motor dealer in Dumbartonshire, was an enthusiastic amateur motorbike racer and his older brother, Jimmy, whom he idolised, was prominent on the sports car racing circuit and competed in the 1953 British Grand Prix.

Jackie was best known in his youth as a champion clay pigeon shooter, but satisfied his lust for speed by joining the Tyrrell Formula Three team.

As well as Tyrrell, he drove in F1 races for BRM, Matra and March. He won his first F1 Grand Prix race in Italy in a BRM and by the late 1960s had established himself as the number one driver in the world. He was F1 champion in 1969, 1971 and 1973 and had a a great rivalry with suave Englishman Graham Hill.

Stewart held the record for most wins by a Formula One driver (27) for 14 years until overtaken by Frenchman Alain Prost, and the record for most wins by a Brit driver for 19 years until Nigel Mansell won the 1992 British Grand Prix.

He decided to retire as champion in 1973 after the fatal crash involving his team-mate François Cevert in practice for the United States Grand Prix at Watkins Glen, missing what would have been his 100th Grand Prix. He was exhausted after crossing the Atlantic 186 times in a couple of years while keeping up with his racing media and promotion work. When he hung up his helmet he could be bracketed with his idol Jim Clark as the greatest of all Scottish drivers. 'Jimmy was THE master,' Stewart acknowledged in later years. 'What he achieved in that Lotus was unbelievable. I raced against him many times and only saw his backside. His driving was so delicate, so convincing. He was so modest – very much the quiet farmer.'

I have had the pleasure of meeting Sir Jackie on the celebrity circuit and am in awe of his achievements. He has chronic dyslexia (as does Jimmy Greaves, incidentally) and he dictated his autobiography *Winning Is Not Enough*. He feels that being dyslexic forced him to think outside the box. 'I have always wanted to prove I could match the intelligent people,' he says, conveniently hiding the fact that he has a brain the size of Mars.

In recent years he has thrown himself into promotional work for his charity Race Against Dementia, after his wife and childhood sweetheart, Lady Helen, was diagnosed with the illness.

Sir Jackie is an astonishing one-off ... Formula One, of course.

JACKIE STEWART FOR THE RECORD:

- Born: 11 June 1939, Milton, Dunbartonshire
- Career span: 1965–73
- World champion: 1969, 1971, 1973
- Teams: Tyrrell, BRM, Matra, March
- Races: 99
- Victories: 27
- Pole positions: 17
- Podiums: 43
- BBC Sports Personality of the Year: 1973
- Knighted: 2001

70

BEN STOKES

*'Big Ben strikes for England
but pays a heavy price'*

JUST FOR his sizzling performances in the summer of 2019 alone, Ben Stokes deserves his place in my *Eighty at Eighty*. He won the World Cup and an Ashes showdown for England with two out-of-this-world displays that made old sportsmen like me shake our heads in wonder and amazement.

When I was a young batsman dreaming of one day taking the Aussies apart I never thought I would see the feat achieved by Ian Botham at Headingley in 1981 and then Freddie Flintoff in the 2005 series.

Then along came Stokes, first dragging England to a nail-biting super-over victory against New Zealand at Lord's in the World Cup Final. Six weeks later he played the innings of a lifetime on that same Headingley ground where Botham lifted himself into the land of sporting legend 38 years earlier.

He had this retired batsman jumping around in front of his television set as he launched a blistering solo assault on the Aussie attack. Targeting an England record chase of 359, there were still

73 runs needed when Stokes was joined at the wicket by last man Jack Leach, who repeatedly rubbed his spectacles as nervous tension went off the Richter scale.

Stokes dispatched off-spinner Nathan Lyon for three sixes and followed up by hitting Josh Hazlewood for four, six and six in three consecutive balls, bringing up a hurricane century with the first of those boundaries.

With 17 needed to win, all of us spectators roared as Ben was dropped by a diving Marcus Harris. In the next over, with two runs needed, Leach should have been run out but the ball was fumbled, and off the next delivery Stokes looked lbw but Australia were out of reviews.

Leach scrambled a single in the next over and, with one to win, Stokes slammed through the covers and sank to his knees – 135 not out – in exhausted celebration as England clinched victory by one run. All those of us spectators, at the ground and the millions watching on television, felt exhilarated just to have witnessed of one of the great innings.

Ben was born in New Zealand to a rugby league professional father, Ged, and an English mother, and moved to the northeast at the age of 12 when his dad landed a job as head coach at Workington Town. A fiery red head with a rugby player's physique, he has made headlines as much for his off-field adventures as his cricketing feats that include England's fastest ever Test double hundred, the fastest Test match 250, and the highest score for a Test batsman batting at number six.

Ben also holds the record for the most runs scored by an individual batsman in the morning session of a Test match. He bats left-handed and bowls right-handed, continually changing matches with his at times devastating seam deliveries.

Stokes became the highest-paid overseas player in the history of the Indian Premier League in 2017 and won the Most Valuable Player award during that season. In 2020, he was awarded the Sir Garfield Sobers Trophy for Best Cricketer of the Year and collected the prestigious *Wisden* World Cricketer of the Year trophy.

To all of us looking on everything seemed wonderful for Ben, but in the summer of 2021 he announced that he was taking an 'indefinite break' from cricket. He decided to prioritise his mental wellbeing, and (temporarily I hope) gave up the game he plays better than almost anybody in history.

'In my day' we used to be told to 'pull yourself together' and just got on with the game. Now I am happy to see proper attention being given to the psychological as well as physical side of sport.

My best wishes go to Ben and I congratulate him on having the courage to speak out about the mental pressures he was under. He must be given as long as he needs to get himself in the right frame of mind to play the game at the highest level. The times of bottling it up are, I'm glad to say, over.

Nobody will ever be able to take away from Ben that summer of 2019. He played cricket from another planet.

BEN STOKES FOR THE RECORD:

- Born: 4 June 1991, Christchurch, New Zealand
- Teams:
  - Durham (2009–present)
  - Melbourne Renegades (2014–15)
  - Rising Pune Supergiant (2014–15)
  - Canterbury (2017–18)
  - Rajasthan Royals (2018–present)
- Tests: 71
  - Runs 4,631 (37.04)
  - Wickets 163 (31.38)
  - Top score: 258
  - Best bowling: 6/22
- First-class career: 148 matches
  - Runs: 8,414 (35.39)
  - Top score: 258
  - Wickets: 338 (29.34)
  - Best bowling: 7/67
- ODI matches: 101
  - Runs 2,871 (40.43)
  - Wickets: 74 (41.59)
- Best bowling: 5/61
- BBC Sports Personality of the Year: 2019
- ICC Sir Garfield Sobers Trophy for Best Cricketer of the Year: 2020
- *Wisden* Leading Cricketer in the World: 2020

Jason Kenny: Jason Kenny and his wife Laura (née Trott) have the Midas touch on their Olympic bikes. They have twelve gold medals between them, and the Paris Games of 2024 are in their sights. They will have more gold than the Bank of England.

Jim Laker: Did I tell you about the time I played a County cricket match with 19-wicket legend Jim Laker? He and his Surrey and England 'spin twin' Tony Lock could be unplayable on any accommodating pitches ... which the Aussies claimed were doctored. As if ...

Brian Lara, the batting Prince who scored a Lara Lara runs for West Indies. His 501 not out for Warwickshire against Durham in the summer of 1994 remains the pinnacle of all first-class innings. Sheer class.

Rod Laver, the Rockhampton Rocket who was a grand Grand Slammer. He more than anybody turned me into a tennis fan with his majestic play in the 1960s.

Denis Law, everybody's favourite footballer. He always liked to remind me of how my World Cup hat-trick ruined his round of golf. So sad to hear as we were preparing this book that the fiercely proud Scot is the latest victim of the old footballer's curse of dementia. We'll never forget the Electric Heel.

Carl Lewis became the modern Jesse Owens at the 1984 Olympics but did not win friends and influence people with his arrogant attitude. But time has healed and the world now recognises that he was one of the greatest all-round athletes ever to race round a track or jump into a sand pit.

Jonah Lomu was the All Blacks colossus who used England's defenders like doormats in the 1995 Rugby World Cup semi-final. He was built like a back-row forward but had the speed of an Olympic sprinter. Getting in his way at full pace must have been like being hit by Chopper Harris and Bites Yer Legs Hunter at the same time.

Diego Maradona: I was a stunned witness to Diego's shameless 'hand of God' goal in the 1986 World Cup quarter-final in Mexico. Four minutes later I marvelled at his stunning skill as he waltzed through the England defence for what was voted 'the goal of the century'. Diego never did things in halves.

Rocky Marciano: The REAL Rocky remains the only unbeaten world heavyweight champion, 49 fights, 49 wins. He did not pay much attention to the Marquess of Queensberry rules and bludgeoned his hapless opponents to painful defeat. Here he is delivering his 'SuzyQ' punch to end the reign of Jersey Joe Walcott in the 13th round of their 1952 world title fight.

Stanley Matthews, the Wizard of Dribble who played First Division football at 50! His father was the famous Fighting Barber of Hanley, and Stanley could feint with his feet as his Dad did with his fists.

Peter May, the Classics master known simply as P.B.H., made much more than an initial impact. He was described by Aussie cricketer/commentator Richie Benaud as the *only* great England batsman to emerge in the immediate post-war years. Richie clearly never saw me in action for Essex!

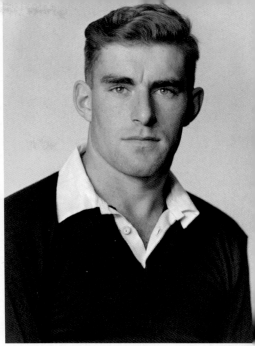

John McEnroe's Superbrat talent trumped his tantrums. He stole the headlines with his behaviour but he could really play the game with his inventive shot-making and volleying skills. He has established himself as one of the most authoritative television pundits, making you wonder how he could have been so argumentative in his young days.

Colin Meads, known throughout rugby as Pinetree, packed awesome power for New Zealand. He and his younger brother, Stan, used to toughen up by carrying a sheep under each arm on their father's farm in King Country. A friendly giant off the pitch, he was a ferocious opponent once the game started.

Lionel Messi, now the toast of Paris after becoming a legend at Barcelona, gave a juggling exhibition when I first met him at the 2006 World Cup draw in Leipzig. I told my wife, Judith: 'I've just met the new Maradona.' He was 16.

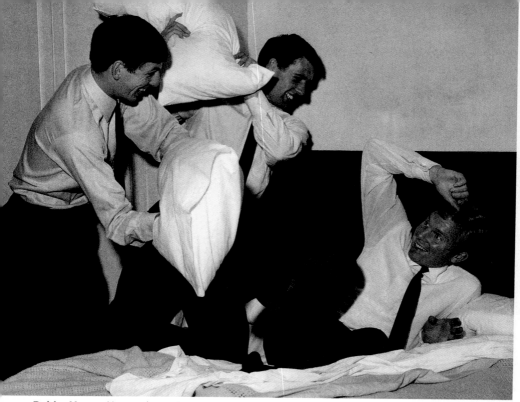

Bobby Moore: Happy days: I join Martin Peters in giving Bobby Moore a pillow bashing during the week leading up to the 1966 World Cup final. My pal Bobby was the world's greatest defender and should have been given an ambassador's role. Somehow he became the Forgotten Hero until rediscovered following his tragic passing at the age of 51 in 1993.

Gerd Muller was famed and feared as Der Bomber who had an unquenchable thirst for goals. Unfortunately for many years he could not say 'no' to that next drink. He sadly passed on as we were preparing this book in the summer of 2021.

Rafael Nadal: I could easily have been writing about Rafa the international footballer. He had to choose between football and tennis for a career. His uncle was an outstanding player with Barcelona. Rafa chose tennis, and he has established himself as an all-time great, particularly on clay where he is almost unbeatable.

Jack Nicklaus, the Golden Bear, was a powerful force on the world's fairways. His record of 18 major victories at one time looked in danger as Tiger's career rocketed but it's safe to say nobody is going to overtake it in the foreseeable future. Nicklaus still rules.

Pelé: Pelé and Bobby Moore, acknowledge each other after the classic match between England and Brazil in the 1970 World Cup in Guadalajara. Pelé's 1,216 goals in 1,254 matches says everything about his impact on the Beautiful Game. Untouchable.

Martin Peters: It's the eve of the last match at the old Wembley in 2000 and my best friend Martin Peters and I make a nostalgic return with a replica of the Jules Rimet trophy to make us feel at home. Martin was known as the footballing Ghost, because he could appear from out of nowhere to score vital goals. I miss him desperately.

Lester Piggott, the 'Long Fellow' of racing who was said to have a face like a well-kept grave. He rode 5,300 winners across 47 years and never seemed to, uh, find it taxing despite living on a starvation diet to control his weight.

Ferenc Puskás: Hungary's Galloping Major who had a rifle of a left foot shot. After Russian tanks rolled into Budapest in 1956, he reinvented himself at Real Madrid as a striking partner feeding off the precise passes of Alfredo Di Stéfano. They formed an unforgettable footballing duo.

Sir Steven Redgrave: I'm glad nobody took up Steven Redgrave's challenge after the 1996 Atlanta Games to shoot him if they saw him back in a boat, as he went on to become an Olympic legend at Sydney four years later. He is the Miracle Man of sport because throughout his career he has battled against ulcerative colitis and type 2 diabetes. A golden hero.

Sir Vivian Richards, the Master Blaster who brought bowlers to their knees whether batting for Somerset or the West Indies. For me, the most exciting cricketer ever to wield the willow.

Sugar Ray Robinson, who is often described as – pound for pound – the greatest boxer of them all. There was plenty of evidence to support the argument until he went to the well too often at the back end of his 202-fight career. At his peak, he was a ring master.

Cristiano Ronaldo: Made in Madeira, Cristiano Ronaldo has become football's first billionaire. I never thought I would see a better wide player than George Best but here he is, a magical footballer with self confidence in abundance.

Ian Rush, the Liverpool and Wales goal-scoring legend, reminds me of me. We had the same work ethic and both put the needs of the team ahead of personal targets. He and Kenny Dalglish together for Liverpool were dynamite.

Peter Snell, the flying Kiwi who showed his rivals a clean pair of heels. He was setting times for the 800 and 1500 metres in the 1960s that would have him well placed in today's major races. For four years he was never beaten in global competition. Snell was no snail.

Sir Garfield Sobers was born with twelve fingers, which came in handy when counting his hundreds of runs and wickets. Arguably the greatest all-rounder ever to hit or bowl a cricket ball, and he was also a stunning fielder. He had it all.

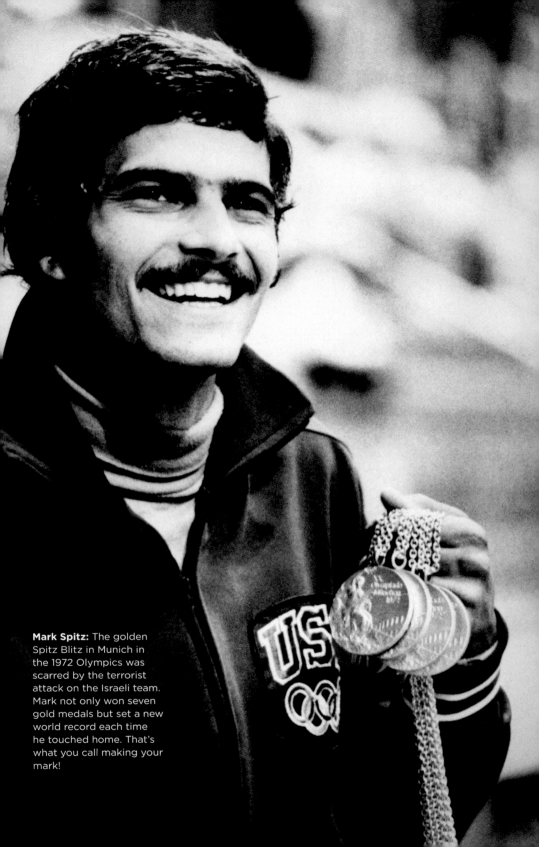

Mark Spitz: The golden Spitz Blitz in Munich in the 1972 Olympics was scarred by the terrorist attack on the Israeli team. Mark not only won seven gold medals but set a new world record each time he touched home. That's what you call making your mark!

Jackie Stewart was the thinking man's world champion racing driver. The Flying Scot won three world titles and was runner-up twice. He held the record for most wins by a Formula One driver – 27 – for 14 years until overtaken by Frenchman Alain Prost.

Ben Stokes – 'Big Ben' – did a Botham on the Aussies at Headingley and was the most dominant cricketer to emerge in modern times. Sadly, the flame of fame burned him and he was forced to take a break because of the mental pressures of always being in the spotlight. At last they are accepting in sport that the mind has to be treated as carefully as the body.

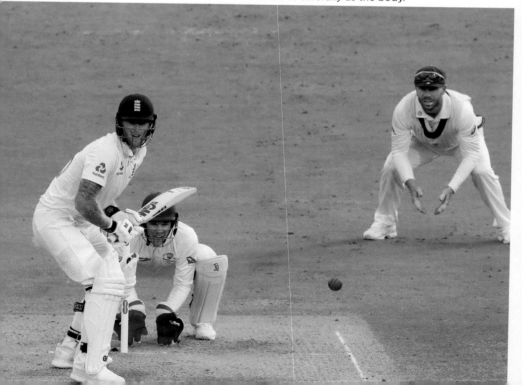

Sachin Tendulkar was a beautifully tuned run machine who became a cricketing god in India. He played 200 Test matches and at the end of his glorious career held the record for most Test runs and most hundreds in both Tests and ODIs. Yes, the Little Master.

Daley Thompson was the Daley express on the track, a force in the field – particularly the long jump pit – and won back-to-back Olympic gold medals in the decathlon. He also had the Fastest Tongue in the West, which often drew him into controversy. But nobody could deny his talent and commitment to being the very best across ten disciplines.

Torvill and Dean provided sporting perfection on ice. Their sensational Bolero routine brought maximum scores from the Olympic judges, and they went on to become worldwide stars with their dancing on ice. They won four world titles to go with their 1984 Olympic crown. They provided sheer bliss for this old footballer.

years the 'meanest man on the planet' until his career and life went into a tailspin. It's been like helplessly watching a car smash since he became the youngest world heavyweight champion at 20 in 1986. At the peak of his power, he seemed unbeatable but he was brought down by self-inflicted demons. His adventure has been a compelling spectacle.

Shane Warne is a spin master who could confuse and bemuse the best of batsmen. Nobody who saw it will ever forget his first ball bowled in a Test match in England in 1993 when he totally baffled Mike Gatting with a ball that spun eighteen inches. It has gone down in cricketing folklore as 'the Ball of the Century'. He has been causing headlines and headaches ever since, and even as a cricket commentator has you sitting on the edge of your seat. He has 708 Test wickets to say 'Warnie was here.'

Jonny Wilkinson: Jonny is my World Cup-winning twin and we both know about last-minute goals for England. He has admitted struggling with mental issues when the public spotlight was swung on him, but I gloried in my 15 minutes of fame that has somehow stretched to 55 years! But Jonny got it together and has had stellar success on the rugby fields of England and France.

Tiger Woods was the only player with an outside chance of catching the 18-major success of Jack Nicklaus but that is now a distant dream after a series of earthquaking scandals, injuries and accidents. As he battles with the consequences of his latest car smash, we just know we will never see his like again.

Emil Zátopek, the 'Bouncing Czech', completed the 'Impossible Treble' in the 1952 Helsinki Olympics, and here he is on his way to victory in the 5,000m. That's Britain's Chris Chataway on the floor after hitting the curb bidding for the lead. French Algerian Alain Mimoun took the silver and Germany's Herbert Schade the bronze. Chataway got up to finish fifth, a stride behind team-mate Gordon Pirie. Zátopek also won the 10,000m and the marathon.

Zinedine Zidane – Sizzling Zizou – was the Real deal as player and coach in Madrid, and was outstanding for France but often on a short fuse. He infamously got red carded in the 2006 World Cup final for headbutting an Italian defender.

Gianfranco Zola is the player I would most like to have had serving me with passes on a platter. How different my management career might have been if I could have called on Zola when I was in charge at Chelsea. He admits to learning many of his box of tricks when playing as understudy to the one and only Diego Maradona at Napoli. Always learn from the best.

71

SACHIN TENDULKAR

'The little artist with the power
of a Sherman tank'

WE MOVE from the belligerence and aggression of Ben Stokes to
the artistry and technical genius of Sachin Tendulkar. I have often
used the word 'god' in previous selections, but with Tendulkar
that is exactly what he is considered in his native India. He is
worshipped by an army of disciples who have no doubt that he
was the greatest batsman of them all, even ahead of Bradman,
Richards, Hobbs, Headley and Lara.

He could not have been more removed from a player like
Stokes, who was beefy and very physical. Tendulkar was a 5ft 5in
bantamweight, as light on his feet as a ballet dancer with perfect
balance and an economy of movement that made you wonder
how he could make the ball fly to the boundary as if shot from a
Sherman tank. He had the full range of shots in his armoury, could
play all around the wicket and with a grace and style that suggested
his runs should have been delivered on a silver salver.

As a batsman of note (okay, a bum note), I could not see a
single weakness in Tendulkar's game. We knew he was something

special when at the age of 19 he played an innings against Australia at the WACA that veterans agreed had never been bettered at the renowned old Perth ground.

The watching Don Bradman paid him the ultimate compliment. 'Young Tendulkar,' he said as an aside to his wife, 'reminds me of me.'

Those watching Tendulkar in his schooldays in India reckoned that by the age of 12 he was already exceptional, and he made his Test debut just four years later. He proved he had character and courage to go with his skill when he continued to bat in that first Test while blood seeped from his mouth after he had been struck by a bouncer from Waqar Younis.

He conjured his first match-saving Test century against England at Old Trafford at 17, and by the time he was 25 he had added 16 more Test hundreds. In 2000 Tendulkar became the first batsman to amass 50 international centuries and in 2008 overtook Brian Lara as the leading Test run-scorer.

Folklore has it that scorers got writer's cramp trying to keep up with his scoring as he shot past 13,000 Tests runs. As I prepare this tribute book to my heroes, Sachin holds the record for the most hundreds in both Test and ODIs, which is an astonishing statistic considering he did not register his first ODI ton until his 79th match.

Just before his 37th birthday he broke a 40-year-old barrier by scoring the first double hundred in one-day cricket. Then in 2012, when just one month short of his 39th birthday, he became the first player to score 100 international centuries, which like Bradman's batting near-100 average is likely to be a mark that is never challenged.

The Little Master retired from Test cricket in 2013 after a hugely emotional 200th appearance, on his home ground at the Wankhede Stadium against West Indies. There was not a dry eye in the house. Like so many outstanding sportsmen I have come across in my life time, Sachin is ambidextrous. He batted and bowled with his right hand, threw with either and did most other things, such as writing, with his left.

In cricket-mad India the popular saying is, 'Cricket is my religion and Tendulkar is my god.' He cannot lead an ordinary life in his homeland and when he goes out has to wear disguises so that he is not continually mobbed. Aussie Test star Matthew Hayden said during a series in India, 'I have seen God. He bats at number four for India.'

As I was preparing this book, Tendulkar tested positive for Coronavirus. India held its breath until they heard the little man was recovering. No sportsman on earth has a bigger following. Truly a god of cricket.

SACHIN TENDULKAR FOR THE RECORD:

- Born: 24 April 1975, Bombay, (now Mumbai)
- Teams:
  - Cricket Club of India (1988)
  - Mumbai (1988–2013)
  - Rest of India (1989–90)
  - Yorkshire (1992)
  - East Bengal (1994)
  - Rest of World XI (1998)
  - Asia X1 (2000)
  - MCC (2014)
  - Sachin's Blasters (2015)
  - India Legends (2020–21)
- Tests: 200
  - Runs 15,921 (53.78)
  - Top score: 248 not out
- First-class career: 310 matches
  - Runs: 25,396 (57.84)
  - Top score: 248 not out
- ODI matches: 463
  - Runs 18,426 (44.83)
- *Wisden* Cricketer of the Year: 1997
- *Wisden* Leading Cricketer in the World: 1998, 2010
- ICC Sir Garfield Sobers Trophy for Best Cricketer of the Year: 2020
- Bharat Ratna, India's highest civilian award: 2014

72

DALEY THOMPSON

'The complete all-rounder and
Fastest Tongue in the West'

MANY GOOD judges rate Daley Thompson the greatest all-round athlete the world has ever seen, yet he does not get the recognition he deserves for a long procession of performances that left his rivals gasping in his wake. He tackled the decathlon with a swagger and cockiness that upset some members of the Establishment, but that was his way of getting a psychological advantage over his opponents in the toughest of sporting challenges.

Thompson's early ambition was to go down the professional football road, but his athletics potential was spotted by Newham and Essex Beagles coach Bob Mortimer who persuaded him to give the decathlon a go. Six feet tall and with a physique from the Greek gods, he took to the punishing test with such enthusiasm and expertise that he was unbeaten in the ten-discipline challenge from 1978 to 1987.

He won gold medals in the 1980 and 1984 Olympics and became the first decathlete to hold the European, World Championship, Commonwealth and Olympic titles simultaneously. It was consistency on an extraordinary scale. But he struggled to win everybody over because of an attitude that bordered on the arrogant.

Daley's best haul of 8,847 points in the 1984 Olympics in Los Angeles remains a UK record to this day, but he made foes as well as friends with his supremacy across the ten events: 100m, long jump, shot putt, high jump, 400m, 110m hurdles, discus, pole vault, javelin, 1500m.

Thompson, who broke the world record four times, had a piercing sense of humour that some found offensive. His quip about hoping to have a baby with fellow Olympian Princess Anne sent an electric shock through the Establishment, and he riled American ace Carl Lewis by wearing a T-shirt that carried the question, 'Is the world's second greatest athlete gay?'

After blitzing the opposition in the 1984 Olympics on the way to retaining his championship, Daley irreverently whistled on the victory rostrum while the national anthem was being played. He just did not care what people thought and reigned over the decathlon world with a confidence that was unshakeable.

Asked by an American television reporter how he felt after his victory in Los Angeles, Daley caused indigestion by responding, 'I haven't been this happy since my grandmother caught her tit in the mangle.'

But all the joking aside, he took his sport seriously to almost fanatical levels and trained harder than just about anybody to stay on top. He was the son of a Scottish-born mother and a Notting Hill-based Nigerian cab driver who was murdered when Daley was 12. He was sent to a boarding school for, let's say robust, children and was a rebel without a pause.

Never slow to make withering comments on the racism issue, he was driven by a career-long rivalry with outstanding West German decathlete Jürgen Hingsen. Much to Hingsen's frustration, he was never able to get the better of his taunting nemesis.

Daley was forced to retire in 1992 with a recurring hamstring injury, and returned to his first love of football but without making the breakthrough beyond reserve team experience with Mansfield Town and Reading, plus a brief spell of non-league action. A fitness coach and motivational speaker, Daley also dabbled with motor racing and opened his own gymnasium in Upper Richmond. He remains close friends with Lord Sebastian Coe and was an ambassador for the Coe team that brought the Olympics to London in 2012 with such resounding success.

Never short of controversial comments, the 'Fastest Tongue in the West' named as his hero his predecessor as Olympic champion, Bruce Jenner. When the American publicly came out as a trans woman called Caitlyn Jenner in 2015, Daley said, 'She must be the toughest person I know because if you have to live as somebody else for 60 years it can't be easy. I'm cool about it.'

Whether running, jumping, hurdling, throwing or leaping, Daley was an extraordinary athlete and comfortably makes it into my list. He would not win a gold medal for diplomacy, but he always competed with a sparkle in his eyes and for more than nine years was just unbeatable.

The complete all-rounder.

DALEY THOMPSON FOR THE RECORD:

- Born: 30 July 1958, Notting Hill, London
- Full name: Frances Morgan Ayodélé Thompson
- Career span: 1975–1992
- Club: Newham and Essex Beagles
- Olympic gold medals: 1980 (Moscow), 1984 (Los Angeles)
- World Championship gold medals: 1983 (Helsinki)
- European Championship gold medals: 1982 (Athens), 1986 (Stuttgart)
- Commonwealth Games gold medals: 1978 (Edmonton), 1982 (Brisbane), 1986 (Edinburgh)
- Personal bests:
  - 100m: 10.26s (Stuttgart, 1986)
  - Long jump: 8.11m (Edmonton, 1978)
  - Shot putt: 15.73m (Stuttgart, 1986)
  - High jump: 2.11m (Austria, 1980)
  - 400m: 46.86s (Austria, 1982)
  - 110m hurdles: 14.04s (Stuttgart, 1986)
  - Discus: 47.62m (France, 1986)
  - Pole vault: 5.10m (Toronto, 1983)
  - Javelin: 64.04m (Seoul, 1988)
  - 1500m: 4m 22.8s (Czechoslovakia, 1978)
- Best score: 8,797 points (Los Angeles, 1984; still UK record)
- BBC Sports Personality of the Year: 1982

73

TORVILL AND DEAN

*'Sporting perfection on ice
from a golden couple'*

ICE SKATING leaves me pretty cold (another weak attempt at humour – I shall shut up). But along with the rest of the nation I warmed to the stunning exploits of Torvill and Dean, and my Judith insisted I include them even though doing so lifts my total of sporting heroes to 81. You have to be made of ice (there I go again) not to have melted at their performance to Ravel's Boléro in the 1984 Sarajevo Winter Olympics. It is impossible to hear that beautiful music without thinking of their equally beautiful routine, and the fact that it was staged on Valentine's Day added romance to their presentation.

They achieved what all sports competitors strive for and rarely manage: complete perfection. Christopher and Jayne scored an unprecedented maximum nine sixes for artistic impression. It was incredible to watch even if – like me – you didn't know a Mohawk from a Salchow.

While researching for this book, I took time out to study clips of Torvill and Dean in action and I strongly recommend you take the same course. You will thank me. They were absolutely mind-blowing with their skating routines which, while entertaining, also contained athleticism, stamina, technical skill and gymnastic artistry of the highest order.

And to think that Christopher had been a bobby on the beat in their native Nottingham and Jayne an insurance clerk while working at their ice skating craft in their spare time. As you will see on YouTube, I doubt there have ever been British sports competitors gathering more applause and admiration across the globe.

The 1984 gold medal performance captured the interest and imagination of millions of viewers across the world, and laid the foundation for Torvill and Dean to become household names and have a career in which they have travelled to dozens of countries with their spectacular ice shows.

After their overwhelming victories at the Olympics and the subsequent 1984 World Championships, the golden couple – a platonic partnership off the ice – turned professional. Under Olympic Games rules at the time they were ineligible to participate in 'amateur' competition. The rules were later changed as shamateurism was smashed and they made a comeback to the Olympic rink in the 1994 Winter Games in Lillehammer, winning a bronze medal that many experts said should have been gold.

Lucrative years lay ahead for them both, mainly as globetrotting show promoters and performers, in-demand coaches and expert choreographers before they again became household favourites as judges on ITV's phenomenally popular *Dancing on Ice*.

On the 30th anniversary of the 1984 Olympics in 2014 they recreated their Boléro routine in the same Sarajevo arena where they had touched perfection, and four years later Christopher was back in the Olympic picture when he choreographed the gold medal-winning performance of Aljona Savchenko and Bruno Massot in South Korea.

Torvill and Dean had taken on the baton of a golden generation of British ice skaters, with the balletic John Curry and the powerful but graceful Robin Cousins ruling the rinks of the world.

And this old ex-footballer looked on with admiration and awe at their talent. I wonder if they could have done it with Bites Yer Legs Hunter or Chopper Harris trying to kick them up in the air? I am joking, of course. Torvill and Dean represented the best of British. Perfection.

TORVILL AND DEAN FOR THE RECORD:

- Jayne Torvill born: 7 October 1957, Nottingham
- Christopher Dean born: 27 July 1958, Nottingham
- Competitive career span: 1975–1996
- Olympic gold medal: 1984 (Sarajevo)
- Olympic bronze medal: 1994 (Lillehammer)
- World champions: 1981, 1982, 1983, 1984
- European champions: 1981, 1982, 1984, 1994
- British champions: 1978, 1979, 1980, 1981, 1982, 1983, 1994)
- World Professional Championship: 1984, 1985, 1990, 1995, 1996
- BBC Sports Personality of the Year: 1984

74

MIKE TYSON

'The rise and fall of a mean fighting machine'

THERE WERE three or four years when Mike Tyson could claim to have been the most powerful, dangerous and ferocious heavyweight in the history of boxing. But he lost his way when hitting the self-destruct button and went from being feared to being pitied and shamed as his career nose-dived.

It was like being a helpless witness to a car crash as Tyson's life came apart after he had established himself as a mean, merciless fighting machine. There was a $10m divorce and suicide attempt when he was briefly married to Hollywood actress Robin Givens, a savage knockout defeat by 20/1 underdog James 'Buster' Douglas, a prison sentence for rape, the scandal of biting off part of Evander Holyfield's ear during a championship fight, drug abuse, alcoholism and a bankruptcy in which the man who had earned $300m was declaring debts of more than $23m.

Yet for all the turmoil 'Iron Mike' remained a favourite of the masses, who were entranced by his rollercoaster adventures that not even a Hollywood scriptwriter could have invented. I was one of those hooked on his unbelievable journey.

Like everybody else, I looked on from outside the ring as he rose from being a street-gang bully to become the youngest ever world heavyweight champion in 1986, when he knocked out title holder Trevor Berbick in two rounds of naked savagery. The 20-year-old Tyson had been mentored and managed by wily Cus D'Amato who 30 years earlier had steered 'Freudian' Floyd Patterson to the title.

D'Amato was able to control Tyson, but when he died shortly before his protege ripped the championship from Berbick, the Brooklyn brawler started to go off the rails.

Tyson makes it into my list because of his sheer magnetism. It was compelling looking on as he knocked out every challenger who dared get into the ring with him, and even more gripping as everything started to unravel.

Standing just over 5ft 10in and weighing around 15st 8lb at his peak, Tyson was short and squat by the standards of the new generation of dreadnought heavyweights, but he had such fast fists and potent power that he cleared the decks of a procession of opponents including James 'Bonecrusher' Smith, Pinklon Thomas, Tony Tucker, Tyrell Biggs, Tony Tubbs, Larry Holmes, Michael Spinks and British hero Frank Bruno.

After his stunning tenth-round knockout defeat by Buster Douglas followed by his prison sentence for raping a beauty queen, Tyson went into freefall. In a second fight with Holyfield he was disqualified in the third round for twice biting Holyfield's ear and had his licence taken away. Living up to his nickname of the 'Baddest Man on the Planet', he was sent back to prison after assaulting two men following a road-rage incident.

He was allowed back into boxing on his release and earned a title fight with Lennox Lewis that the British/Canadian won on an eighth-round knockout.

Soon after that, Tyson filed for bankruptcy with debts approaching $23m. He then reinvented himself as an author and on-stage performer, talking candidly about his life and times. In July 2020 he fought an exhibition draw with former four-weights champion Roy Jones Jnr in what was billed as a legends fight. Mike was 55 and still with lots of headlines to come.

I now need to sit and get a rub down with a copy of *Sporting Life*.

MIKE TYSON FOR THE RECORD:

- Born: 30 June 1966, Brooklyn
- Amateur career: 1982–84
  - Fights 35
  - Wins: 30
- Junior Olympic champion: 1982
- New York State Golden Gloves champion: 1983
- Professional career: 1984–2003
  - Fights: 58
  - Wins: 50 (44 inside the distance)
  - Defeats: 6
  - No-contests: 2
- Aged 20, youngest fighter to win the world heavyweight title by beating Trevor Berbick in 1986
- Title defences:
  - James 'Bonecrusher' Smith, 7 March 1987, Las Vegas; won on points after 12 rounds
  - Pinklon Thomas, 30 May 1987, Las Vegas; won by stoppage in sixth round
  - Tony Tucker, 1 August 1987, Las Vegas; won on points after 12 rounds
  - Tyrell Biggs, 16 October 1987, New Jersey; won by stoppage in seventh round
  - Larry Holmes, 22 January 1988, New Jersey; won by stoppage in fourth round
  - Tony Tubbs, 21 March 1988, Tokyo; won by stoppage in second round
  - Michael Spinks, 27 June 1988, New Jersey; won by knockout in first round
  - Frank Bruno, 25 February 1989, Las Vegas; won by stoppage in fifth round

- Carl Williams, 21 July 1989, New Jersey; won by stoppage in first round
- James 'Buster' Douglas, 11 February 1990, Japan; lost by knockout in tenth round
- Other title fights:
  - Frank Bruno, 16 March 1996, Las Vegas; won by stoppage in third round
  - Bruce Seldon, 7 September 1996, Las Vegas; won by stoppage in first round
  - Evander Holyfield, 9 November 1996, Las Vegas; lost by stoppage in 11th round
  - Evander Holyfield, 28 June 1997, Las Vegas; lost by disqualification in third round
  - Lennox Lewis, 8 June 2002, Memphis; lost by stoppage in eighth round

75

SHANE WARNE

'The Aussie maestro who
could spin a great yarn'

IT WAS Shane Warne who likened his life to a soap opera, and certainly it was more *Home and Away* than *Neighbours*. He made headlines wherever he went, mostly with his deadly spin bowling but sometimes with a lifestyle that was too often playboy centred for the taste of the cricket establishment.

He makes my list purely for his bowling feats, and in particular for being the first to break the magical 700-wicket barrier. Warnie was never less than entertaining and was a leg-break bowler without equal, challenging batsmen with Freddie Trueman-type competitive spirit but without being able to back up his sledging with ferocious speed.

Nobody who saw it will ever forget the Australian's first delivery in Test cricket in England. Mike Gatting, the man on the receiving end at Old Trafford, definitely didn't see it. The ball was a fizzing leg break that seemed to be threatening Gatting's leg stump and spun 18 inches and hit the off stump instead. The baffled batsman had to wait to see television replays before he knew what had happened.

That was our introduction to the wiles of Warne, and it was tremendous fun for us cricket lovers following his career over the next 14 years. He had us riveted to the screen with his bowling and raising our eyebrows over events in his private life that included lots of sex scandals, suspension for taking illegal substances, fraternity with a bookmaker, and adventures at the poker tables of the world.

I played with probably the greatest off-break bowler of all time in Jim Laker, whose path crossed mine when he was winding down his career with Essex. Jim was a silent assassin, rarely saying a word and just getting on with his job of taking wickets. Warne was all energy, emotion and as chirpy as a canary, getting under the skin of batsmen with his comments while confusing them with his spin. He could have got the ball to turn on the M1.

As well as his bowling he was in the record books for his batting, setting an offbeat record with the most runs accumulated in Test cricket – 3,154 – without scoring a century. He once made 99 and got a roasting for a suicidal shot that cost him his wicket and the magic three figures.

Even though he was playing for the 'enemy', I used to love watching Warne trundle in to bowl leg breaks that we thought had become a forgotten art. Many think he was at his best at the back end of his career after he had served a 12-month ban for swallowing forbidden diuretics in a bid to control weight that continually ballooned.

In 2004 he claimed a world-record 96 victims, 40 of them England batsmen who were continually bewildered by his pitch and pace. Sometimes I swear the ball was so slow that a tortoise could have beaten it down the wicket, but the spin as it landed was wicked. The next ball could be almost medium pace and then it could be a straight-on delivery. He was never predictable. It would definitely have been G.C. Hurst bowled S.K. Warne 0.

Warne talked a foreign language, referring to his zooter, slider, toppie, flipper and back-spinner. Whatever he bowled it certainly brought dividends in a career that took in key contributions for Victoria, the captaincy of Hampshire and a haul of more than 1,000 international wickets in Tests and one-day internationals. His 708 Test wickets put him second in the all-time list to the Sri Lankan magician Muttiah Muralitharan.

In the autumn of his career, Warne became the poster 'boy' for the IPL as a swashbuckling skipper of Rajasthan Royals and earning the sobriquet 'the greatest captain Australia never had'. Since switching to the TV commentary box with always interesting observations, he has made it clear that his one regret is that he was never trusted with leading his country.

Shane was too much of a gambler for the selectors. But what fun it would have been for we spectators.

You beauty, cobber.

SHANE WARNE FOR THE RECORD:

- Born: 13 September 1969, Upper Ferntree Gully, Victoria, Australia
- Teams:
  - Victoria (1990–2007)
  - Hampshire (2000–2007)
  - Rajasthan Royals (2008–2011)
  - Melbourne Stars (2011–2013)
- Tests: 145
  - Wickets 708 (25.41)
  - Runs 3,154 (17.32)
  - Best bowling: 8/71 v. England (Brisbane, 1994)
  - Ten wickets in a match: 10 times
  - Top score: 99
- First-class career: 310 matches
  - Wickets: 1,319 (26.11)
  - Runs: 6,919 (19.43)
- Best bowling 8/71 (v. England, Brisbane 1994)
  - Top score: 107 not out
- ODI matches: 184
  - Wickets: 293 (25,73)
  - Best bowling 5/33 v. West Indies (Sydney, 1998)
  - Runs 1,018 (13.95)
- *Wisden* Cricketer of the Year: 1994
- Voted one of the five *Wisden* Cricketers of the Century (along with Don Bradman, Garfield Sobers, Jack Hobbs and Viv Richards): 2000

76

JONNY WILKINSON

'Jonny, my World Cup-winning 'twin''

JONNY WILKINSON and I are twinned together in sporting history in that each of us has scored a last-minute, World Cup-winning goal for England. In case I have forgotten to mention it, mine came in the last seconds of extra time against West Germany in 1966. Jonny's was much more nerve-wracking, a precision dropped goal from 40 yards in the last seconds of extra time against Australia in 2003. Same sensation, different-shaped balls.

I have a vivid memory of gleefully watching the moment Jonny's kick won the game on television, as does Judith. We just happened to be lying side by side in a hotel bed in Weybridge while on a break, and I jumped out of bed and did a jig when the ball went over the bar. What a finale. It really was all over! I was then questioned surely more than a hundred times by the media about what it was like to score a last-minute winning goal in a World Cup Final. Only Jonny and I know!

My hat-trick brought me more fame than I deserved, but for the then shy, introverted Jonny his goal gave him unwanted celebrity. He has admitted to having had to fight mental pressures to the point where he would hide in his hotel room rather than face well-meaning but pestering people. He should try hearing them ask, 'Was it over the line?' At least his drop goal was clear cut and delivered with the coolness of, dare I say, a Bobby Moore.

It's fair to say I gloried in my World Cup success because it was so unexpected. Don't forget that neither Martin Peters nor I had played for England before 1966 dawned, so every moment came as a bonus. My co-writer of this book, Norman Giller, interviewed me shortly after the World Cup victory and asked me in his then role as chief football writer for the *Daily Express* how I felt. When I said, 'Ten feet tall,' he organised a photograph in which I stood on the table in the kitchen of our chalet-bungalow in Essex and the cameraman, Bob Stiggins, took a shot from below my feet making me look like a giant.

Jonny on the other hand shrunk away from publicity. But he gradually came to terms with the flame of fame and in a stellar career won four Six Nations titles with England and, after helping Newcastle to Premiership and Powergen Cup titles, joined RC Toulon, where he won French league titles and the European Cup.

What was remarkable about Wilkinson's victorious drop goal is that he usually favoured his left foot but he instinctively took aim with his right. That memorable moment was the highlight of a record-breaking rugby career in which this fleet-footed fly-half of huge heart and inventive mind cemented himself as one of the legends of his sport.

Surrey-born but Newcastle-based, Wilkinson made his international debut at the age of 18 in 1998 and over the next 13 years played 91 Tests for England and amassed a record 1,179 points.

An ultra intelligent boy (Judith just said 'unlike you'), Jonny dropped out of Durham University to become a full-time player with Newcastle Falcons, making the most of the long overdue switch from amateur to professional rugby. Mentored by former

England fly-half maestro Rob Andrew, he repaid his debt to Rob by wiping all his records out of the rugby books.

He was famously teetotal and followed Buddhist principles. Me? I have always drunk in moderation, and follow the principle of always doing what Judith tells me.

After the dramatic drop goal in Sydney in 2003, Wilkinson's career was haunted by injury. Knee ligament, arm, shoulder and kidney problems stopped him playing again for England until their opening game of the 2007 Six Nations Championship against Scotland. In his comeback performance he scored a Calcutta Cup record of 27 points in a man-of-the-match performance. The following week against Italy, he became the highest point-scorer in the history of the Five/Six Nations Championship.

Injury problems returned later that year but he battled back to be part of England's Rugby World Cup squad, who surprised many by powering into the final where they were beaten by the Springboks.

'Wilko' scored a record 29th Test drop goal against France in the 2008 Six Nations – surpassing the tally he shared with Argentine hero Hugo Porta. He holds the Rugby World Cup points record with 249, capturing the figure previously posted by Scotland's Gavin Hastings during England's 2007 quarter-final victory over Australia. He is also the only player to score points in two World Cup finals – kicking four penalties and that famous drop goal in the 2003 victory over Australia and two penalties in the 15-6 loss to South Africa in 2007.

Jonny retired in 2014 after steering Toulon to the double of Heineken Cup and French league (Top 14) titles. He is now a motivational coach and a forthright television pundit, lives with his wife Shelley and family in Berkshire, and has got rid of all those mental demons that often attacked him in his playing days. It's a privilege to be so often twinned with him.

He will always be remembered for that last-minute World Cup-winning goal. I know how he feels!

JONNY WILKINSON FOR THE RECORD:

- Born 25 May 1979, Frimley, Surrey
- Position: fly-half
- Major club teams:
  - Newcastle Falcons (1997–2009): 182 games, 2,049 points
  - Toulon (2009–2014): 141 games, 1,884 points
- French Top 14 championship: 2014
- European Cup: 2013, 2014
- English Premiership: 1998
- Powergen Cup: 2001, 2004
- Test career: 1998–2011
  - Caps: 91
  - Points: 1,179
- Six Nations championship: 2000, 2001, 2003, 2011
- British Lions: 6 caps, 67 points
- BBC Sports Personality of the Year: 2003
- International Rugby Board Player of the Year: 2003

77

TIGER WOODS

'Major problems that handicapped the Tiger'

YOU WOULD have put your house on Tiger Woods eventually overtaking Jack Nicklaus as the all-time winner of the most golf majors and then, overnight in December 2009, his world exploded with a spate of salacious revelations about his private life. When you're as big and as famous as Tiger there is no privacy and soon the world and its brother were devouring him in a gossip-eating frenzy.

Suddenly the best-protected and promoted brand image in sport was shattered and there was talk of billions of dollars being lost by shareholders in the Woods empire. As he sought urgent psychiatric treatment, his marriage ended in a headline-hitting divorce and you wondered how on earth he could come back from this carnage.

But we are talking Tiger Woods, golfer supreme and up there with the likes of Muhammad Ali and Pelé for transcending sport with his fame and achievements. A forgiving world saw him battle back to win the US Masters in 2019, but the stress of competition had taken its toll physically and after four serious back operations we knew we would never again see the peak-years Tiger.

Then, in the awful Covid-19 pandemic winter of early 2021, he was involved in a car crash that left him with multiple injuries and the likelihood of never playing golf again. But remember, we are talking Tiger Woods.

This is a book about sport and my greatest heroes, so I have no comment to make about Tiger's personal life. What he (or anybody) does once the door is closed should be purely their business. Speaking for myself, I have always held the view that if you have earned celebrity status you have a responsibility to set the right example when in the public spotlight, but that does not mean you should be owned and shackled by fame.

Let's just summarise Tiger's astonishing golfing record to underline why he was considered the master of the fairways.

After an outstanding junior, college and amateur career, he was the top-ranked golfer in the world from August 1999 to September 2004 (264 consecutive weeks), and again from June 2005 to October 2010 (281 consecutive weeks), accumulating 13 major championships.

He tumbled to number 58 in the rankings following his private problems and back surgery, then fought back to take the top spot again in 2014. He won the PGA Player of the Year award a record 11 times, and headed the money list in ten different seasons, eventually raking in more than $120m just in prize money. His sponsorship, endorsement and appearance money made him one of the biggest earners in sporting history.

Tiger won 15 majors, trailing only the Golden Bear Nicklaus. He has finished first in 82 PGA Tour events, tying the record set by 'Slammin'' Sam Snead. On his travels he has won 41 European tournaments and also 24 other events around the world.

He is also the second golfer (after Nicklaus) to achieve a career Grand Slam three times, has won 18 World Golf Championships and was a member of the victorious USA team in the 1999 Ryder Cup.

Tiger had a distinctive style, not only with the way he played with his whiplash swing but the way he dressed, influencing golfers worldwide with his fashion dress and cool appearance. He was also the first black player to dominate the game.

Let's face it, there will only be one Tiger Woods.

TIGER WOODS FOR THE RECORD:

- Born 30 December 1975, Cypress, California, USA
- Name at birth: Eldrick Tont Woods (nickname Tiger)
- Career span: 1996–ongoing
- Prize money: $120,851,706
- US Amateur champion: 1994, 1995, 1996
- PGA Tour victories: 82
- Major victories: 15
    - US Masters: 1997, 2001, 2002, 2005, 2019
    - US PGA Championship: 1999, 2000, 2006, 2007
    - US Open: 2000, 2002, 2008
    - Open Championship: 2000, 2005, 2006
- European Tour victories: 41
- Rest of the world victories: 24
- PGA Player of the year: 1997, 1999, 2000, 2001, 2002, 2003, 2005, 2006, 2007, 2009, 2013
- Presidential Medal of Freedom: 2019

78

EMIL ZÁTOPEK

'Bouncing Czech who completed
the 'Impossible Treble''

WHEN I was a lad growing up in Essex we did not have television as a window on the sports world and had to rely on the wireless, the common name then for a radio. I clearly recall listening with my father Charlie, a retired footballer, to the commentaries on the Olympic Games from Helsinki where every day they were referring to a Czechoslovakian runner called Emil Zátopek. I was an 11-year-old schoolboy and starting a lifetime love of all sports. Zátopek: it had a magic ring to it. Like Superman or Zorro. Zátopek.

Zátopek was one of the first names that stuck in my head, and no wonder when you realise what he achieved in those 1952 Games in Finland. He completed the 'Impossible Treble', winning the 5,000m and 10,000m and then the marathon, a race he was running for the first time.

Crack British road runner Jim Peters was the favourite for the marathon and was setting what he thought was a 'killer' pace at 12 miles when Zátopek came up to his shoulder and asked in his broken English, 'Mr Peters, are we going fast enough? Should I go to the front?'

With that, Zátopek accelerated and the rest of the field only saw his back from then on. Our hero Jim watched the bouncing Czech disappear into the distance and eventually dropped out in a state of exhaustion.

Emil was idolised by track and field fans, and wherever he competed he was accompanied with rhythmic chants in time with his strides of 'Zátopek, Zátopek, Zátopek.' He was an almost frightening sight to behold when running, grimacing as if in deadly pain and rolling his head from side to side. One reporter described him as 'a running corpse.'

He had first come to prominence in the immediate post-war years when serving in the Czech Army and revolutionised training with exhausting interval running that involved sudden lung-bursting sprints. Zátopek – fluent in seven languages – said he based his training schedule on that followed by 1920s Finnish running master Paavo Nurmi, 'only twice as hard'.

The athletics world was buzzing about Zátopek's performances in his homeland and in the London Olympics of 1948 he lived up to his potential when he won a silver medal in the 5,000m and raced away with the gold in the 10,000m, lapping all but two of his rivals.

My writing partner Norman Giller scripted and produced a TV series with his good friend Brian Moore called *The Games of 48*, and they brought Zátopek over from Prague to recall his races. He showed them the women's hostel where he recalled shinning over the forbidden wall to meet up with his then girlfriend Dana Ingrová, who later became his wife and Olympic champion in the javelin in 1952. She unleashed her winning throw just an hour after Emil's victory in the 5,000m.

In each of his track victories in Helsinki, French-Algerian Alain Mimoun was runner-up to Zátopek, as he was in the 10,000m in London. Emil was handicapped by a groin injury at the 1956

Games in Melbourne and finished sixth in defence of his marathon title. The race was won by his old rival Mimoun, who was waiting to hug him as he crossed the line. 'At long last,' Mimoun told him, 'I did not have to stare at your back.'

The Zátopeks joined the protests against Russian occupation of Czechoslovakia in 1968, and when the uprising was put down they had all their privileges removed and Emil was expelled from the Army and sent to a manual labour camp. With the end of the Cold War, they received a public apology from the government in 1990.

In races ranging from 5,000m to 30,000m, Zátopek – nicknamed the Czech Locomotive – set 18 world records over the course of his career. He and his wife were born on the same day and in the same year. Their love affair captured world headlines and they were noted for the humour in their marriage. At the press conference after her victory in the javelin, Emil interrupted and said with tongue in cheek, 'I deserve some of the credit for inspiring her with my win in the 5,000m.' Dana responded, 'Really? I challenge you to go and inspire another girl to throw over 50 metres.'

I've put up with that sort of cutting tongue from Judith for almost 60 years. She says she wants a gold medal!

Emil Zátopek. A name the athletics world will never forget.

EMIL ZÁTOPEK FOR THE RECORD:

- Born 19 September 1922, Kopřivnice, Czechoslovakia
- Career span: 1938–57
- Clubs: Gottwaldo (Zlin), Dukla Prague
- Olympics gold medals:
  - 5,000m: 1952 (Helsinki)
  - 10,000m: 1948 (London), 1952 (Helsinki)
  - Marathon: 1952 (Helsinki)
- European Championships gold medals:
  - 5,000m: 1950 (Brussels)
  - 10,000m: 1950 (Brussels), 1954 (Berne)
- Set 18 world records, including:
  - 5,000m: 13m 57s
  - 10,000m: 28m 54.2s
  - Marathon: 2h 23m 04s
- Pierre de Coubertin medal for 'True Spirit of Sportsmanship' in 1975
- *Runners World* 'Greatest Runner of All Time': 2013

79

ZINEDINE ZIDANE

*'Sizzling Zizou was the Real
deal as player and coach'*

DID I tell you that I was one of the former 'stars' who made the draw for the 2014 World Cup? It was in Brazil at the beautiful Costa do Sauípe Resort on 6 December 2013, two days before my 72nd birthday, and standing alongside me on the stage was none other than one of my all-time favourite footballers: Zinedine Zidane.

I had last seen Zizou – his affectionate nickname throughout the game – when he was ignominiously sent off in the 2006 World Cup Final after deliberately headbutting his Italian opponent Marco Materazzi for verbally insulting him. I made sure I was very polite to the still wonderfully chiselled Frenchman!

There has never been a footballer quite like Zizou. In all my years playing and watching the game I have not seen anybody play with his style and technique. He shielded the ball in a unique way, dribbled as if the ball was glued to his feet, and made it all seem as easy and effortless as a walk in the park. This supreme playmaker had just one weakness – a short-fuse temper that was likely to explode at any second.

How sad that one of the few European footballers who can challenge even Pelé and Maradona for the greatest-of-all-time accolade will be as much remembered for his anger as his artistry. It was famously said of him that he 'smiles like Saint Teresa and grimaces like a serial killer'. I promise it was not me who said it.

One of the theories about Zidane is that he was driven throughout his football career by an inner rage, and was always sensitive to racist comments about his Algerian ancestry.

He was sent off 14 times, and often the trigger that made him lose his temper could be traced to an opponent making an taunting remark about his family background. It became common knowledge in the game that he could be easily wound up, and players with a quarter of his ability would make him lose his concentration – and often his rag – by verbally insulting him.

When in the right restrained mood, he would punish them with football that was almost supernatural, but on the bad days a red mist would descend and he would answer the verbal comments with physical retribution.

There was no more telling or sadder evidence of this than in the last game of his career, when the eyes of the world – including mine – were on him. A billion television viewers saw him explode with anger during extra time when France took on Italy in Berlin. Suddenly he charged at Materazzi and headbutted him in the chest like a billy goat with its unmentionables on fire.

Materazzi went down and Zidane went off, apparently after the referee had been told in his earpiece what the fourth official had seen on the television action replays. Lip-reading experts claimed that what Materazzi said to detonate the Zidane temper was, 'You're the son of a terrorist whore, so just f*** off.'

It was well known that Zidane was ultra sensitive to any mention of terrorism, because his father had been falsely accused by French fascists of being a Harki (an Algerian who fought for the French during the War of Independence).

Zidane's version was that Materazzi kept tugging his shirt, and he claimed, 'I told him if he wanted my shirt that much he could have it after the game, but he said he would rather have my sister.'

That hardly justified the moment of madness that brought sudden shame to Zidane, who had been head and shoulders above any player in the tournament as he held his passing-out parade in front of the biggest audience in sport.

It was nothing new for Zidane to self-destruct in a major match. He was red-carded for headbutting Hamburg's Jochen Kientz during a Champions League match when he was at Juventus, and he was in trouble for stomping on Fuad Amin of Saudi Arabia during the 1998 World Cup.

He used his head much more intelligently in that year's final against Brazil, nodding in two superb goals from corner kicks to put France on the way to a stunning 3-0 victory.

As the final whistle blew, I received an instant text message from my eldest grandson, Jack. It read, 'You've still got the record, Grandpa, Jack xx' Now you know what it means to the Hurst family. Proud or what.

Many football followers throughout France, Italy and Spain will tell you that Zidane was the greatest playmaker of them all. We might have seen more of him in England because Kenny Dalglish had him on his wish-list of players when he took over at Blackburn, but Jack Walker, the chairman bankrolling Kenny's ambitions, reportedly looked at the list and asked, 'Why do we want this fella Zidane when we have Tim Sherwood?'

Those who witnessed Zidane's early performances for Bordeaux claim he played better football while he was there than he did anywhere else in the future, because he performed without pressure and was always making the impossible look possible.

Heavy responsibility at Juventus robbed him of some of his adventurous spirit. The Italian media, who had previously fallen in love with the charming, outgoing Frenchman Michel Platini, were unhappy that Zidane was so reclusive off the pitch. He avoided the celebrity roundabout and was happiest at home with his Spanish dancer-wife, Véronique and their four sons.

But this basically shy man still produced enough magic on the pitch for Juventus to persuade Real Madrid to part with a world record £47.2m for him in 2001. He repaid a lot of the huge fee with the winning goal – a spectacular volley – in the 2002 Champions League Final against Bayer Leverkusen at Hampden Park.

David Beckham got to play in the same Real attack (they became close friends) and described him simply as 'the greatest footballer in the world'.

In 2004, a UEFA jubilee poll put him ahead of all the footballers who had performed with European clubs throughout the previous 50 years. That left Johan Cruyff, Eusébio, Di Stéfano, Puskás and George Best trailing in his wake. Another poll in France had him voted the most popular of all Frenchmen. It seemed that everybody loved Zizou, but he had still not conquered those inner demons.

Zidane ended his last game with Real in tears as the capacity crowd at the Bernabéu continually chanted 'Merci' throughout the last club match of his career.

Then it was on to Germany for World Cup 2006 and his final shots. He managed to get himself booked and suspended in the second match for petulantly pushing a South Korean defender, but after missing one game he returned to steer France through to the Final with a series of match-winning performances against Spain, Brazil and Portugal.

He put France into a 1-0 lead against Italy in the Final with a penalty that crashed against the underside of the bar and crossed the line by inches. Sound familiar? That goal made him only the fourth player (along with Pelé, Paul Breitner and Vavá) to have scored in two World Cup finals.

Everything was set for him to make a glorious exit from the world stage. Then came the red mist and a headbutt that overshadowed all that had gone before.

After hanging up his boots, Zidane switched to coaching and had even more success than in his playing days. He became the first coach to win the Champions League three times consecutively, won the UEFA Super Cup and FIFA Club World Cup twice each, as well as a La Liga title and a Supercopa de España. This success led to Zidane being named Best FIFA Men's Coach in 2017. He resigned in 2018 but returned to the Bernabéu in 2019 and proceeded to win another La Liga and Supercopa de España, but was soon off for a third time after accusing Real of losing faith in him.

Mean, moody and magnificent, Zizou comfortably makes my *Eighty at Eighty* for his footballing and coaching skills. He was a one-off, and I would tell him that to his face.

ZINEDINE ZIDANE FOR THE RECORD:

- Born: 23 June 1972, Marseille, France
- Career span: 1988–2006
- Clubs:
  - Cannes 1988–92 (71 games, 6 goals)
  - Bordeaux 1992–96 (179 games, 39 goals)
  - Juventus 1996–2001 (214 games, 31 goals)
  - Real Madrid 2001–06 (230 games, 49 goals)
- France: 108 caps, 31 goals
- Playing honours include:
  - Serie A: 1997, 1998
  - La Liga: 2003
  - Champions League: 2002
  - World Cup: 1998
  - European Championship: 2000
  - Serie A Foreign Footballer of the Year: 1997, 2001
  - European Footballer of the Year: 1998
  - Player of Tournament: 2006 World Cup, Euro 2000
  - UEFA Golden Jubilee Poll – Best European Player: 2004
  - FIFA World Player of the Year: 1998, 2000, 2003
  - Ballon d'Or: 1998
- Coaching honours include:
  - La Liga: 2017, 2020
  - Champions League: 2016, 2017, 2018
  - UEFA Super Cup: 2016, 2017
  - FIFA Club World Cup: 2016, 2017
- Voted Best FIFA Best Men's Coach: 2017

80

GIANFRANCO ZOLA

'The player I would most liked
to have had serving me'

HOW APPROPRIATE that the final sportsman in my list is the player I would most liked to have had serving me his passes on a platter. Of all the overseas footballers who have decorated our game since the doors were thrown wide open, Gianfranco is the one who made my old competitive juices run. I reckon I would have doubled my goals output if the little Italian artist had been threading the ball through to me. 'Just get into space, Geoffrey, and Zola will find you.'

I wonder if Gianfranco (what a name to roll off your tongue) realises that he was born in the same week that the 1966 World Cup kicked off at Wembley? It was fitting then that 30 years later he should join Chelsea and help steer them to two FA Cup final victories at the old Wembley.

More wishes: how different my stay at Stamford Bridge as manager would have been with the Zola magic box of tricks and the Abramovich money! How contrasting a world was it back then? Well, I was on an annual salary of £28,000 a year, which would be pocket money today. I would have loved to have had the zillions to spend that seems to flow like water under the Stamford Bridge today. As I am preparing this chapter Chelsea have just signed Romelu Lukaku for around £97m. Goodness, what would Zola have been worth at his peak? The mind boggles.

Let me tell you that it was no accident that much of the magic Zola produced at Chelsea bore a startling resemblance to Maradona's bag of tricks. He had come under the influence of the Argentinian master while playing understudy to Diego early in his career at Napoli.

I got to know the charming Gianfranco quite well and he told me, 'I used to spy on Diego at every opportunity. Every time he was in training I would be in the background, watching like a hawk. I studied the way he curled balls at free kicks, how he dribbled and how he made space for himself with his acceleration. Then I would practise all the things I had noticed. As you can imagine, I am a great admirer of Maradona. He remains the best footballer I have ever seen.'

While all the good things rubbed off on Gianfranco, he was wise enough not to take on any of Maradona's dubious baggage. Off the pitch, they were as alike as grass and granite. Zola's lifestyle could not have been more different. A teetotaller, he quickly settled into his London home with wife Franca and their three children. Away from the football crowds, he loves nothing better than playing Beethoven on the grand piano in his lounge.

He eventually got to take over Maradona's number ten shirt, and his goals and passes helped Napoli win the Serie A championship in 1989/90. A £1.4m move to Parma in 1993 coincided with him taking over from Roberto Baggio as a key man in Italy's attack. He was a major influence on the Parma team that developed from a domestic force in Italy to a power in Europe.

Standing a haircut taller than Maradona at 5ft 5in, Zola was always an Anglophile and he jumped at the chance when Chelsea player-manager Ruud Gullit came calling for him in November

1996. He made such an impression in his first season in England that he was voted the Football Writers' Association Footballer of the Year. The move had revitalised his game just as he was losing his appetite at Parma.

The enchanting little man told me, 'My first season in English football was just unbelievable. The memories of it will live with me forever. It was very important to me that I should help Chelsea win something after Ruud [Gullit] had put so much faith in me. Our victory against Middlesbrough in the FA Cup was unforgettable. To be part of that wonderful occasion was fantastic. I have never known anything quite like the atmosphere of a Wembley cup final. It sent shivers down my back. Two days earlier I had been honoured to be presented with the Footballer of the Year award. It was an overwhelming experience, particularly as the legendary Sir Stanley Matthews handed it to me. That was just awe-inspiring. My father was there on his first visit to England and for the entire trip he kept saying, "I have met Stanley Matthews." Even to this day, there are few bigger names in football. In Italy he is known as Mister Football. I was privileged to have a long talk with Sir Stanley, and he told me that he used to play for £20 a week. Today he would be worth all the money in the Bank of England!'

Zola was the first player to win the Footballer of the Year award without playing a full season, and was the first Chelsea player to win the accolade.

He had seven wonderfully happy and satisfying seasons at Chelsea before heading into the sunset by holding his passing-out parade with Cagliari on his home island of Sardinia. Chelsea supporters went into mourning when they heard that the player known as 'Magic Box' was leaving Stamford Bridge, where he had such a rapport with the fans that he was voted by fans as the best-loved Chelsea player in the club's history.

Many of his 80 goals for Chelsea were conjured – back-heels, volleys, side-foots after dazzling dribbles and scissor kicks. One FA

Cup goal against Norwich – a back-heel delivered while he was in mid-air – was described as 'pure fantasy'.

Roman Abramovich took over at Chelsea just after the little man had committed himself to Cagliari and did all he could to persuade him to change his mind and stay at Stamford Bridge. But Zola is a man of his word, and refused to break his verbal promise to join his home-island club. Everywhere he went, Abramovich heard people saying how Zola was the greatest player Chelsea had ever had. He went to the lengths of trying to buy Cagliari – as you do – so that he could lay claim to Gianfranco, but his offer for the club was rejected.

Zola was a magnificent ambassador for his country and for the whole of football, and is the perfect role model for any young professional just coming into the game.

Even at 38, he still had the power to influence matters on the pitch and – in the role of skipper and schemer – he steered Cagliari back to Serie A before hanging up his shooting boots.

I remember the then Chelsea manager Claudio Ranieri – once Zola's coach at Napoli – saying that he had never known a player get a reception like Gianfranco did at away grounds. 'They applaud him as he steps off the coach and again as he comes on to and leaves the pitch,' he said. 'It is extraordinary how he has won the hearts of everybody.'

His off-the-field charity work at Chelsea was rewarded with an OBE, a rare honour for an overseas player.

'My greatest satisfaction is the way people respect me,' he said on hearing of his OBE honour. 'Many people excel in games but when you have achieved that level of respect, it is something extra special. Money can give you many things but respect cannot be bought. What I have achieved in the way people regard me, in my mind, is remarkable. I will always have a little of London and a lot of Chelsea in my heart.'

What a way to finish my journey through 80 years of sporting memories, wishing that we could reopen Gianfranco's magic box.

GIANFRANCO ZOLA FOR THE RECORD:

- Born: 5 July 1966, Oliena, Sardinia
- Career span: 1984–2005
- Clubs:
  - Nuorese 1984–87 (31 games, 10 goals)
  - Sassari Torres 1987–89 (88 games, 21 goals)
  - Napoli 1989–93 (136 games, 36 goals)
  - Parma 1993–96 (149 games, 64 goals)
  - Chelsea 1996–2003 (311 games, 80 goals)
  - Cagliari 2003–05 (81 games, 27 goals)
- Italy: 35 caps, 10 goals
- Serie A: 1990
- UEFA Cup: 1995
- UEFA Super Cup: 1993, 1998
- FA Cup: 1997, 2000
- League Cup: 1998
- European Cup Winners' Cup: 1998
- FWA Footballer of the Year: 1997

EXTRA TIME

GEOFF HURST

'A fortunate footballer in the right place at the right time'

IT'S NOT quite the end. Or should I say, 'Some people think it's all over'? The publisher has insisted I add myself to the *Eighty at Eighty*, with a For the Record entry on Geoff Hurst, plus an honest self appraisal of the player and the man.

Well, it's been quite a journey, during which a bit-better-than-ordinary footballer got lucky and found global fame by becoming the only player in the history of the game to score a World Cup final hat-trick. Okay, for some cynics out there, two and three-quarter goals. I will always say it was over the line. Look at the result in the record books.

It was a classic example of being in the right place at the right time. Wembley was the place, Saturday, 30 July 1966 was the time.

I kicked off life in a little market town called Ashton-under-Lyne in what was then Lancashire, moved to Chelmsford in Essex at six when my football professional-father Charlie was transferred there, and spent my school days in the two happy worlds of football in the winter and cricket in the summer. I got my work ethic from my dad, who combined football with his job as a skilled toolmaker. He taught me right from wrong, left foot from right foot and the importance of being two-footed. Due to his coaching and cajoling, to this day people cannot say whether Geoff Hurst preferred left to right. My controversial hat-trick came from head, right foot on the swivel and then left foot with all my might. Thanks, Dad (note to those still saying it was two and three-quarter goals … I shall set Judith on you!).

All those people of a certain age will confirm that football now is on a different planet to when I came into the game as a 15-year-old, £7-a-week apprentice at then Second Division West Ham United. Our top players at the club – the likes of Noel Cantwell, John Bond and Malcolm Allison – were on the maximum weekly wage of £20, the same as the superstars Stanley Matthews at Blackpool, Jackie Milburn at Newcastle and Billy Wright at Wolves.

Pitches in midwinter were mud heaps, footballs were leather panelled and not water resistant, our boots were like clodhoppers compared to the slippers of today, there were no substitutes, no red and yellow cards, European football was very rare and heavily rationed action on television, and there was not an overseas player or club owner in sight. Goalkeepers could be shoulder charged, and the sometimes legal tackling meant you took your life in your hands trying to negotiate through defences that were iron clad and manned by unforgiving players who were paid to try to kick you over the stand.

Now we watch Premier League football being played by foreign footballers, at clubs largely owned by foreign investors, on pitches like billiard table tops, playing with 'beach' balls, squads rather than teams, much of the game non-contact, substitutes galore and wages that have turned our players into among the richest young men in the world (good luck to them).

I was so fortunate early on to play with footballers of exceptional talent who were making a name for themselves; the young, majestic Bobby Moore in defence, the magical Martin Peters appearing from out of nowhere to create chances for me, Johnny 'Budgie' Byrne the nearest we ever got to producing a Di Stéfano. This was all at West Ham, while coming through at other clubs were the likes of Bobby Charlton and George Best at Manchester United, a young whizkid called Jimmy Greaves at Chelsea, slimline genius Denis Law at Huddersfield and a soprano Clitheroe kid by the name of Alan Ball at Blackpool.

The game was changing out of sight, and I was so lucky to come under the influence of a gentleman and scholar of the game in our West Ham manager Ron Greenwood. He was the one who spotted my potential as a goal-getting forward rather than a plodding midfielder, and he also taught me much about life, a good Christian man who put dignity, honesty and high morals at the top of his shopping list. He was the first person I ever heard say, and mean, 'black lives matter' when he introduced among the first black players to the league in Clyde Best, Ade Coker and John Charles (not THAT one; a lovely, smoothly talented player from Canning Town), plus his brother Clive. I used to look on embarrassed as morons bombarded Clyde with bananas as he ran on to the pitch. The balanced, tolerant Greenwood preached, 'We must judge players by the colour of their shirt, not the colour of their skin.'

Ron not only taught us how to play but how to behave. He gave a discipline to my life on and off the pitch and it was thanks to him that I had a career that was fairly successful, and – along with Bobby and Martin – I learned to play football the modern way. Those apparently instinctive moves that we three Hammers stitched into England matches were created on West Ham's Chadwell Heath training ground by the coaching genius that was Ron.

Only one other person had a bigger influence on my life: my gorgeous wife, good companion and best mate Judith. She has always been there to hold my head above water when threatened with being submerged by the slings and arrows of outrageous fortune.

And we have had more than our fair share of heartache and worry to balance the luck of those three goals. Worst of all was losing our darling first daughter, Claire, to a brain tumour in 2010 after a brave ten-year battle. It was Claire I left in the pram after being hero-dazzled by meeting Jimmy Greaves in the supermarket all those years ago, and it was Claire who along with wonderful sisters Charlotte and Joanne brought laughter and love into the Hurst household.

Losing her was the worst thing that happened to us, and put in perspective nasty things like being conned out of money by scammers and scoundrels, having our home burgled several times with footballing and life trophies stolen, not being given a fair crack at management by Chelsea plus the aches and pains that so many of we old footballers suffer. Also scarring my life was the suicide of my four-years-younger brother, Robert, who threw himself under a train at Chelmsford when I was playing for Stoke in 1974 during one of his dark depressions which, thankfully, never engulfed me.

Judith wonders if I should mention such melancholy things in a celebration book like this, but I have always believed in being candid. Trying to hide heartache merely leads to more grief. Speak up, speak out, speak from the soul. I think I can hear Ron Greenwood's influence in those words.

On the positive side, at 80 I have all my marbles ('some of them,' says Judith), a proudly held knighthood, I enjoyed a long and successful career in motor insurance which is much less boring than it sounds, have two smashing daughters and grandchildren who put a bounce in my step despite the plastic hip, have Judith pouring love into my life, and – conceit alert – I can still boast that I am the only footballer to have scored a hat-trick in a World Cup final.

It's mostly been fun. I wish I could do it all again. Stay safe.

SIR GEOFF HURST FOR THE RECORD:

- Born: 8 December 1941, Ashton-under-Lyne, Lancashire
- Two younger siblings: sister Diane and brother Robert
- Father Charlie Hurst was a professional footballer with Bristol Rovers (1938–43), Oldham Athletic (1943–46), Rochdale (1946–47), Chelmsford City (1948–50), Sudbury Town (1950–51)
- Moved to Chelmsford, Essex: 1948
- West Ham ground staff: 1956–58
- Professional footballer career span: 1958–79
- West Ham first-team debut: 15 December 1958 v. Fulham (Southern Floodlit Cup)
- League debut: 27 February 1960 at Nottingham Forest
- FA Cup: 1964
- European Cup Winners' Cup: 1965
- Joint record 49 League Cup goals with Ian Rush
- Clubs:
    - West Ham (1958–72): 500 games, 242 goals
    - Stoke City (1972–75): 130 games, 39 goals
    - Cape Town City (1973, loan): 6 games, 5 goals
    - Cork Celtic (1976): 3 games, 3 goals
    - Seattle Sounders (1976): 23 games, 8 goals
    - Total: 674 games, 299 goals
- England record:
    - Youth internationals: 6 games, no goals
    - Under-23 (1963–64): 4 games, 1 goal
    - Full internationals (1966–72): 49 games, 24 goals
- Teams managed:
    - Telford United (1976–79)
    - Chelsea (1979–81)
    - Kuwait SC (1982–84)
- Cricket:
    - Right-hand bat, wicketkeeper
    - Essex (1962–64)
    - Only first-class appearance: May 1962, v. Lancashire
    - First innings 0, second innings 0 not out (did not bat)
- Knighted: 1998

Thanks for your company. Next up, how about my *Ninety at Ninety*?

Also available at all good book stores

9781785317927

9781785316470

9781801500067

9781785314995

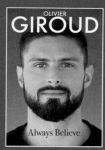

9781801500098

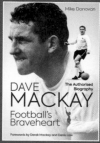

9781785317910

9781785318580

9781785314407

9781785315510